DIFFERENCE AND DISAVOWAL

The Trauma of Eros

ALAN BASS

STANFORD UNIVERSITY PRESS

Stanford, California

2000

Stanford University Press
Stanford, California

© 2000 by the Board of Trustees of the
Leland Stanford Junior University

Printed in the United States of America
on acid-free, archival-quality paper.

Library of Congress Cataloging-in-Publication Data

Bass, Alan.
Difference and disavowal : the trauma of Eros / Alan Bass
p.   cm.
Includes bibliographical references and index.
ISBN 0-8047-3827-0 (alk. paper) —
ISBN 0-8047-3828-9 (paper : alk. paper)
1. Psychoanalysis.
2. Freud, Sigmund, 1856–1939.
I. Title.
BF173 .B2147 2000
150.19'52—dc21   00-057323

Typeset by James P. Brommer in 10.5/13 Bembo

Original Printing 2000

Last figure below indicates year of this printing:
09   08   07   06   05   04   03   02   01   00

CONTENTS

PREFACE   vii

Introduction   1

1. Concreteness and Fetishism   11

2. Narcissism, Thought, and Eros   53

3. A Dialogue with Hans Loewald: The Two Realities   91

4. The Part Object, Depressive Anxiety, and the Environment   146

5. Analysis of Surface, Analysis of Defense   210

Afterword   267

NOTES   275

REFERENCES   297

INDEX   303

Is an identifiably Freudian psychoanalysis on the verge of extinction? Many today seem to hope or fear that it is. No contemporary Freudian would disagree with a diagnosis of chronic crisis. Nevertheless, my years of practice, supervision, teaching, and writing about Freud —and a wide spectrum of psychoanalytic theories—have convinced me that the Freudian tradition can be renewed from within. Such renewal can only occur if the most difficult questions, at the limits of theory and practice, are confronted. I am attempting such a confrontation here, from several very particular points of view.

I came to psychoanalysis almost twenty-five years ago. I was already a first-generation student of deconstruction, a perspective that continues to inform me. Deconstructive analysis generally proceeds by very close readings in order to show how texts are marked, or even made possible, by difficulties their own presuppositions cannot encompass. This is an implicitly psychoanalytic approach. It works to show how contradictions, exclusions, and impasses are resources for new ways of thinking. The day-to-day practice of psychoanalysis itself is inevitably deconstructive. It does not fail to produce encounters that push against received clinical knowledge. This book, in fact, has grown out of a sustained effort to grapple with a clinical dilemma that also demands a deconstructive approach to theory. Throughout this work I attempt to show how Freudian theory and practice are marked by contradictions which themselves are the most important resources for understanding a major clinical problem. The entire effort in turn contributes to the renewal of Freudian theory and practice.

No prior knowledge of deconstructive theory on the part of the reader is assumed or necessary. However, I do wish to give some account of the converging paths that led me to write this book. In one of Derrida's most challenging works, *Glas*, he devoted a few pages to Freud's article on fetishism. As always, he was demonstrating how certain elements of Freudian theory intersect with the deconstruction of metaphysics. Derrida's emphasis was on Freud's description of the oscillating structure of the fetish, part of his own long-standing effort to develop a theory of undecidable structures. Indeed Derrida proposed a generalization of fetishism from a philosophical point of view.

These ideas stayed with me for a long time. I did not do anything with them until, as a member of a study group on psychoanalysis and literature, I encountered Wallace Stevens's poem "The Snow Man." This poem is a meditation on mind, nature, thing and nothing, and has an intricately oscillating structure. It seemed ideally suited for an integration of the theory of fetishism and a psychoanalytic approach to literature. As I began to reread Freud's late work on fetishism, I was quite surprised to find that Freud himself, at the very end of his life, had also begun to propose a generalization of fetishism. Freud, however, based this generalization on a radically inconsistent argument. My efforts to sort out the inconsistency, in order to extend Freud's thinking, produced a theory of disavowal of difference as the foundation of defense. Anyone familiar with deconstructive thought knows that repudiation of difference is its major concern. So I had arrived at a generalization of fetishism in which there was also a clinical basis for thinking deconstructively. The first version of this integration was presented in "Fetishism, Reality, and 'The Snow Man'" (1991).

I cannot say exactly when it began to dawn on me that this theory was clinically relevant in a much more specific way. I began to see it as an explanation for a very vexing problem—the prolonged encounter with patients who strenuously defend against what one presumably goes to an analyst for: interpretation. As I began to do research for an article that would integrate my understanding of fetishism with this clinical problem, I was happy to discover that some elements of my theory had been anticipated by other analysts. The clinical and theoretical integration of this material became "The Problem of 'Concreteness'" (1997), which is a version of the first chapter of this book. The rest of the volume consists of new material.

The psychoanalytic literature is incredibly rich. I am painfully aware that there is both too much and not enough discussion of it here. There are many significant omissions in the discussions of the past literature relevant to my clinical problem—for example, no Bion, no

Lacan. The current literature that deals with the problem of resistance to interpretation has been expanding rapidly, but I could not survey it all adequately. Close consideration and synthesis of all these contributions is eventually mandatory. I hope that at least it will become clear why I think that resistance to interpretation has become a central preoccupation of analytic practice. In some ultimate work, this clinical thinking would have to be integrated with the thinking that treats inevitable repudiation of difference (Nietzsche, Heidegger, and Derrida, to begin with). However, the ideal book for the ideal reader with the ideal insomnia would have been impossible—not that I was not tempted.

But I was very fortunate to have nearly ideal readers for my first drafts. My profound thanks first have to go to Dr. Louise Kaplan. The world knows her for her own writings; I know her as a superlative psychoanalytic editor, scrupulously devoted to the most generous reading and rigorous in her editorial advice. I am equally indebted to Dr. Donald Moss and Richard Rand, whose appreciations and critical remarks were invaluable. I also owe it to Rand that this book came to be published by Stanford University Press. At a decisive moment I met Elizabeth Rottenberg, who graciously prepared the index.

I am especially grateful to the patients, supervisees, and colleagues who permitted their clinical material to be used. Just as I had to winnow the literature, so I had to winnow the vast amount of clinical material so many people have shared with me. But without all this material I would never have reached the conclusions I offer here. I hope that all such readers will see their invisible hands at work.

My wife, Erica, constantly encouraged me to take whatever time I needed to devote to this work, and my daughter, Chloe, provided indispensable technical assistance. I am also very grateful to Guillaume des Forêts and Danielle Memoire for their endless summer hospitality at *la Folletière*, where much of the writing and rewriting of this book was done—including these words set down in August 1999.

A.B.

Does not disavowal . . . found human reality?

—Laplanche and Pontalis,
Vocabulary of Psychoanalysis

As soon as the economy of the undecidable secures for
the fetish its greater stability, as Freud recognizes, its
lesser stability already presupposes some liaison to
opposed interests. So the measure of solidity or stability
would be the ligament between the contraries, this
double bond and the undecidable mobility of the fetish,
its power of excess in relation to opposition.

—Derrida, *Glas*

Introduction

Freudian psychoanalysis is synonymous with interpretation. Do we always remember how unusual it is as a therapeutic measure? Interpretation emerged out of Freud's initial integration of theory of mind and theory of treatment. For example, in his 1896 paper "The Aetiology of Hysteria," he wrote that the clinical problem in neurosis was to explain why earlier experiences retain their traumatizing power. The solution was a theory of unconscious memory. Freud immediately realized, however, that the theory of unconscious memory demanded a new psychology, "of a kind for which philosophers have done little to prepare the way" (1896, p. 219). This new psychology synthesized the specific theory of neurosis with the universal theory of dreams (Freud 1900). Once dreams became the key to theories of mind and psychopathology, they also became the key to the theory of treatment. The title alone of Freud's magnum opus, *The Interpretation of Dreams*, makes the point: interpretation is the bridge between the theory of mind and the therapy of neurosis.

The central clinical-theoretical position of interpretation evolved slowly and unevenly from 1894 to 1900. Freud's first psychoanalytic publications famously centered on recall of repressed traumatic seductions through hypnosis. Nonetheless, he understood dreams as wish fulfillments, and began to comprehend their relation to unconscious memory, before the full abandonment of hypnosis and before the postulation of the seduction theory. This is evident in the 1895 manuscript called the *Project for a Scientific Psychology*. The 1896 paper on the aetiology of hysteria put forward the strongest version of the seduction theory but also advocated an interpretive technique. Freud notoriously alleged that all hysterical symptoms are due to the repression of infantile seductions. Therapy consists of reversing such repressions. Hypnosis, however, does not do so reliably enough. This clinical problem is resolved by means of what Freud already knew about the method of dream interpretation—following chains of associations to their intersecting nodal points, where interpretation imposes itself. Since symptoms, like dreams, contain intersecting chains of associated memories, they, too, can be interpreted. Interpretation becomes the most reliable means to reverse psychopathology. Even the relation to the therapist can be interpreted, as it inevitably becomes an expression of the repressed (an idea already elaborated by Freud in his chapter on psychotherapy in *Studies on Hysteria* [1895b]).

During Freud's lifetime more and more mental disorders were investigated psychoanalytically, with no change in the fundamental assumption about interpretation. For example, the innovative theory of depression ("Mourning and Melancholia," 1917), the revised comprehension of perversion in relation to unconscious guilt and repressed fantasy ("'A Child Is Being Beaten,'" 1919), and the insight into inhibitions of ego functioning in terms of anxiety and compromise formation (*Inhibition, Symptom, and Anxiety*, 1926) made these disorders as interpretable as the classical neuroses. The domain of what was interpretable expanded as Freud could demonstrate the unconscious content and mechanisms of various forms of pathology. This is not to imply that he thought that all forms of psychopathology should yield to interpretation. He had specific ideas about its limits. To mention only three, he thought that effective interpretation could only occur if a patient were capable of forming a transference to the analyst, thereby excluding from an interpretive approach those who were so narcissistically withdrawn that transference was impossible ("On Narcissism," 1914b); he saw the reactions to traumas that breached the stimulus barrier as "beyond the pleasure principle," implying that interpretable structures demanded the dominance of certain regulatory principles (*Beyond the Pleasure Principle*, 1920); and he was frank that certain kinds of ego deformation could produce "infantilisms" whose modification by interpretation was questionable (*Analysis Terminable and Interminable*, 1937a). None of these limiting factors, however, led to any questioning of the basic assumption that interpretation, especially in the transference, is the central technique for psychoanalytic treatment.

The basic theory and the interpretive technique did not have to change because both were derived from the concept of repression. Freud always said that repression is "the cornerstone on which the whole structure of psychoanalysis rests" (1914a, p. 16). The notion of unconscious memory, and indeed of "an unconscious," is synonymous with repression. In the great summing up of 1915 ("Repression," "The Unconscious"), Freud explained the clinical manifestations of repression in terms of a theory of primal repression. His most general conception is that representatives of mental processes may either never enter consciousness at all (primal repression) or can be withdrawn from it (secondary, or clinical, repression). Interpretation works to reverse the process of secondary repression; primal repression creates the possibility that what is most meaningful may never have been conscious. Whether primary or secondary, repression concerns meaningful, if unconscious, mental content. Apparently meaningless dreams and symptoms are actually substitutes for repressed meanings. To make these meanings conscious by interpretation is to reverse the effects of repression.

As psychoanalysis became increasingly therapeutically ambitious, various challenges to the primacy of both repression and interpretation arose. Given the intrinsic link between repression and interpretation, one might have predicted that a challenge to one would lead to a challenge to the other, but such was not always the case. Repression does not play a central role for either Klein or Lacan, for example. Nonetheless, both develop theories of treatment in which interpretation remains central, which is one reason why both always insisted that their practices were Freudian. Starting with Rank and the later Ferenczi, there was another major line of development that did challenge the repression/interpretation model. Alexander's "corrective emotional experience," Balint's conception of "the basic fault," Winnicott's ideas about environmental impingement, and Kohut's notion of narcissism derived from failures of empathic attunement all brought the noninterpretive, experiential aspects of treatment into the foreground. These analysts challenged basic tenets of Freudian theory, as had those innovators who remained convinced of the primacy of interpretation.[1] But the modifications of theory and practice sometimes did, and sometimes did not, modify the commitment to interpretation. Moreover, the commitment to "experience" or "interpretation" does not necessarily reflect a commitment to a specific therapeutic format. Some innovators, such as Ferenczi, Lacan, and Alexander, modified elements of the basic format of psychoanalytic therapy (frequent sessions of regular duration, the use of the couch, the long treatment, the focus on the patient-analyst relation), while others, such as Klein, Winnicott, and Kohut, did not.[2] There has been no consistent development of psychoanalysis guided by the question of how theory of mind, theory of treatment, and format of treatment are integrated.

In general, the innovators who stress the experiential, noninterpretive factors in psychoanalytic treatment argue in terms of understanding early phases of psychic development, nonneurotic forms of psychopathology, and difficult transference situations. Therapeutic and scientific realism always demand flexibility in order to understand and treat an expanded patient population—the way Freud himself began with his novel treatment of neurosis. There has been a more or less tacit assumption, however, that Freud generalized a theory and method of treatment that went very far to explain neurosis but did not necessarily "fit" analytic work with other disorders. Such an assumption can seem inarguable. But it does not promote looking at the relations between theory of mind and theory of treatment comprehensively, including neurosis. Instead, clinical techniques or new insights into psychodynamics effective in the treatment of nonneurotic patients are incorporated into the clinical repertoire without examining the relation between theory of treatment and theory of mind.

This clinical empiricism avoids the most fundamental questions: what forms of psychopathology and what clinical techniques derived from them tell us most about a general theory of mind and treatment? How do the answers to such questions inform the use of a given therapeutic format? For Freud, hysteria initially served such a function. Once its dynamics could be amalgamated with the dynamics of universal dreaming, an integrated theory of mind and treatment was possible. Should the interpretive stance derived from the generalization of the treatment of hysteria be questioned? Does a questioning of interpretation demand a questioning of therapeutic format? Are there specific forms of psychopathology that hold the answers to these questions? To complicate such questions further, what larger assumptions about science, knowledge, and therapeutics are built into them?

Freud's own assumptions about science, knowledge, and therapeutics are well known. Psychoanalysis was to be a science of empirical observation guided by the commitment to truth, which inspires all the natural sciences. This thinking was intrinsic to the theory of repression. Not only does the focus on repression suggest that psychopathology results from not knowing the truth about oneself, it also implies a relation to the truths to be found in nature. As Freud put it in a letter from his early psychoanalytic period, the question of defense led him into "the very core of nature" (1985, p. 136). One cannot make such a statement without some ideas about what nature is, what it means to investigate it scientifically, and what the situation of mind in relation to natural forces might be. Interpretation is intrinsic to Freud's conviction that he had discovered the "natural" force of mind (repression) that treats "natural" (sexual) wishes in pathological ways. Freud would never have insisted on the primacy of interpretation had he not thought it the result of a natural science type of investigation. Thus, more difficult questions have to be added to those about science and knowledge. What conception of nature is implied in a theory and practice whose basic model is always repression? What role would such a conception play in the general approach to theory building and clinical practice?

In today's climate of uneasy relativism, such questions seem anachronistic. But the result of not asking them is the current organization of psychoanalysis into various groups with commitments to various theories. This kind of splintering is characteristic of a postmodern age, which suspects universal, all-encompassing narratives. Yet it leaves psychoanalysis looking more and more like a set of beliefs with no particular rationale to hold it together. While there can be many salutary effects from no longer having one central theory and practice of psychoanalysis, there can also be an aggravation of an ad hoc empiricism that engages in therapy for therapy's sake and clinical experiment for the market's sake. The integrative vision of nature, science, theory, and practice that characterizes Freud are all too easily rationalized away in such a climate. The greater challenge is to rethink Freud's original vision, taking into account all the critiques of such integrative efforts. Interpretation needs to be reapproached from such a perspective.

This book will attempt such a rethinking, based upon a clinical anomaly. There is a group of patients who seek out analytic treatment, who appear to be the kind of patients for whom analysis is indicated, and yet whose treatments do not advance with interpretation. There is something about interpretation itself that such patients resist. To understand their psychodynamics is necessarily to reopen the question of interpretation in relation to the theory of mind. Further, once one begins to investigate this problem one comes upon a striking phenomenon: analysts in fact have always dealt with such patients. There is a subterranean but unintegrated tradition of describing them, and clinicians of diverse schools have written about the difficult work with these patients in astonishingly similar terms.

Any scholarly investigation would have to take these descriptions and their theoretical analyses as essential resources, of course. By tracing the themes that consistently emerge in this relatively unintegrated literature, one can begin to elaborate a theory of the resistance to interpretation. These writings, however, will serve an additional purpose. All these descriptions grapple with a limiting factor for a theory of unconscious processes linked to an interpretive technique. They demonstrate what happens when psychoanalysts, knowingly or not, engage with issues that test their most fundamental presuppositions. Analysis of these texts—some by very well known figures (for example, Freud, Klein, Abraham, Winnicott, Loewald, Jacobson) and some by lesser-known writers who have reflected upon the anomaly—will be just as important as analysis of clinical data. Such analysis will show how psychoanalytic theory and practice themselves break down and have to be rethought when their limits are encountered.

It is not usual to read clinical texts in this way. The justification for doing so is that all the authors who describe resistance to interpretation delineate a pathology of what can be called (after an early paper of Ferenczi's) the "sense of reality." But, unbeknownst to themselves, the analysts who treat and describe these patients mostly share the same "sense of reality." Analysis of the clinical texts can show how theory itself is constructed on the same basis as the pathology it describes and how clinical technique can replicate the problem. This is not a version of the old barb that psychoanalysis is the disease of which it purports to be the cure. Rather, it is an attempt to show where scrupulous analysts have encountered a problem that their own presuppositions could not explain. The "symptomatic" contradictions of these descriptions can be analyzed in order to delineate the "sense of reality" that limits traditional interpretation.

To explain the dynamics of the sense of reality that produces resistance to interpretation is inevitably to reopen the question of defense. The theory of repression led to a new conception of the reality of mind and to a therapy well integrated with that reality. Once the pathology of certain reality organizations can be shown to be a defensive operation, one can begin to formulate other views of reality, mind, and treatment. Freud actually started to consider this question at the end of his life. It remains mostly unappreciated that in some of his very late texts he began to rethink the centrality of repression in favor of a theory based on disavowal and splitting. These new ideas grew out of his renewed interest in fetishism. Several contemporary writers have already seen that the theory of fetishism is essential to the problem of resistance to interpretation and that Freud was initiating a fundamental revision of his thinking in his late works. What I believe to be novel in my approach is a modification of Freud's theory of fetishism, placed in the context of his beginning generalization of disavowal and splitting. This revision is centered on the question of defenses against differentiation. It leads to a conception of defensively dedifferentiated reality organizations on both sides of the couch, in basic theory construction and in interpretive technique.

Each of the chapters develops this thesis from a different point of view. The first chapter develops a theory of the concrete patients who resist interpretation in relation to Freud's theory of fetishism. It also includes the kind of analysis of related clinical texts just described. The second chapter deals with the question of defensive reality organizations from the perspective of narcissism. The revision of the theory of fetishism developed in the first chapter will be integrated with an expanded conception of primary narcissism, emphasizing Freud's cryptic discussions of unconscious thought and unconscious time. The third chapter is an extended encounter with Loewald, the most important theoretician of primary narcissism. He has also written trenchantly about unquestioningly adopted defensive reality organizations in psychoanalytic theory and technique. In addition, his clinical concept of "enactive remembering" is crucial for understanding defenses against differentiation. However, there will also be emphasis on a critical problem in Loewald's thought—his conspicuous failure to relate his theory of primary narcissism to a theory of anxiety and defense.

The idea of the part object is essential to the theory of fetishism and to defenses against differentiation. The fourth chapter will begin with Abraham's introduction of the part object and his prescient description of narcissistic resistances to interpretation. Klein, at first Abraham's most important disciple, greatly expanded the understanding of the part object with her theory of depressive anxiety. As a conception of the anxiety intrinsic to reversal of splitting defenses, depressive anxiety can be applied to the theory of defenses against differentiation. Klein's theorizing is also a prime example of the replication of a defensively dedifferentiated sense of reality. Depressive anxiety has to be reconfigured so that it takes into account the role of dedifferentiated reality organizations in theory and practice. Winnicott's revision of the depressive position moves in just this direction and will be discussed in the last section of the chapter. His appreciative critique of Klein, his comprehension of the role of environment in the depressive position, and his conception of transitional space are all central to understanding defenses against differentiation. But Winnicott, too, has his own unquestioned view of reality, which has to be factored into his concept of environment.

All these analyses lead to a new theory of the anxiety intrinsic to differentiating processes. Such anxiety sustains primal defenses, which themselves produce resistance to interpretation. The last chapter will examine the theory of technique in this light. It will reconsider two basic tenets of interpretive technique—analyze from the surface, interpret defense before content. The general thesis is that the possibility of interpretation can be a differentiating trauma, which fetishistic or concrete patients defend against. Interpretation itself, then, can be linked to extreme anxieties and primal defenses. The point, however, is not that the interpretive stance has to be abandoned in favor of an experiential one where interpretation arouses intense anxiety. Rather, the understanding of interpretation in terms of repression, interpretation of meaning, has to be revised. The patients who specifically resist interpretation in fact demonstrate why interpretation is an essential function of the therapeutic environment, or frame.

This position implies that patients who defend against the possibility of interpretation have unconsciously registered it, have been made anxious by it, and defend against it. If interpretation is intrinsic to the analytic environment, then such patients demonstrate an unconscious registration of this environment, of reality. The idea of unconscious registration of reality has to change our conventional sense of reality as much as the theory of repression changed our conventional sense of mind. This is my most general theme.

CHAPTER I

Concreteness and Fetishism

THE CLINICAL PROBLEM:
EXAMPLES AND FIRST EXPLANATIONS

There is a troubling encounter that can occur within the traditional analytic setup. One reads about or works with a group of patients who seem to fall within the usual parameters for psychoanalytic treatment and who often seek it out but whose analyses do not seem to advance with interpretation. The literature on these patients contains a compelling fact: analysts of differing theoretical persuasions, who nevertheless hold interpretation to be the primary technique of analysis, find it necessary to develop new forms of intervention in order to resolve the patients' difficulties with interpretation itself. All the analysts who work with these patients find themselves having to reexamine the way they interpret.

Three vivid, but typical, examples illustrate this clinical dilemma.

1. A student analyst begins to work in supervision on a case that he has had in analysis, four times a week, on the couch, for years. He reports, however, that the patient is very frustrating, because she seems to reject almost all interpretive efforts to understand her. For example, the patient is late for an early-morning session, which she knows to be the first of her analyst's day. She begins the session by saying, "I know that you're mad at me for being late." The student analyst, thinking of recent sessions in which the patient had struggled with

defenses against anger, wonders whether her lateness could be related
to anger at him. The immediate interpretation is ill advised, more a
product of the his long-term frustration with the patient than anything else. However, the patient *has* been in analysis for a long time
and does not seem able even to consider the interpretation, which
was indeed tied to recent sessions. Instead she says that by thinking
she could be angry at him, the analyst is actually rejecting her. What
use is it to come to an analyst who rejects her? The analyst tries to
explain his reasoning, linking her fear of rejection to the previous
work on her fear of aggression. His thinking, of course, is that resolution of the transference resistances against aggression will be helpful
to the patient. The patient, however, lapses into silence and remains
silent for the rest of the session. In the next session, the analyst in-
quires about the patient's reactions to the protracted silence of the
preceding day. The patient says she is not interested. She brushes him
aside and goes on to speak of other issues. The student reports that
much of the patient's treatment proceeds in this way.

2. A patient was late for a session. When I went to the waiting
room, he was still hanging up his coat, with his back to me. I greeted
him and as usual ushered him into the consulting room. He was
clearly distressed at the beginning of the session. Like the student in
the first example, I of course assumed that his distress was related to
his lateness, but the patient said that this was not so. When I asked
what was wrong, he blurted out, "You didn't make eye contact with
me." The patient explained that he was upset that I had opened the
door to my office too quickly for him to hang up his coat and then
sit down so that I would greet him from his usual chair in the waiting room. I had deprived him of the eye contact that had initiated
each of his previous sessions. Without the eye contact, he said, he felt
so deprived that he did not think he could speak to me. Until that
moment, I had been unaware of the patient's gratification from the
waiting-room routine. Typically, I had all kinds of thoughts about the
possible sexual or aggressive meanings of the gratification. But like the
patient in the previous example, he was not interested in understanding the event. Either he had the eye contact or he did not. If not, then
there was no point in talking about something that he would not
have that day. This patient startled me some time later when he finally

explained why he was so often in the habit of playing with the plastic tissue box case next to the couch. This habit had eluded resolution through any efforts of my own to interpret his associations to it. It was simple, he finally said. The box was shiny enough to show a reflection, and when he held it at a certain angle he could see me behind him.

This patient had come specifically for analysis and had seemed to be doing reasonably well in the treatment, with nothing beyond the usual problems of character neurosis. I learned from these events that the patient had created certain conditions for being in analysis—receiving inevitable gratifications from my greeting him, being able to see me at will while on the couch—that were subtle enough to escape immediate detection but which actually vitiated the entire process. The patient finally made clear that the interpretive work I assumed I had been doing was enframed by actions that, from his point of view, were not to be interpreted.

3. Caper (1994), a contemporary Kleinian, gave a vivid description of a similar configuration. In her initial consultation, a patient described a feeling of always having to serve other people for whom she was never doing enough. Over the first two and a half years of treatment, the patient experienced similar reactions to her analyst. The patient seemed to "accept" interpretation of them "as 'transference' from past experiences with her mother" (p. 905), but the analyst noticed that such interpretations did not seem to change the patient's conviction that she was now obliged to make the analyst's work less demanding. Caper's eventual grasp of what was occurring in the sessions is consistent with the constellation I have been describing:

> despite her interpretation about her experience of me being a
> carry-over from the past, she still took it as an unquestionable
> *present* [author's emphasis] fact that I was exhausted. In this light,
> her attempts to lighten my burden were then the only possible
> way that she could hope to help me . . . she was not just confus-
> ing me with a past figure, or having a fantasy (in the ordinary
> sense of the word) about me in the present, but actually experi-
> encing me in the present as exhausted and overwhelmed by her.
> I now realized that what had been irritating me was that this

experience carried with it a sense of conviction so strong that it
seemed to admit literally no doubt, *rendering the interpretations I
made about it completely impotent: in so far as they did not support this
picture of me, she simply ignored them.* (p. 906; my emphasis)

Caper describes an intervention different from the usual kind,
which presumes that to make meaning conscious will modify defenses. He told the patient that her "certainty about my exhausted
state . . . was so fundamental and undoubted that it made serious consideration of any alternative impossible" (ibid.). The patient fell silent
and eventually said that the entire treatment *had* been governed by a
belief that was not affected by the *experience* of the analysis. Caper
writes that following this session, it "was as though the analysis itself
had suddenly emerged through a film into the real world: the patient
was in contact with how she made her internal objects *different* from
her external ones, and this enabled her to see the *difference* between
them and therefore to be in contact with her *real, external* analyst" (p.
906; my emphases). Caper quite pertinently states that the two and a
half years it had taken to help the patient establish contact with him
was a "blow to his therapeutic omnipotence." It made clear that "'being in analysis' was not in itself any guarantee of progress or development" (ibid.). One sees the obvious parallel with the patient who used
the reflecting tissue box to see me at will: the assumption that a normal analytic process was unfolding turned out to be unwarranted.

Again, we have an analyst who maintains the usual classical analytic
framework. He interprets according to Kleinian conceptions of unconscious processes but discovers that the very process of interpretation itself has been subtly but strenuously defended against. He finds
himself having to intervene in such a way that fantasy taken as un-
questionable fact can become questionable. In all the examples, knowledge, conviction, and illusion are central concerns: the first patient
knew that the analyst was angry at her for being late; the second was
fundamentally *convinced* that he had to have control over visual contact
in order to tolerate the analysis; and the third was using the analysis to
maintain an *illusion* from which she theoretically wanted relief.

Such patients are often called "concrete." In 1957, Edith Jacobson
described a group of patients who "treat their psychic strivings as if

they were concrete objects" (p. 80). They seek out analysis and seem to begin it satisfactorily—in contrast to the chaotic beginnings of other nonneurotic patients—but quickly show themselves resistant to the project of understanding themselves via interpretation. The analytic presupposition that troubling behaviors, thoughts, and fantasies have meanings other than their apparent ones—the basic presupposition of the theory based on repression—provokes prolonged defensive reactions in these patients. Surprisingly, however, this resistance does not seem to make them break off treatment. Rather, they can stay in analysis for a long time while fending off the analyst's interpretations. Typically, their analysts will attempt to interpret this very difficulty in terms of the transference—again, according to the basic presupposition that the patient's most powerful fantasies, defenses, and anxieties have to be reexperienced in the transference in order to be modified. But just as typically, when approached in this way such patients become dismissive, grow agitated, or, even worse, frankly admit that they are really coming to sessions for certain repetitive patterns of gratification. Many analysts come to feel distressed working with such patients. There seems to be an unbridgeable gap between the analyst's commitment to therapeutic change via understanding and the patients' refusal to consider such a question at all. Is it even justified to continue an analysis in such circumstances? Should one switch to a noninterpretive approach? A moment's reflection shows that if these patients could benefit from the experiential aspects of analysis, stressed by those who do not see interpretation as the major vehicle for psychic change, they would have done so. They are often treated by devoted analysts willing to struggle with this perplexing situation and their own possible countertransference contributions to it. Why, then, does one not see improvement based on a long-term regular relation with a devoted therapist, even if the therapist's interpretations are systematically rejected?

In rough terms, it is clear in every example that the patients take something that comes from inside (an affect, an idea, a memory, a fantasy) and treat it as an indisputable perception of something that comes from the outside. It is tempting to call this process "projection." However, projection creates a rigid boundary between inside and outside that affects reality testing as conventionally conceived. Interpretation of projection is fraught with danger because the patient can experience the analyst as an enemy attempting to disarm him or her. Concrete patients do something else. They seem to blur the boundary between inside and outside affectively, without losing at least an intellectual knowledge of it. This is why they appear to meet the usual criteria for psychoanalytic treatment. While they may certainly become resentful, angry, anxious, or overwhelmed if their boundary blurring is confronted prematurely, they do not experience the analyst as an enemy. Rather, they paradoxically want to stay in analysis on the condition that their boundary blurring *not* be modified. The problem is to explain a syndrome that has evident affective and cognitive components. Is there a defensive conflict at the root of concreteness? Should it be explained as a developmental disorder?

Jacobson's 1957 explanation of concreteness is multifaceted, drawing on developmental and defensive considerations, as well as dream theory. In essence, she argues that the conflation of reality and fantasy in concreteness depends upon the hypercathexis of perception that makes every dream a hallucinatory experience (p. 77). In waking life, too, one can deny an unpleasurable perception by replacing it with a pleasurable wish raised to almost hallucinatory, perceptible intensity. What makes it possible to do so is regression to a "'concretistic' infantile stage where the child, though already aware of the difference between the internal and external world, between the self and objects, still treats them both in the same manner" (p. 80). In analysis, interpretation becomes the equivalent of an unpleasurable perception. It can be denied *"en bloc"* (p. 81) by regression to the "concretistic" stage. This developmental-defensive mechanism would explain an apparent contradiction: such patients are aware of the difference between internal and external and yet do not let it count. The global rejection of the analyst's interpretations depends upon the ability to conflate one's wishful repudiation of them with a perceived reality.

There are other aspects of Jacobson's argument to which I will return. On the whole, her fine-grained argument about concreteness has not received the attention it deserves. Nonetheless, her developmental-defensive explanation sets the tone for other explanations of the same phenomenon. There is something evidently right about conceiving concreteness in terms of a conflation of fantasy and reality. Such conflations would seem to be derived from problems in the differentiation between self and object. The patients who both know that this differentiation exists and can act as if it does not seem to provide evidence for an intermediate phase between nondifferentiation and fully internalized differentiation, Jacobson's postulated "concretistic" stage.

Nearly thirty years later, Brown (1985) reached similar conclusions. He defined concreteness as the inability to lift oneself out of the immediacy of the moment, leading to a refusal to "take in" interpretations (p. 379). Brown elaborated a developmental explanation, also emphasizing cognitive and affective factors. Like Jacobson, he begins with the idea that in dreams "an actual perceptual event (hallucination) substitutes for obtaining the desired object through action in waking life" (p. 381). Brown emphasizes Freud's idea that hallucination as a substitute for gratification is inherently regressive. One way to understand concreteness is to generalize this tendency to substitute a "lower mode of experiencing an event for a higher mode" (ibid.). Because concreteness so dramatically affects communication between patient and analyst, Brown proposes a semiotic version of what Freud calls "topographical regression" in dreams:

semiotic concreteness describes a mode of functioning in which an abstract thought is replaced by the perceptual data to which it originally referred, resulting in confusion between the signifier and the signified. . . . In the primary process the word and its perceptual identity are equivalent (semiotically concrete), whereas the secondary process implies a distance or separation between the word and its perceptual identity. (p. 382)

Like Jacobson, Brown understands semiotic concreteness in terms of ego boundaries. It depends upon "an interpersonal mode in which the usual boundaries between self and object are either vague, absent, or obliterated" (ibid.). Since the separation of signified and signifier implies toleration of the space between them, concreteness most generally derives from problems related to the "gradual separation of the self and nonself" (p. 399). The painful affects warded off by blurring the boundaries between self and nonself are potentially repeated in the transference. Patients who are usually intelligent can appear "to be dense and thick-headed, unable to understand the clinician's interventions" (p. 383).

Brown gives an example of a patient who appeared to understand quite well the relation between her current interpersonal problems and her past reactions to her father's remarriage after her mother's death. But when the analyst announced an upcoming week's vacation, the patient grew scattered. The analyst interpreted her anxiety about the separation, but his words had no meaning to her. Brown comments that his interpretation presumed that the patient could think abstractly, when she was actually in a state of semiotic concreteness. It was only when Brown said that his impending absence was experienced as "a removal of something that held her together and that her mind was now experienced to be as useless as I was to her" (p. 395) that the patient was gradually able to return to her more usual mode of functioning. Brown integrates Piaget's theory of maturation of cognition with Mahler's theory of separation-individuation, Klein's transition from the paranoid-schizoid to the depressive position, and Winnicott's idea of transitional space to explain semiotic concreteness.[1] Like Jacobson, he postulates a specific stage of development at which the child cognitively registers its separation from mother but affectively rejects boundary formation (p. 392).

Frosch (1995) combines Freudian theory with similar cognitive-developmental considerations to understand his perplexing experience with an apparently analyzable patient. The patient seemed to be quite involved in her analysis, although Frosch was typically troubled by his inability to interpret certain "intransigent" configurations effectively. Over time and apparently as usual, the patient grew increasingly aware of erotic feelings during sessions. However, as sexual excitement during sessions intensified, the patient panicked. She said she was convinced that if she spoke of her fantasies, the analyst would become as excited by them as she was. Unable to control himself, he would behave abusively, and she would then have to stop the analysis. Since she did not want to stop, she could not talk about her fantasies. She said she knew that the analyst was ethical and would never really abuse her. She also understood that the analyst would want her to talk about these fantasies and her fear of his sexual abuse in order to understand the transference. Despite this, she could not change her conviction that to talk about her fantasies was to threaten her analysis. Like Caper's and Brown's patients, Frosch's patient sometimes grasps the ideas of transference and interpretation but powerfully conveys that, to continue her treatment, she must operate from within a frame of reference different from the analyst's.

Frosch begins to articulate the patient's frame of reference in terms of the problem of symbolism and interpretation. He understands his patient's conviction of his inability to control himself should she speak of her sexual fantasies as a "preconceptual organization of emotion." The organization is preconceptual because it "does not endow a piece of reality with some secret meaning that could appropriately be called symbolic" (p. 438). Instead, when a person has difficulty moving between psychic and material reality, he or she must create "belief structures" that define what is experienced as "real and as not real." However, these "belief structures" accommodate the difficulty in distinguishing between inner and outer reality.

Like Brown, Frosch applies Piaget's understanding of the difference between the preconceptual and representational organizations of the child's mind to understand resistance to interpretation. For the preconceptual child, "things are as they appear to be at any given moment; three year olds shown a white stimulus that is then put behind a blue filter cannot correctly distinguish between the object's real and apparent color" (p. 426). Thus, as Frosch's patient became entrenched in her conviction that she had to control her sexual excitement and fantasies in order not to threaten her treatment, she came to see the analyst through the "filter" of their joint success in exercising this control. Frosch reports that if he said something that appeared to his patient not in line with this project, she would wonder how she could let herself be involved with a person who was as deficient as she, like the late patient who wonders why she comes to an analyst who rejects her. Frosch quotes his patient as saying, "'You're a jerk, just like me. That feels real. Don't tell me it's transference . . .'" (p. 441). He understands such "belief structures" to be organized according to the "preconceptual" formula that whatever provokes an intense feeling in the moment must be so (p. 443). Such intense conviction is actually "an integral part of pathological compromise formations which ward off the expectation of intolerable

emotion. . . . The person lives in a world that can be tolerated emotionally, but little or no maturation or *differentiation* occurs in the areas affected by these compromise formations. This is particularly clear
in the transference" (ibid.; my emphasis). I have emphasized "differentiation" to link Frosch's most general sense of the problem to Caper's. Frosch also contends that the analysis could not become "real"
until the patient became aware of the "difference" between her "internal" and "external" objects. In Freudian terms, Frosch says, one can
understand the patient's active dismissal of the difference between her
"picture" of the analyst and her knowledge of his ethical neutrality as
disavowal of reality together with hypercathexis of fantasy. Such a
process creates a "fantasy construction that is *not symbolic* in the usual
sense" (p. 437; my emphasis).

Frosch has articulated what will be my major focus—the disavowal
of reality and the creation of nonsymbolic forms of psychopathology.
Jacobson, in her 1957 paper, had already said that the patients who
treat "their psychic strivings as if they were concrete objects perceived" (p. 80) employ the defenses of disavowal and ego splitting
which Freud introduced to understand fetishism. In a similar vein, in
"Use of the Analyst as a Fetish" (1992) Renik gives a detailed example of a patient who seeks out traditional analysis after several previous analytic treatments. It soon became evident that the patient was
seeking out analysis again because she derived direct gratification from
actually being in the room with the analyst. The patient had no wish
to understand this configuration, as in all the examples so far.

Like Frosch, Renik draws on an understanding of how disavowal
permits a persistent conflation of reality and fantasy, such that the patient's seeming awareness of reality has no impact upon the living out
of a fantasy. Renik writes: "One way to understand the problem of
persistent unrealistic expectations in analysis is to conceptualize the
crucial issue in terms of the kind of thinking the patient applies to
a fantasy he or she enacts at length within the treatment relationship . . . " (p. 543). This "kind of thinking" is the "specific cognitive
mode" (p. 544) Freud described in his analysis of fetishism, where disavowal permits the maintenance of two contradictory ideas without
the one's influencing the other. Renik sees the fetishistic mode as neither neurotic nor psychotic. Rather, it is "an intermediate form of

thinking" (p. 547) that permits "an unusual degree of conviction about the reality of a reassuring idea" (p. 545). The conviction derives from the conflation of fantasy with the actual physical presence of the analyst, just as the fetishist is assured of potency if his or her chosen object is present. Renik, like Frosch and like Jacobson before both of them, gives strong reasons for returning to Freud's conception of fetishism in order to understand concrete patients.

At first glance it could appear that the overall theory and technique elaborated by Freud would have little to say about the dynamics of the concrete patient. He was famously dismissive about patients who "are accessible only to 'the logic of soup, with dumplings for arguments'" (1915b, p. 167). The entire edifice built on the original theory of neurosis and dreams, with repression as its cornerstone, assumes that psychopathology has a symbolic, interpretable structure. One finds variations of Frosch's statement that such patients do not "endow a piece of reality with some secret meaning that could appropriately be called symbolic" in all the literature on them. Jacobson and Brown independently reached the same conclusion to explain this phenomenon: concrete patients use topographical regression, the basic dream mechanism of hallucinatory satisfaction of wishes, in waking life. To be transiently or persistently concrete is to impose some sort of wish fulfillment upon external reality, as was the case in all the clinical examples.

Is the use of this dream mechanism in waking life the result of regression to a "concretistic" stage between nonseparation and separation? Is it primarily a developmental, affective-cognitive problem? Or is the use of dream mechanisms in waking life a compromise formation due to conflict? If concreteness, like fetishism, depends upon the defense of disavowal, what does disavowal defend against? To answer such questions one has to return to Freud's early idea of hallucinatory wish fulfillment to see if it illuminates his late thinking about fetishism and disavowal. Freud's very early theory explains wish fulfillment and defense in terms of primary process repudiation of real trauma. His late theory of fetishism reopens the entire topic of defense against reality. A return to Freud's early and late theories sheds new light on what reality is for the patients who defend against interpretation.

FROM WISHES AND PRIMARY DEFENSE
TO FETISHISM AND DISAVOWAL

In the *Project for a Scientific Psychology*, Freud first defines primary process as the wishful, hallucinatory revival of the memory of a previous satisfaction (1895a, pp. 319, 326–27). Hallucinatory recall of memories of previous satisfaction is a perceptual experience. Thus, it is like the experience of dreams, which Freud already understood as wish fulfillments (pp. 335–40), a good five years before *The Interpretation of Dreams*. Freud is quite aware of the problem built into his conception: without some inhibition of the primary process, there is no way to distinguish between the perceptual experience of hallucinatory recall and the reality of the external world. His answer is that the ego's secondary process carries out this inhibiting function (p. 327). We already find here the bases for a theory of psychic reality, real because it is perceived in dreams and hallucinations and yet unreal because it can eliminate the reality of the external world if left unchecked.

What is so important for the rest of the theory is that Freud conceives what he calls "primary wishful attraction" at the origin of defense. This aspect of Freud's early thinking is often lost today, but it will be indispensable for a dynamic explanation of concreteness. The basic principle is that wishes primarily replace pain with images of gratification, and defenses prevent energic investment in painful experience itself: "The wishful state results in a positive *attraction* towards the object wished for, or more precisely towards its mnemic image; the experience of pain leads to a repulsion, a disinclination to keeping the hostile mnemic image cathected. Here we have primary *wishful attraction* and primary *defence*" (p. 322). This theory shows clearly why Freud defined primary process in terms of the pleasure-unpleasure principle: wishes replace unpleasure with pleasure; defenses are the attempts to eliminate the registration of unpleasure per se. Thus, there is a basic conflict between the primary and secondary processes. The primary wishful-defensive process tends toward inertia (p. 312). It attempts to eliminate whatever is dissonant, painful, or traumatic. The secondary process inhibits this functioning, allowing energic investment in the dissonant reality.

The basic principle of psychopathology—primary wish and defense complement each other to eliminate the traumatic—also produces the theory of a mental apparatus that inevitably resists knowledge of the painful or dissonant. When Freud calls "primary defense" the "first biological rule" (pp. 370–71), he wants to situate the pathological processes at the juncture of mind and body because they seem to occur autonomously. (Perhaps this is why he stated during this period that defense was a problem from "the core of nature.") Certainly, such processes are framed in terms of a particular conception of mental energy: a tendency to inertia is given a "biological" cast. There are many more questions raised than answered by such a conception, which in fact plays a problematic role in all of Freud's theorizing. However, the original formulation does attempt to explain two major aspects of psychopathology. First, the hallucinatory perception of wishes can defensively substitute for the perception of whatever raises tension. Second, wish and defense working together produce considerable mental inertia. Therapeutically, this inertia has to be overcome if the secondary process is to perform its function of distinguishing between internal hallucinatory recall and external perception. Only then will the ego carry out its secondary process activity of including the traumatic within itself. The profound idea that informs Freud's original conception of mind and psychopathology is that unconscious memory can substitute for external perception in the interest of defending against undue tension. This point is crucial. It explains that unwelcome tension-raising knowledge can be treated as traumatic and can be warded off by primary wish fulfillment and primary defense.

At the end of *The Interpretation of Dreams*, Freud refines his initial conception of wish fulfillment. He evokes the familiar model of the hungry baby who links memories of previous satisfactions with the need to relieve current tension. The proto-wish is the hallucinatory revival of the memory of the breast in an attempt to alleviate hunger without waiting (1900, pp. 542–44). Two very important complementary aspects of wish fulfillment are stressed here: temporal immediacy and perceptual identity. Throughout the book on dreams Freud stressed that wishes have only one temporal mode, the present. Here he explains the "nowness" of wish fulfillment and the primary process in terms of the attempt to relieve tension immediately. Although there is no longer a discussion of what was called "primary defense" in the *Project*, the idea is implicit. The hypothetical infant attempts to relieve tension by substituting visualization for relief. By that very act, the infant attempts not to attend to its own distress in the moment. For the same reason, Freud also emphasizes that the wish creates what he calls a perceptual identity with the memory of the tension-relieving object. The hallucinatory nature of wish fulfillment—the fact that dreams are perceptual experiences that excite the visual apparatus in the same way as any other visual experience —allows dreams a positive discharge function and a negative defensive function that is convincing.

Opatow (1997), discussing the positive discharge function of wishes, similarly emphasizes that the dream is a conscious lived experience that activates the memory of an object that is "seemingly present" and thus convincing. There is no dream without an implicit "affirmation" of what Opatow calls "an illusory truth," that is, that the distinction between "perception and memory" can be overcome. According to the model of the *Project*, this distinction itself depends upon the inhibiting secondary process of the ego. For the dreamer, who exemplifies the universal potential for psychopathology, seeing is believing. To see now even the manifestly distorted image of an object perceptually identified with satisfaction can potentially discharge the disturbance of increased tension.

There is an important echo of the link between the positive function of wish fulfillment (the replacement of tension with an image of satisfaction) and its negative, defensive function in Freud's "A Metapsychological Supplement to the Theory of Dreams" (1917). He again takes up the question first raised in the *Project*, "the great practical importance of distinguishing perceptions from ideas, however intensely recalled. Our whole relation to the external world, to reality, depends on our ability to do so" (1917, p. 231). The intrinsic paradoxes of his theory of mind are that hallucinatory wish fulfillment "consists in a cathexis of the system *Cs. (Pcpt.)*, which however, is not effected—as normally—from without, but from within," and that "a necessary condition for the occurrence of hallucination is that regression shall be carried far enough to reach this system itself and in so doing *be able to pass over reality testing*" (p. 232; my emphasis). In other words, dreams reveal that there are certain organizations of what appear to be the sine qua non of reality testing—consciousness and perception—which eliminate reality testing. At this point Freud has a thought about this regressive cathexis of consciousness, which he puts in a footnote: "I may add by way of supplement that any attempt to explain hallucination would have to start out from *negative* rather than positive hallucination" (ibid., p. 232, n. 3).

Freud is once again thinking about the negative, defensive function implicit in every positive wish fulfillment. Essentially, he is reformulating the early notion of primary defense as the complement of wish fulfillment. As the explanation of positive hallucination, negative hallucination in fact has two functions: it prevents investment in whatever raises tension (for example, hunger), but it would also have to eliminate the distinction between perception and memory so that one is convinced by the apparent reality of the positive hallucination in every dream. Negative hallucination makes possible Opatow's point: every dream confirms the illusion that the distinction between memory and perception can be overcome. Without such a mechanism, there would be no explanation of the apparent paradox that in dreams consciousness is aroused but reality testing is unquestioningly suspended. In dreams, then, perception is used in the service of both negative and positive hallucination.

To return to the problem of concreteness, negative hallucination would also explain the dreamlike, regressive cathexis of perception described by Brown and Jacobson. The analyst's interpretations are treated as tensions that can be eliminated by negative hallucination—denial "*en bloc*," as Jacobson calls it. Simultaneously, the distinction between perception and memory is overcome in consciousness. As a result, something that is strictly speaking a memory of something from within (an affect, an idea, a wish, a fantasy) is taken as a perception coming from without. Concreteness, then, to employ Freud's early reasoning, would be a way of overcoming secondary process by substituting for it the dream mechanisms of perceptual identity and temporal immediacy. The intense resistance to modification of concreteness is a result of the domination of consciousness by primary process, with its tendency to inertia. The therapeutic task of overcoming this inertia would have to be directed at the global use of negative hallucination, the basis for this dreamlike state of consciousness.

There is, however, an obvious question. Why would the analyst's interpretations be experienced as something one would have to defend against? What is the nature of the anxiety that leads to the global use of negative hallucination? To begin to answer such questions, we must reconsider Freud's late theory of anxiety itself. In the late revision (1926), Freud famously reverses his long-held conviction that anxiety is an aftereffect of repression. Until this point the neurotic was understood to be anxious about a previously repressed wish. Anxiety is now reconfigured as a signal. A forbidden but pressing wish can take the ego into a dangerous situation, for example, the threat of punishment. As a signal of impending danger, anxiety initiates repression, which is an attempt to "flee" a danger of internal origin. It is often forgotten that this rethinking of anxiety depends upon a return to some of the earliest thinking about tension regulation. Freud defines the original danger situation as one of helplessness in the face of "growing tension due to need. . . . When the infant has found out by experience that an external, *perceptible* object can put an end to the dangerous situation . . . the content of the danger it fears is displaced from the economic situation on to the condition which determined that situation, viz., the loss of the object . . . " (1926, pp. 137–38; my emphasis).

As in the dream theory, Freud again shows how perception can be used to relieve tension. Now, however, perception of possible loss is the prototype of the transition from panic (overwhelming tension) to signal anxiety. Freud does not specifically compare the role of perception in signal anxiety to the role of perception in dreams. Nonetheless, he has given us another insight into a paradoxical function of consciousness. Not only does seeing a dream convince one that tension has been relieved during sleep, to see an external object identified with relief convinces the waking baby that all is well. Not to see it signals that the baby could be overwhelmed by tension.[2] This may often be so from the baby's point of view. However, it creates the possibility that we may continue to be convinced that perception of an external object can relieve tension and that nonperception of it is a signal of distress.

Perception in the moment can create not only convincing illusions of relief, as in wish fulfillment, but of danger as well. Signal anxiety displaces the basic danger situation from the economic one of being overwhelmed by tension to the fear of the absence of the relieving object. Thus, it is an important form of tension regulation. One can begin to understand just this kind of defensive use of signal anxiety in concreteness. Each patient insisted on the reality of his or her perception, while warding off the analyst's interpretations. One can hypothesize that the analyst's interpretations are experienced as a dissonant or traumatic reality. The tension created in this situation is close to panic, to the primal anxiety of being overwhelmed. This anxiety can be defensively regulated by being displaced onto illusions of danger or relief. In other words, the patient's insistence on the reality of his or her perception creates the illusion of relief, while the questioning of the perception creates the illusion of danger. For example, the patient who "knew" that the analyst was mad at her for being late is paradoxically relieved by her perception, which preempts any interpretation. The tension provoked by the possibility of interpretation is eliminated by the two functions of negative hallucination: the attempt to eliminate registration of the tension altogether and the suspension of the distinction between perception and memory.

However, this entire process would not occur if the threat of the tension tied to interpretation had not been registered. As a compromise formation, rather than as a developmental disorder, concreteness would be a defensive warding off of the registered reality of interpretation. Freud's revision of the theory of anxiety in fact had led him to reconsider what he called the "loss of reality" in all compromise formations (1924a, pp. 186–87). In psychosis there is defense against a piece of external reality. Hallucinations or delusions substitute for the lost reality. In neurosis the symptom is the substitute for the lost internal realities of wish and anxiety. This is why Freud now says that in both neurosis and psychosis there is always a substitute for the reality lost to defense. The crucial point is that there is always some loss of a registered reality in any substitute formation. If the external or internal reality had not been registered, it would not have led to conflict.

Fetishism led Freud to new ideas about apparent loss of registered reality. As is well known, he understood the fetish as a substitute for the missing maternal phallus. According to the familiar logic of the castration complex, the little boy becomes anxious about the mother's lack of a penis when he links it to fantasies of the penis' having been removed. One possible outcome is a compromise between what Freud calls the boy's "unwelcome perception" of the absence of the penis and "the force of his counter-wish" to see the missing penis in order to assuage his castration anxiety (1927b, p. 154). Thus, the fetish, the concrete, visible thing that has to be perceived in order for the man to be potent. Freud does not say so, but this analysis is an extension of the theory that all is potentially well for the baby who sees the mother. For the man with a powerful fantasy that the penis could be separated from the body, all is well if he can see a replacement for it in a sexual situation. The fetish can be understood in relation to the basic principles of signal anxiety. Perception of the presence of the object is conflated with relief from anxiety, because of belief in the danger of the absence of the object. But this analysis is not exactly the same as Freud's. Its implication is that the dangerous absence of the relieving object—that is, castration anxiety—has a regulatory, defensive function. It would counter a registered possibility of overwhelming tension. How would this work in fetishism?

In a later discussion Freud points out that the fetish is a "compromise formed with the help of displacement, such as we have been familiar with in dreams" (1940a, p. 203). The dream is the hallucinatorily real, if defensively distorted, perception of wishful fantasy; analogously, the real perception of the fetish as a form of convincing reassurance implies that the fetish has fantasy content attached to it.[3] The fetishist, like the dreamer, creates a perceptual identity between tension relief and the memory of fantasy: there is a straight theoretical line from the original hallucination of the breast to the fetishist's having to perceive the objectified equivalent of the maternal phallus. The fetishist, unlike the dreamer, of course, creates a perceptual identity between an actual object and fantasy in waking life, just as the baby conflates absence and presence of the mother with danger and reassurance. If dreams did not awaken consciousness through their stimulation of the visual apparatus, then something like fetishism— the conviction that the presence of a certain object eliminates the danger—would not be possible. Something like fetishism also would not be possible unless the fetishist were employing a mechanism akin to negative hallucination, which makes every hallucinatory wish fulfillment seem real. In other words, the fetishist uses perception in the paradoxical way Freud outlined in the idea of a regressive cathexis of consciousness. Once the distinction between perception and memory is eliminated via negative hallucination, the fetishist can use perception in waking life the same way the dreamer does. He or she attempts to gain relief in two ways: first, via the initial negative hallucination of the distinction between memory and perception, so that perception of fantasy can eliminate tension; and second, via the positive perception of a concrete, relieving object actually conflated with fantasy. This is the same process that creates concreteness through the use of dream mechanisms in waking life.

The comparison of fetishism to dreams is illuminating in another way. The baby attempts to eliminate real, registered tension of hunger via the hallucinatory revival of the experience of satisfaction. What real, registered tension does the fetishist attempt to eliminate? Although he does not ask this question specifically, Freud implicitly takes it up but in a confused way. His idea is that extreme castration anxiety cannot be totally relieved by a wish-fulfilling perception, just as the tension of hunger finally cannot really be relieved by hallucination. The fetishist's insistence that the fantasy-endowed thing be there, present, and visible, what can be called his "concreteness," reveals that he is always anxious that the woman *is* castrated. The fetishist actually has what Freud calls a "divided attitude . . . to the question of the castration of women" (1927b, p. 156) and constantly oscillates between the belief that the woman is castrated and not castrated. This "divided attitude" and oscillation are the specific result of the defense mechanism Freud calls "disavowal." Disavowal is newly understood to create a split in the ego, such that the ego both acknowledges a piece of reality and rejects it and then oscillates between the two states.[4]

Conceptually, a mechanism like disavowal is intrinsic to the idea that defensive substitutes are created to avoid a registered reality. While the operation of defense always implies an attempt to convince oneself that something disturbing has not been registered, the defense itself always implies that the disturbance has been registered. In the same way, negative hallucination accounts for the process of repudiation of something registered; positive hallucination accounts for the replacement of what has been registered by fantasy. Since consciousness is involved, one can then accurately compare the fetishist's waking sexual experience to the dreamer's sleeping experience. In both, consciousness and perception produce a reality effect that actually eliminates reality testing.

Despite the depth of understanding gained from Freud's description of disavowal and ego splitting, one also has to attend to a major inconsistency within it. Disavowal allegedly creates a split in the ego such that one side acknowledges and one side rejects what Freud calls reality. The fetishist's oscillation between the woman's castration and noncastration, however, is an oscillation between two fantasies. *Perceived castration is a fantasy*. It would be very simple to chalk up Freud's unnoticed inconsistency here to his own confusion about reality and fantasy as concerns the "castration" of women. The oxymoron "fact of castration" runs throughout his late reconsideration of female sexuality (for example, "Some Psychical Consequences of the Anatomical Distinction Between the Sexes" [1925], "Female Sexuality" [1931], "Femininity" [1933]) and has given rise to decades of criticism from inside and outside psychoanalysis. This psychobiographical explanation has its own validity, but it does not sufficiently take into account some of the further elaborations of disavowal and ego splitting in relation to psychopathology and wishful substitute formation in general.

In terms of the theory of anxiety, Freud has understandably conflated the absence of the perceivable fetishistic object with the absence of the mother. Both signal danger and inevitably reinforce the conviction that to see the potentially absent object is to relieve tension. In terms of fetishism, this still leaves one wondering about a splitting of the ego such that reality is both registered and repudiated. We understand that the baby is still in the realm of illusion if it conflates a momentary perception of the mother's absence with the possibility of being overwhelmed by tension, but we easily grasp the basis of this fantasy. This is not so readily the case in later development. What is the repudiated reality, if the perception of absence the fetishist fears—castration—is a fantasy? How does one explain the obviously valid clinical finding that, as Freud says, the fetishist oscillates between the ideas that the woman can be castrated or not castrated? On this level, the fetishist does seem to treat castration as an unbearable fact.

In his paper on fetishism, Freud describes what he calls a "very subtle" instance. He speaks of a patient whose fetish was an athletic support belt that signified that both men and women could be castrated or not castrated because it "covered up the genitals entirely and concealed the distinction [*Unterschied* (1927a, p. 316)] between them" (1927b, p. 156). In this particular example, castration and noncastration are both clearly fantasies. This "very subtle" instance can actually be generalized in a way that makes Freud's analysis of fetishism and disavowal more consistent: the reality the fetishist disavows is the reality of sexual difference. Sexual difference is the dissonant reality whose registration would provoke something like panic, near traumatic levels of anxiety. The fetishist's visible oscillation between the absence and presence of the phallic substitute has been preceded by a much less visible registration and repudiation of difference. Here one can accurately say that via disavowal there is an oscillation between reality and fantasy: sexual difference is replaced with the fantasy of phallic monism. Within the fantasy of phallic monism castration is a perceived "fact." As a result of this initial process, there is subsequent oscillation between the two positions implicit in phallic monism— castrated, not castrated. The two positions intrinsic to phallic monism, therefore, function as perceptual, wishful-defensive substitutes (Bass 1991). They use the relieving-presence/dangerous-absence structure of signal anxiety to keep a more overwhelming anxiety at bay.

Freud, then, did not distinguish between a primary split in the ego produced by disavowal—registration of difference, its replacement by wish fulfillment altogether—and a secondary split between two fantasies that substitute for the differentiation lost to defense. Part of the problem is that the primary split has to do with a process of registration and repudiation, while the secondary split is more concerned with the subsequent fate of fantasy content. Such primary splits, as in Freud's "very subtle" instance, always use perception in a wishful, quasi-hallucinatory way to substitute for a differentiation that has become too anxiety provoking. In fetishism per se, the oscillation between two convincingly "real" possibilities—either I see "it" or I don't

—affirms an illusion, that is, that the concrete presence or absence of the phallic substitute determines the level of anxiety. To explain the dynamics that permit the use of perception to conflate reality with fantasy, one also has to include the process that suspends reality testing, precisely the function of negative hallucination.

Primary disavowal describes the way in which negative hallucination makes the apparent, illusory repudiation of registered sexual difference seem real. Once the suspension of the difference between perception and memory has taken place within consciousness, the presence of the fantasy-endowed concrete object determines whether the fetishist can feel enough relief from anxiety to be potent or whether the absence of the object causes increased anxiety. Neither possibility shakes the fetishist's conviction that the fantasy of phallic monism—the thing is either there or not there—has replaced sexual difference. Therefore, the structure of fetishism is more complicated than in Freud's description. There are two levels of oscillation. The clinically apparent, conscious oscillation between the possibility of the woman's "real" castration or noncastration substitutes for the unconscious process of oscillation between registered difference repudiated by fantasy altogether.

CONCRETENESS AND THE DISAVOWAL
OF DIFFERENCE

Concreteness in general is a result of the process that produces the primary split, the split between any differentiation that has become too anxiety provoking and the defensive use of hallucinatory wish fulfillment to substitute for it altogether. This is the level at which one finds the oscillation between registration and repudiation of reality. This is also the level at which negative hallucination first has to suspend the difference between perception and memory, so that the apparent reality of the perception of fantasy can be maintained.

The emphasis on differentiation per se, however, requires further explanation. We have seen two major instances of defense against differentiation: the elimination of the difference between perception and memory through negative hallucination and the "very subtle" example of the fetishist who eliminates sexual difference through the fantasy of phallic monism. Are these examples intrinsically linked? A complete answer to this question will be elaborated in all subsequent chapters. One can begin to understand defense against differentiation by looking at Freud's ideas about difference as hostile and threatening and difference as traumatic tension. In "The Taboo of Virginity" (1918b), he introduced his famous phrase, "the narcissism of minor differences" (p. 199). The model for "the narcissism of minor difference" is related to the problem of fetishism: the "primitive" dread of woman "based on the fact that woman is different from man" (p. 196). Freud comments: "it is precisely the minor differences in people who are otherwise alike that form the basis of feelings of strangeness and hostility between them" (p. 199). Sexual difference, then, becomes the model of a narcissistic threat. If the psychic apparatus inherently resists registration of dissonant realities, then the inherent strangeness of sexual difference will always tend to be repudiated.[5] Two years later, Freud links differentiation to raised tension in *Beyond the Pleasure Principle* (1920). There he defines Eros as the tension-raising introduction of "vital differences" into the psyche. He uses an analogy to processes within unicellular organisms to define the basic psychic conflict between the tension-raising introduction of differences and the tension-lowering tendency to inertia (p. 55).

The "vital" but strange, threatening, and tension-raising qualities of differentiation make it potentially overwhelming. It can provoke levels of anxiety close to, but not quite the same as, the fear of being overwhelmed by need. As Freud makes clear in the revised theory of anxiety, the basic response to undue tension is to conflate the presence of a perceptible object with relief and the absence of the object with danger. As in fetishism, this can create a rigid structure of oscillation between two fantasies. However, both possibilities prevent internalization of the repudiated differentiation. Unconsciously, the repudiated difference then becomes the greatest danger of all, because it would unbalance the primary process inertia gained by replacing it with the structure of opposed fantasies.[6] It comes to represent the threat of destabilizing tension, strangeness, and loss of narcissistic equilibrium. The tendency to inertia of primary process described in the *Project* (primary wish fulfillment and defense) can be integrated with the tendency to inertia and dedifferentiation of the death drive. Secondary process is the overcoming of this inertia, the tension-raising internalization of differentiation—Eros.[7]

Clinically then, the concrete patient uses the temporal immediacy of perceptual identity to convince himself or herself that the tension of differentiation can be eliminated on a moment-to-moment basis. To make intrapsychic conflict into a "concrete object perceived" (Jacobson) requires a compromise between differentiation, on the one hand, and primary wish fulfillment and defense, on the other; or between the elimination of difference via negative hallucination and its replacement with the positive hallucination of the presence or absence of the relieving object. This is why the late patient in the first example so tenaciously clings to her "knowledge" that the analyst is angry at her. She defensively maintains a perceptual identity between her internal and external pictures of the analyst, starting in the "now" of her encounter with him. She thereby creates a rigid fetishistic structure: I have to "see" your anger "now"; if I do not, what I am convinced I need to see will not be there, and I will be anxious about its absence. Although fetishism itself is related to conflicts about sexual differentiation, concreteness can result from conflicts over differentiation at any level of development. Despite its apparent "primitiveness," concreteness is not necessarily tied to primitive conflicts nor only to problems of separation. Rather, for the concrete patient, separation itself becomes something like a "fact of castration." It is the illusion (taken as perceptual reality) of separation as disastrous absence. (Recall Brown's patient who concretely made her mind stop functioning when he announced a week's vacation.) Such illusions are explicable in terms of a revised understanding of primary disavowal. Primary disavowal is an ongoing process of using the basic properties of wishes—temporal immediacy and perceptual identity, negative and positive hallucination—to repudiate unconsciously registered differentiation.

The word "process" is essential here. In his last discussion of disavowal, Freud began to discuss "the splitting of the ego in the *process* of defense" (1940b). (He had already used the term "defensive process" to describe the response to anxiety in 1926.) He now overtly says that this thinking goes back to his earliest ideas but is also "new and puzzling." There are several reasons for the novelty and the puzzle, one of them being the concept of "process" itself. Process is less apparently visible than content. When the student analyst of the late patient speaks of how frustrating his patient is, he knows that something is amiss but cannot quite articulate what it is. The problem is not at the level of content and yet seems to be going on all the time. Clinically, one is always impressed by the tenacity of concreteness, by the typical way in which concrete patients will stay in treatment but not be able to use the analyst's interpretations. Theoretically, even a hallucinating baby can stop generating fantasy once its tension is relieved by feeding. As a defense, concreteness makes it clear that there is no such possible relief from the tension of differentiation. Every new moment renews the threat for the simple reason that time itself implies possible change. Thus, the fetishist for Freud and the concrete patient in general lead one to think about the process of defense directed against what can be called the processive aspects of reality. Such processes produce real effects but are not perceivable. The most salient example is time. Time, again, is intrinsic to all change, to all differentiation. The idea that wish fulfillment implies perceptual identity is so important because it allows one to understand that by using negative hallucination to conflate reality and fantasy in the "now" of perception, wish fulfillment can be used defensively to ward off the process of differentiation over time.[8]

As many contemporary authors have pointed out, most prominently among them Gray (1994), defensive process itself is more difficult to perceive than fantasy content.[9] Defenses work silently and invisibly, to use Anna Freud's memorable phrase (p. 8). The silent and invisible way in which hallucinatory wish fulfillment can defend against equally silent and invisible differentiating processes means that the analyst has to understand concreteness in terms of two not readily perceivable processes. The entire problem is situated at the level of a regressive, defensive cathexis of consciousness and perception themselves. This is why clinical technique is so difficult with concrete patients. What looks like an insistently "primitive" kind of thinking is actually the result of complicated interactions between the process of differentiation and the processive use of wish fulfillment as primary defense. To be effective, interventions have to be geared to such processes. Hypothetically, one might address the late patient's anxiety over differentiation by wondering with her whether she gains some relief from "knowing" that the analyst is angry at her. With this kind of intervention the analyst conveys an understanding of how crucial it feels to the patient to maintain the inertia of her rigid oppositional structure, because the unconscious alternative to it is the threat of de-stabilizing tension. Or one might address the defensive conflation of perception and fantasy by wondering whether she uses her thoughts in such a way as to make the analyst part of them. Here one would begin to address the anxiety over differentiation in the transference. The analyst's questioning attitude is important. It implies a processive investigation of wish fulfillment operating in the moment, not an interpretation of meaning in a symbolically structured situation. (McLaughlin [1991] and Smith [1993] make similar recommendations about the technical approach to enactments.)

Perhaps the greatest technical difficulty of such work is the general necessity of thinking in terms of process rather than content. The model of mind and psychopathology centered on repression prejudices the analyst in favor of meaning. One's working assumption is that everything the patient says is meaningful, even if in a defensively distorted way. Analysts are quite comfortable discerning the rich variations in meaning in the content of the fantasy material. The meaningful compromise formations produced by repression show wish and defense in conflict with each other, producing symbolic structures. Symbolic, content interpretations specifically address such conflicts. They can have the desired liberating effect as long as they are integrated with an understanding of anxiety and resistance.

The possibility of distorted but meaningful compromise formation implies enough distinction between perception and memory for one thing to mean another: what I perceive now may be significant because it indirectly expresses my past. Consciousness cannot be entirely dominated by negative hallucination when wish and defense are in conflict.[10] But in the compromise formations produced by primary disavowal, wish and defense work together against the tension of differentiation. There is an ongoing attempt to eliminate the distinction between perception and memory in the "now" of perceptual identity. Symbolic, content interpretations do not address the subtle, ongoing processes that maintain the inertia of the concrete compromise. They bypass the defensive maintenance of a state of consciousness in which meaning, differentiation, and reality testing are replaced by illusions of relief or danger. In such illusions the absence or presence of fantasy-laden perceptions is all. Therefore, in order to reach the patient on this regressed yet acutely conscious level, the analyst must become comfortable with intervening in terms of the process that actively works to prevent meaning.

When the patient says, "I know that you're mad at me for being late," the temptation is to attend to the content in the second half of her statement. One then would think about the possible meanings, especially transference meanings, of her fantasy of the analyst's anger at her for being late. To do so, however, would be to ignore the negative hallucination that dominates her consciousness when she says "I know. . . . " Her "knowledge" expresses her compelling defensive need to make sure that whatever fantasy she imposes upon the analyst can be taken as a reality in a way that brooks no alternative, no difference in apparent meaning. If one does not address this process and if one assumes, as the student analyst did, that interpretation of meaning other than an apparent one will have therapeutic effect, the patient simply feels as if she is engaged in a power struggle—and so does the analyst. In the examples given previously, recall Caper's description of the "blow to his therapeutic omnipotence." He realized that interpretation as usually conceived did not modify his patient's nondifferentiation of her fantasy about his exhaustion from the reality of his functioning. But a processive intervention produced clinical results. As Caper says, it was not until he interpreted that her conviction was so strong as to admit no alternative that the patient began to change.

The typical countertransference danger for the analyst in such situations is to share the patient's conviction that seeing is believing. The analyst would then attempt to convince the patient that what he or she sees has to be believed. Both would operate from within the assumption that perception guarantees objectivity.[11] As Freud emphasized, perception can only be linked to objectivity if the distinction between perception and memory is maintained. Moreover, one can hypothesize that when the late patient claims that the analyst is rejecting her, what she means is that she feels endangered, because the analyst has interfered with the "use of the analyst as a fetish," in Renik's phrase. The patient *was* late for an early-morning session and imperatively needed to make sure that her lateness had no interpretable meaning. She uses a commonsense idea—"You must be angry at having to wait for me so early in the morning"—to create a fantasy picture of the analyst that has to be taken as a reality. Even though she is speaking about the analyst's anger, unconsciously she creates this fetishistic structure in order to feel relieved. As soon as the analyst interprets in terms of content, she feels endangered or, as she puts it, "rejected." Essentially, the power struggle on both sides of the couch becomes one in which the analyst wants to impose meaning where the patient has to defend against it. The patient then experiences herself either as having won a struggle to maintain her conflation of reality and fantasy, and feeling relieved, or as having lost it, and feeling endangered. As in fetishism, however, neither possibility begins to approach the unconscious conviction that differentiation is the greatest danger of all.

The threat of differentiation is implicit in the analyst's neutrality, which brings into question any direct "knowledge" of the analyst's thoughts and emotions. The traditional function of neutrality is to keep open the possibility that one's perception of the analyst may mean something other than it appears to and could be interpretable. Inchoately, what bothered the student analyst was his sense that the patient used the sessions to struggle with him over his neutrality. However, he could not articulate his justified concern that the patient would be content to fight his interpretations of meaning, because he could not conceptualize the moment-to-moment working of primary disavowal. He, too, felt as if he were losing a power struggle. To the extent that he continued to interpret the meanings of the patient's productions, in fact he first "won" and then "lost" the "battle." When he cornered the patient into accepting that her lateness had a hostile meaning, she retreated into total silence. In the next session the patient successfully brushed aside his attempt to investigate her silence of the day before. Whether the analyst "wins" or "loses," he has lost his neutrality.

As the student understood more about the process going on between him and the patient, he became less frustrated by her and less invested in content interpretations. In essence, content interpretations of the form "I am not angry at you for being late, and your lateness implies that you are angry at me" mean: "Do not create a moment-to-moment perceptual identity between your wishes and your picture of me without understanding that it is your fantasy." This is precisely what a concrete patient has to do to defend against differentiation. As the student became less invested in content interpretations and more beneficially neutral in examining the processes occurring in the sessions, the patient actually grew quite uncomfortable. Noting the change in his style, which made the sessions into less of an endless power struggle, she said, "I don't like this. It feels like trees flying in the air." She was for the first time able to articulate her anxiety in the session that had made the analysis into a potentially interminable enactment that would always fend off destabilizing tension—"trees flying in the air." In subsequent sessions, as the analyst was able to interpret the way in which the patient imperatively felt she had to make him fit in with her perceptions, the patient said, "I want to change you. I want you to be more like me and stop being different." This is a particularly clear statement of how the patient had been using wish fulfillment on a moment-to-moment basis throughout her treatment. As long as the student tried to interpret in the usual way, he was essentially doing the same thing as the patient—creating a perceptual identity according to his wish. The patient could accurately feel that she *had* changed him. She had compelled him to adopt a nonneutral position. This was the grain of truth in her "knowledge" that he was angry at her—although not for being late. In essence, she struggled to make him like her, and he struggled to make her like him. The power struggle was more tolerable for the patient than "trees flying in the air."

It is clear that if the analyst persists in interpreting according to the "yes" of positive wish fulfillment when the patient persists in the silent and invisible "no" of negative hallucination and primary disavowal, each can be engaged in a destructively narcissistic struggle to make the other an extension of himself or herself. Both patient and analyst are threatened by the strangeness and destabilizing tension of difference. Freedman, in his writings on desymbolization (unpub.; Freedman and Berzofsky 1995), has been particularly attentive to attempts to destroy what he calls the "mental space"—that is, differentiation—

necessary for representation. This destruction of "mental space" can take place on the level of time, when the patient attempts to ensure that every moment of actual contact with the analyst, every "now," is used fetishistically. The analyst can do the same if he or she assumes that the patient should respond to content interpretations and should share his or her frame of reference. The acute problem of potentially endless analysis with such patients, also addressed by Renik (1992), requires a conception of how to address the destructive narcissism implicit in the defense against differentiation over time. Renik himself proposes imposing a termination. He is admirably motivated by considerations of therapeutic integrity and nonexploitation of patients who seem willing to stay in analysis forever. Nevertheless, a forced termination bypasses analysis of the "very subtle" dynamics of narcissistic defense against differentiation, like the analyst who would continue to interpret in terms of content rather than process.[12]

As one continues to think about the clinical example in these terms, one returns to the question of what forms of differentiation the patient has registered and repudiated. It would require a detailed exposition to demonstrate the intricate workings of oral-phase differentiation of self and other, anal-phase differentiation of degrees of autonomy and power, and oedipal-phase sexual differentiation with which the patient was struggling. What becomes important is that the patient's concrete compromise formations also created a transference of defense in which the possibility that her analysis could be a differentiating process was subject to primary disavowal. She would not have been engaged in such an intense defensive process to make the analyst conform to her picture of him if she were not threatened by something else, the something else of his being "different" than she is. Analogously, the patient who had been using the tissue box to see me at will began a session one day saying that he was too exhausted by the rest of his life to "deal with" what he called my "penetrating interpretations." After complaining for a while about the rigors of analysis, he "interpreted" what he had been saying in terms of his own fears of sexual penetration. Then he began to complain that the problem with analysis is that it demands total compliance on the part of its patients. Analysts want their patients to "return to the womb" and thus foster total dependence. When I said to the patient that it seemed important to him to see me in mutually contradictory ways—as both penetrating and engulfing—in order to ward off whatever was troubling him in the moment, he immediately replied: "That's the last thing I want to hear you say. As soon as you did say it, I felt this terrible dizziness, and I won't allow that in my sessions." Here again we find a structure of "thoughts" that are actually oscillating fantasies— "I can make you into a penetrating phallus or an engulfing womb at will"—which repudiate a registered sense of traumatic unbalance (a "terrible dizziness," like "trees flying through the air"). To keep this unbalance out of the session the patient caricatured the process of free association and interpretation. He unconsciously equated interpretation with his fantasies, actively disavowing what was troubling him. Analysis, then, would "make no difference."

In the end, though, what does make the analyst different from the patient? The concrete patient shows us that the possibility of interpretation can be a destabilizing tension. But this possibility is intrinsic to the framework of analysis. Clinically, the analyst's maintenance of the framework always serves a silent and invisible differentiating function. Framework means not only the arrangements about time, money, schedule, location, and physical environment, as crucial as all of these are, but also the neutrality necessary for an interpretive stance. Loewald (1980) elaborates a theory of the analytic environment—the frame—in which the most crucial element is that the analyst maintains a different level of psychological organization than the patient. Loewald understands the "therapeutic action of psychoanalysis" as the internalization of this different level of organization.[13] When the late patient tries to make the analyst more like her and "not different," in essence she is attacking the environmental, or frame, aspect of the analyst's different level of organization. Instead, they are both involved in the same power struggle and are both defensively using perception in the same way. Similarly, Frosch's patient claims that he is a "jerk," *just like her*; from within her frame of reference this is not transference.

The concrete patient cannot permit the analyst to be different than he or she is via maintenance of the framework. Internalization of difference represents the overwhelming tension that the patient has unconsciously come to analysis to avoid. But unconscious registration of the possibility of interpretation also provides the motivation for analysis. Being in analysis is itself a compromise between this unconscious motivation and the overwhelming anxiety that accompanies it—thus, again, the striking phenomenon of endless or repeated analyses with concrete patients. Renik's patient was on her third round. The student's late patient tried every variety of adjunct treatment—medication, yoga, acupuncture, rolfing, among others—while in analysis. She gave up each in turn while strenuously resisting interpretation of the fact that analysis was the only form of treatment she did not give up. Not to understand that the struggle against interpretation is the defensive expression of exactly what makes the concrete patient stay in analysis leads to enactment on the analyst's part. In the extreme, the analyst persists with traditional interpretations that do not work and then may impose a termination.

Effective intervention in the ongoing process of concreteness must modify primary disavowal as it occurs. If the patient is ever to tolerate any intervention that raises tension levels, the analyst must gradually help the patient achieve some consciousness of the traumatizing disequilibrium warded off at almost every moment. The basic therapeutic aim articulated by Freud in *Project* remains valid: overcoming the inertia of primary process. But the assumption that interpretation of symbolic structures will produce this result has to change, of course. In general, interventions have to be aimed at the patient's unconscious attacks on the analyst's maintenance of the differentiating framework of the treatment—especially the frame element of his or her own mind at work at a different level of organization. Such interventions help to make conscious the intense anxiety that motivates maintenance of primary process inertia. Such primal anxiety expresses the tension of destabilizing a fetishistic structure, a structure that allows the patient to "know" how to gain (illusory) relief.

TOWARD THE GENERALIZATION
OF FETISHISTIC STRUCTURES

The analytic literature is full of contributions that clarify various aspects of concreteness and fetishism. A highly selective integration of some of them will serve as a transition to Freud's surprising generalization of fetishism. Given the dynamic links between concreteness and fetishism, this generalization will have important implications for the overall question of interpretation. In even broader terms, it would have to influence the psychoanalytic theory of mind, that is, the model of psychopathology that gives the greatest purchase on unconscious processes.

In her 1957 article, Jacobson devotes a few dense pages to Freud's inconsistency in talking about the oscillation between two fantasies, when he claims to describe the oscillation between reality and fantasy (p. 77). Jacobson explicitly says that the concrete patient, like the fetishist, defensively conflates perception of reality with perception of fantasy:

> This outstanding example of denial [*Verleugnung*, disavowal], the denial of female castration, illuminates the distortion of reality which is regularly involved in this defense. Actually, *either of the two opposing ideas distorts realistic facts*: even though women do lack a penis, they are certainly not castrated. The child's common misinterpretation of the female genital perceived indeed reveals the direct influence of the id on the initial perception. . . . The immediate, painful distortion of reality in this case is the *concrete*, external reflection and confirmation of the child's own castration fears and wishes. What is important for our comparison between denial and repression is that in denial the opposing idea employed by the ego as a defense against the frightening notion is again an id fantasy, this time a *wishful*, pleasurable one. This pleasurable idea may likewise *use certain perceptions which lend themselves as confirmation*. In summary: the *opposing ideas* are both topically cathected in the ego and distort external reality perceived . . . the pleasurable, wishful idea *serves the denial* of the painful frightening notion. (p. 77; my emphases)

Jacobson has clearly described the structure of oscillating fantasies that serve defensive ends and that can be concretely conflated with reality. We have already seen that she understands "the direct influence of the id on . . . perception" as regression to a "'concretistic' infantile stage where the child, though already aware of the difference between the internal and external world, between the self and objects, still treats

them both in the same manner" (p. 80). Jacobson describes an awareness and repudiation of difference in order to understand concreteness in terms of fetishism and wish fulfillment. The crux of my theory is that fetishism depends not upon conscious awareness but on
unconscious registration and repudiation of difference. Jacobson also
understands concreteness as a regression to a particular stage of development. My contention is that negative hallucination used as a primary disavowal of differentiation is possible at any stage of development. In fact, every possibility of differentiating between internal and
external, self and objects, to use Jacobson's terms, can be experienced
as too traumatically tension raising and can be replaced with a fetishistic structure of opposed fantasies. Jacobson makes the point that
withdrawal of cathexis from painful perceptions and simultaneous
hypercathexis of desirable ones inevitably produces splitting and a
"massive, global . . . generalization of defensive processes" (p. 81). This
is a good description of the paradoxical state of consciousness that depends upon negative hallucination to "pass over reality testing," in
Freud's expression.

   In an article on perceptual identity, Sandler (1976) made a series
of related points. He called "actualization" the process by which an illusion is formed in waking life. This is essentially the way in which
perception of something actual can be the defensive, fantasy substitute for a threatening piece of external reality. Via actualization, perception makes reality correspond to wishes. This is like Jacobson's
idea that concreteness uses "perceptions which lend themselves as
confirmations" of fantasies. Sandler argues that perceptual identity
can operate not only "centrifugally" to create dreams and symptoms
but also "centripetally" to create illusions. He further argues that the
"centripetal" use of perceptual identity implies a process in which
the ego nonconsciously scans the environment to make sure that experience of it is "consciousness syntonic" (p. 35). This nonconscious
scanning of the environment can be conceived—somewhat oxymo-
ronically—as "unconscious secondary process," an idea, Sandler says,
that provokes "great resistance" (p. 35, n.3).[14] Sandler does not link his
findings to the dynamics of fetishism, which of course have everything to do with the maintenance of illusion through the waking use
of perceptual identity. However, his idea of "unconscious secondary

process" can be viewed in relation to primary disavowal, the unconscious registration and repudiation of differentiating processes. It is another way of thinking about the concrete patient's constant scanning of the (analytic) environment and use of perceptual identity to make sure that the "picture" of the analyst is syntonic with the state of consciousness dominated by negative hallucination.

Boesky (1982), in a reconsideration of acting out, gives clinical examples of actions that create "an illusory reality which serves the purpose of defense. . . . " Action, he says, creates verisimilitude in a way similar to that in which "the magician's guile . . . is calculated to create the illusion of reality in part by distracting our most critical perceptual functions. In this respect our patients become magicians when they act out in an effort to recruit the analyst as a witness to a reality which is spurious" (p. 48). To explain the "magic" of illusion used as defense, Boesky invokes the hallucinatory reality of dreams (p. 49). Adair (1993) makes a similar argument about masturbation fantasies. There are many analogous statements in the literature on enactment. Chused (1991), for example, says that during enactments the patient has a strong conviction about the accuracy of his or her perceptions and attempts to make the analyst behave in a way that supports this conviction (p. 617), as in all the clinical examples discussed previously. Should the analyst inadvertently comply with the patient's pressure, there may be an "actualization [pace Sandler] of a transference perception, a realization of [the patient's] fantasies" (p. 638). In a 1992 panel on enactment, there was general agreement about the "immediacy" of enactments, their "nowness," although with no specific mention of the role of temporal immediacy in hallucinatory wish fulfillment (Panel 1992).

Loewald provides the most important summary statement integrating the theory of wish fulfillment with the replacement of primary by secondary process in consciousness. He conceives the global transferences characteristic of what he calls the "enactive form of remembering" in terms of differentiation and temporality. His description of global transferences can be linked to Jacobson's idea of a global generalization of defensive process. In Loewald's view, "mental processes are primary . . . insofar as they are . . . undifferentiated and non-differentiating. . . . The secondary process differentiates . . . "

(1980, pp. 167–68). The "enactive form of remembering" is a generalized, or global, substitution of the "timelessness and lack of differentiation of the unconscious and of the primary process" (p. 165) for the differentiating secondary process. Loewald's conception of enactive remembering can be integrated with a revised metapsychology of fetishism to explain resistance to interpretation per se. States of consciousness dominated by "timelessness and lack of differentiation" are the defensive repudiation of unconscious registration of differentiation, Sandler's "unconscious secondary process."

The other strand in this theory, initiated by Freud, of course, is the link between fetishism as a model of perversion and disturbances of reality testing. Perhaps the most forcefully argued contribution here is Chasseguet-Smirgel's (1984). Her well-known thesis is that perversion represents the replacement of the reality of the difference between the sexes and the generations with idealized anal fantasies (pp. 77–78). Fetishism exemplifies the perverse compromise: it is the result of replacing differentiation with fantasy due to anxiety over the loss of an idealized part object (p. 87). Thus, Chasseguet-Smirgel gives us a theory of the replacement of differentiation with fantasy-laden concrete things. The unconscious aim of perversion is to attack the capacity to think difference and the "law of differentiation" (p. 120).[15] Bach (1994) conceives what he calls "the language of perversion" as "a language of paradox refused and reduced to an either-or choice" (p. 71). Such rigid oppositions, he says, defend against the frightening possibility that "the same reality can be viewed in different ways by different people" (p. 70), the epitome of the narcissistic state of consciousness. Steingart (1995), like Chasseguet-Smirgel and Bach, emphasizes the role of anality and narcissism in understanding the dynamics of patients for whom "seeing is believing" (p. 169). He understands concreteness as an "unconscious sadomasochistic struggle over who is to decide (analyst or analysand) what is to be considered to be real or unreal about the psychoanalytic relationship" (ibid.). Steingart also emphasizes what he calls "the emergence of mind" during the rapprochement stage of the separation-individuation process, which coincides with the anal phase. Because the "achievement of an 'interior' differentiation with respect to self awareness" (p. 201) occurs in the context of the intense ambivalence of the anal-rapprochement phase, this differentiation itself can be subject to "a special sort of anal struggle for control . . . that amounts to insisting that the transference be regarded as real" (p. 204). In agreement with Bach, Steingart states that the "anal-rapprochement, sadomasochistic dynamics [of concreteness] . . . presupposes the establishment of differentiation" (p. 195, n.24). Thus, although he confines the problem to the anal phase (just as Jacobson spoke of a specifically "concrete" phase), Steingart clearly understands it in terms of the "establishment" and battle for control of differentiation. Unlike Jacobson, however, Steingart specifically rejects the idea that concreteness can be understood in terms of dream mechanisms and primary process (pp. 161, 170).

Earlier, Bach (1985) had written that the state of consciousness that defends against a differentiating perspective is one in which patients do "not clearly distinguish illusion from reality precisely in order to maintain their feelings of well-being. In some sense they attempt to reconstruct a kind of waking dream state" (p. 228). There have been many articles on perverse transference along similar lines. Grossman (1996), for example, defines the "perverse attitude to reality" as a pathology of license not to test conclusions, as when all the patients in my examples are unable to test their "conclusions," particularly about the analyst. Addressing the theme that unites all these contributions, including my own, Grossman says that disavowal of an unwanted perception makes it possible to treat dreams as real and perceptions as dreams. He warns that analytic collusion with the disavowal of reality can lead to use of analysis as a fetish, in Renik's sense.

In "Use of the Analyst as a Fetish" (1992) Renik advocates a process-oriented clinical stance. To cite his description again: "One way to understand the problem of persistent unrealistic expectations in analysis is to conceptualize the crucial issue in terms of the kind of thinking that the patient applies to a fantasy he or she enacts at length within the treatment relationship regardless of the particular content of that fantasy" (p. 543). Although there are patients who persistently use only the analyst as a fetish, Renik reminds us that Freud's understanding of the "blurring of reality and fantasy in fetishism" is the "specific cognitive mode" intrinsic to the distortions of reality in all psychopathology (ibid.).

Freud said more about the relations between fetishism and the distortions of reality in all psychopathology than Renik seems to know. In *An Outline of Psychoanalysis*, written at the very end of his life, there is a passage in which Freud starts to expand the new ideas derived from the study of fetishism. The context is the chapter "The Psychical Apparatus and the External World." Freud takes up again the basic psychoanalytic problem of creating substitutes for a disturbing reality. He first says that what looks like denial of reality in psychosis is actually disavowal: the psychotic has always registered the reality replaced by hallucination and delusion. Like the fetishist, only in a more extreme way, the psychotic oscillates between reality and fantasy. Freud goes on to say:

> The view which postulates that in all psychoses there is a *splitting of the ego* could not call for so much notice if it did not turn out to apply to other states more like the neuroses and finally, to the neuroses themselves. I first became convinced of this in cases of *fetishism*. . . . It must not be thought that fetishism presents an exceptional case as regards a splitting of the ego; it is merely a particularly favorable subject for studying the question. . . . Whatever the ego does in its efforts of defense, whether it seeks to disavow a portion of the real external world [psychosis] or whether it seeks to reject an instinctual demand from the internal world [neurosis], its success is never complete and unqualified. The outcome always lies in two contrary attitudes. . . . (1940a, pp.202–4)

Let me reemphasize Freud's words: "*Whatever the ego does in its efforts of defense. . . .* " In other words, the disavowal and ego splitting first elaborated in order to understand fetishism have now become the basis of a changed understanding of psychopathology in general. This may be the principal reason why Freud said that his thoughts about disavowal and ego splitting were both "old and familiar" and "new and puzzling." The specific novelty is that, at the end of his life, we find him moving away from the centrality of repression in his thought. At least two other authors have reached a similar conclusion. Brook (1992) notes: "Freud did not know whether he had something entirely new in this notion of the splitting of the ego, perhaps even as new as a new way to conceptualize the *foundation of all the defenses*" (p. 347). Similarly, Morris (1993) examined Freud's late writings on ego splitting and states that "as Freud tries to situate . . . defenses in a developmental schema . . . the notion of 'original repression' itself seems to give way to something more like original disavowal" (p. 47). Morris also begins to integrate a concept of original or primary disavowal with the clinical problem of concreteness, which can "drain 'understanding' of its therapeutic power" (p. 50).[16]

When Freud begins to conceptualize an intrinsic splitting of the ego in the process of defense such that there are always two contrary attitudes, he means the registration and repudiation of reality. Fetishism is simply a perspicuous example of a process that occurs in all psychopathological substitute formation. The question of the disavowed reality in fetishism takes on new proportions here. If fetishism illustrates the disavowal and splitting intrinsic to all defensive processes and if difference is the reality primarily disavowed in fetishism, then concreteness also would be intrinsic to the "distortions of reality in all psychopathology." This idea would have to lead to a fundamental reconsideration of the symbolic, meaningful nature of psychopathology and to the primacy of symbolic interpretations. From the perspective of the relations between theory of mind and theory of treatment, it is very striking that Freud included neurosis in his generalization of disavowal and ego splitting. He contends that after initial disavowal and ego splitting, such that two contrary attitudes are formed, one of the attitudes may be repressed, leading to neurotic symptom formation; however, the nonrepressed attitude will lead to its own complications (ibid.). This is barely more than the beginning of a revision of the theory of neurosis. Nonetheless, it shows Freud's not falling prey to the ad hoc empiricism that accumulates clinical advances without thinking about their relation to neurosis. In commenting upon the novelty and puzzle of these new ideas, Freud was explicitly aware that they demanded a return to his earliest conceptions. Was he implicitly aware that to make disavowal, instead of repression, the overarching defensive process was also to compel a fundamental revision of the initial theory of mind and inevitably of treatment as well? This question must remain unanswered.

If the dynamics of the concrete patient, like fetishism, can very fruitfully be understood in terms of Freud's earliest ideas about tension regulation and hallucinatory wish fulfillment and his latest thinking about disavowal, then there are compelling reasons to expand upon concrete patients' resistance to interpretation. In one way or another, all the contributions to the analytical literature discussed so far point to the necessity of analyzing the way the patient thinks. This kind of thinking is the intensely anxiety-driven dominance of consciousness by negative hallucination; tension-raising differentiation is replaced by dedifferentiating wish fulfillment.[17] Interventions have to be geared to these processes in order to reopen a collapsed space of differentiation. This space is the condition for meaning.

If we follow Freud's beginning generalization of the processes that create fetishism (concreteness), we also begin to see such processes as the most general ones in psychopathology. They would be the rule rather than the troubling exception. In that case, we would open the possibility of continuing down an innovative path, only barely pursued by Freud, that can greatly expand theory and practice. It takes us into the realm of primary disavowal, where one must begin to think about the relations between the unconscious and processive, nonperceptual aspects of reality. It is as if we begin to have access to a kind of "subatomic" domain within what we habitually take as our basic unit —the wish. To analyze such processes calls for a sea change in basic theory and technique adumbrated in the literature on illusion, fetishism, concreteness, and enactment and powerfully anticipated by Freud in his final works. This is the change from understanding defense directed against fantasy content, the original psychoanalytic stance, to understanding defense against ongoing, silent, and invisible differentiating processes.

Does such a change once more demand that, like the early Freud, we think about defense as a problem from the "core of nature"? So far, I have used the word "reality" or expressions like "processive aspects of reality," as if we already knew what they meant. Such expressions were necessary to begin to describe the dynamics of concreteness. But the registration and repudiation of differentiating processes can also lead to a revised psychoanalytic theory of what such expressions mean. The initial investigations of repression produced the new theory of mind that revealed the unsuspected reality of the repressed.

As the news of Freud's final shift in his understanding of defense begins to reach us—a process that has taken more than half a century—we might again be in a position to understand the unsuspected reality of the primarily disavowed.

Freud himself situated the generalization of fetishism in a discussion of the relations between the psychic apparatus and the external world, what we usually think of as reality. Traditionally, our knowledge of the external world is linked to consciousness and perception. If fetishism and concreteness perspicuously reveal an organization of consciousness that eliminates reality testing, then, as Sandler has pointed out, one has to think of an "unconscious secondary process." The counterpart of the domination of consciousness by primary process in fetishism or concreteness is the unconscious reality testing or secondary process which has to have occurred if the patient so strenuously defends against it. All the clinical examples lead to this inference. It is consistent with the basic psychoanalytic postulate of unconscious registration of whatever is being defended against. The larger postulate, then, is that concreteness leads to thinking about an unconscious process that registers real or external differentiating processes and can initiate complex defenses against them. These defenses can globally, silently, and invisibly come to dominate consciousness such that, in Loewald's terms, it becomes timeless and dedifferentiating.

What does it mean to postulate such unconscious registration of differentiation? What do we learn about real or external differentiating processes if consciousness and perception can be used to defend against them? How must the basic theory of the unconscious be revised if the usual psychoanalytic idea that reality testing is a function of consciousness is not applicable to a process whose implications are so wide? These questions take on new meaning when asked from the somewhat paradoxical position at which we have arrived. The original theory of mind opened the way to understanding primary and secondary processes in terms of the unconscious and consciousness. We now have a generalizable theory of fetishistic structures that puts primary process in consciousness in order to keep unconscious a registered, but repudiated, secondary process. If the question of defense is at the "core of nature" because it produces the basic conception of the unconscious at the juncture of mind and body, then how would a revised understanding of defense, and of primary and secondary processes, affect the understanding of therapeutic action within a more general framework? What would such a framework be, once interpretation, as conceived from within the repression model, is no longer the basic model of what the analyst does?

CHAPTER 2

Narcissism, Thought, and Eros

In describing the "narcissism of minor differences," Freud spoke of the "strangeness" of difference. Clinically, this strangeness compels repudiation. Thus, many of the patients cited in Chapter 1 had to be convinced that their analysts were "just like them." ("You're a jerk, just like me." "I want you to be like me, and stop being different.") They often conveyed that they could only see their analysts as mirror images of their own wishes and defenses. ("I can *only* experience you as exhausted by me.") Theoretically, then, primary disavowal seems to put the narcissism of minor differences at the heart of fetishism or concreteness. If fetishism is also the most general structure of defensive process, then narcissism would have to be a central issue in substitute formation in general. To expand the theory of unconscious registration of difference is necessarily to integrate it with the theory of narcissism.

Freud, however, did not raise the issue of narcissism at all in his late discussions of fetishism, disavowal, and ego splitting. Nor did he make his passing reference to the narcissism of minor differences central to his general conception of narcissism. Today, nonetheless, there is widespread agreement among Freudians that the "narcissistic state of consciousness" (as particularly described by Bach 1985) is preoccupied with the potentially traumatizing impact of otherness or difference. McDougall (1986), for example, states that "narcissistic pathology has its roots . . . in the inevitable trauma of otherness" (p. 221). Everything we have seen about fetishism and concreteness could be reduced to just this formula. In fetishistic transferences the patient potentially feels traumatized by the analyst's otherness. The analyst's difference is unconsciously conflated with whatever form of differentiation the patient disavows, and the patient then does everything possible to protect against it. The "narcissism of minor differences" is particularly significant when applied to the small but powerful difference between analyst and patient in terms of the analyst's interpretive stance. Global defenses against interpretation can also be viewed as attempts to maintain narcissistic equilibrium by controlling or eliminating the difference between patient and analyst.

In its original sense, however, narcissism means self-love, investment of libido in the ego. One of the great problems of the original theory of narcissism is that as Freud deepened his understanding of self-love, he was also moved to postulate a primary narcissism. Primary narcissism hypothetically designates the early state in which there is no difference between oneself and the outer world. It is called narcissistic because all experience seems to come from within. Primary narcissism is distinguished from the secondary narcissism of self-love because it is prerepresentational. For self-love to be possible, the ego has to have been distinguished from the external world, so that its representation is available for libidinal investment. Primary narcissism implies that the difference between the psychic apparatus and the external world is the result of a process that creates a boundary between them. It touches on the idea that psychoanalysis might have something to say about the development of what we generally call "reality." Similarly, the largest implication of the theory of fetishism was that psychoanalysis could have something crucial to say about reality in terms of differentiating processes.

Does the "narcissism of minor differences" have anything to do with a psychoanalytic theory of reality or with primary narcissism? Freud's scattered remarks on primary narcissism do not make it easy to answer this question. The concept has frequently been dismissed as unproven or useless (see Laplanche and Pontalis, pp. 337–38). Moreover, the relations between primary and secondary narcissism have never been clear. In the face of such controversy and lack of clarity, one would have to demonstrate the role of primary narcissism in the psychoanalytic rethinking of reality and of differentiating processes. As in the analysis of fetishism, it will be necessary to integrate elements of Freud's theory in a way that he himself did not, in order both to enrich the theory from inside itself and to resolve certain inconsistencies within it.

AUTOEROTISM, FETISHISM, AND UNCONSCIOUS THOUGHT

Freud's initial ideas about narcissism grew out of the theory of infantile sexuality. That theory was as essential to the overall structure of his thought as was the theory of wish fulfillment—the two are actually consubstantial. The famous dictum that the neurosis is the negative of the perversion (that is, the neurotic defends against what the manifest "pervert" does [1905a, p. 50]) had two major implications. First, the neurotic specifically represses perverse wishes from early childhood. Second, this does not mean that neurotics were already sexually abnormal children. Rather, just as dreams revealed universal infantile wishes, so neurosis reveals a universal, intrinsically perverse infantile sexuality. In the first great phase of Freud's theorizing, the unconscious, as the juncture of mind and body, is essentially a matter of defense, wish fulfillment, and perversion. In *Three Essays on the Theory of Sexuality* (1905b) the essence of perverse infantile sexuality is autoerotism.

Freud understood the autoerotism of infantile sexuality in terms of the separation of aim and object. Conventional theories of love and sexuality emphasized the person, the object. The psychoanalytic theory of love and sexuality took the more radical step of emphasizing perverse, autoerotic sexual aims. In fact, one of Freud's major purposes throughout *Three Essays* is to demonstrate that sexuality as a separate entity begins when the infant uses its own body to experience erotic stimulation. Technically, this "first" moment of autoerotism is not narcissistic. On the whole, Freud contends that there is a development from autoerotism to narcissism, because autoerotism is not initially investment of libido in the ego. But Freud's emphasis on how the infant comes to use its own body for erotic gratification gives a narcissistic subtext to the entire theory of infantile sexuality. In Chapter 1 I de-

lineated the "subatomic" processes at work within the wish. Delin-
eation of the narcissistic subtext of infantile sexuality will reveal analogous processes at work within autoerotism.

We are again looking at the hungry baby. This time, however, the
vantage point is not the relief of tension, as in the earlier derivation
of the wish, but the actual sensations of feeding. These sensations are
the child's "first experiences of . . . pleasure" (p. 181). "Pleasure" here
is not the metapsychological pleasure of tension regulation in terms
of the pleasure-unpleasure principle but "pleasure" as usually understood—erotic stimulation. In Freud's analysis, these first pleasurable
sensations occur before any distinction between the self-preservative
function of feeding and sexuality itself: "The satisfaction of the erotogenic zone is associated, in the first instance, with the satisfaction of
the need for nourishment. To begin with, sexual activity attaches itself to functions serving the purpose of self-preservation and *does not
become independent of them until later*" (p. 182; my emphasis). This de-
tachment occurs when the baby begins to use its fingers to stimulate
its mouth in order to experience remembered pleasurable sensation:

> The need for repeating the sexual satisfaction now becomes
> detached from the need for taking nourishment. . . . The child
> does not make use of an extraneous body for his sucking, but
> prefers a part of his own skin because it is more convenient,
> because it *makes him independent of the external world, which he is not
> yet able to control* and because in that way he provides himself, as it
> were, with a second erotogenic zone. . . . (ibid.; my emphasis)

Freud's thought here is that the intrinsically autoerotic infantile
sexual aims provide a sensation of controlling pleasurable stimulation
oneself. Sexuality "begins" autoerotically, as the young child provides
itself with the "second erotogenic zone" of its own body. Before this
inherently narcissistic moment, sexuality was indistinguishable from
self-preservation, and self-preservation requires contact with the external world. As Freud puts it later in *Three Essays*: "At a time at which
the first beginnings of sexual satisfaction are still linked with the taking of nourishment, the sexual instinct has a sexual object outside the
infant's own body in the shape of his mother's breast" (p. 222). Once

the fingers can also stimulate the mouth, one can feel oneself independent of the breast for pleasurable sensation. *Sexuality is differentiated
from self-preservation by the autoerotic overvaluation of one's own body, which
one can control more readily than the external object.*

Fetishism, quite strikingly, enters *Three Essays* as the major example of autoerotic overvaluation. Freud explains that although fetishism
appears to be a deviation of sexual object, it cannot be understood
until the autoerotic overvaluation of infantile sexual aims is possible.
An extraordinarily rich passage places fetishism at the intersection of
the theory of overvaluation and the general conditions of how overvaluation may become a pathological aberration, that is, an organized
perversion:

> There are some cases which are quite specially remarkable—those
> in which the normal sexual object is replaced by another which
> bears some relation to it. . . . From the point of view of classifica-
> tion, we should no doubt have done better to have mentioned
> this highly interesting group of aberrations of the sexual instinct
> among the deviations in respect of the sexual *object. But* we have
> postponed their mention till we could become acquainted with
> the factor of sexual overvaluation, on which these phenom-
> ena . . . are dependent. What is substituted for the sexual object is
> some part of the body . . . which is in general very inappropriate
> for sexual purposes, or some inanimate object which bears an
> assignable relation to the person whom it replaces and preferably
> to that person's sexuality (e.g. a piece of clothing or underlinen).
> Such substitutes are with some justice likened to the fetishes in
> which savages believe that their gods are embodied. . . . *No other
> variation of the sexual instinct that borders on the pathological can lay so
> much claim to our interest as this one.* The point of contact with the
> normal is provided by the psychologically essential overvaluation
> of the sexual object. . . . A certain degree of fetishism is thus
> habitually present in normal love. . . . The situation only becomes
> pathological when the longing for the fetish passes beyond the
> point of being merely a necessary condition attached to the
> sexual object, and actually *takes the place* of the normal aim, and
> further, when the fetish becomes detached from a particular

individual and becomes the sole sexual object. These are, indeed, the *general conditions* under which mere variations of the sexual instinct pass over into pathological aberrations (1905, pp. 153–54; my emphases).

In sum, fetishism reveals the process of maintaining autoerotic control by overvaluing a "thing." Since overvaluation is intrinsic to love, every loved "object" is to some extent a fetish. Therefore, the overvaluation of the object in "normal love" is essentially autoerotic: it is created by the subject and is easily displaced should the object prove frustrating. Thus, even before the formal introduction of the concept of narcissism, fetishism is a salient example of the potentially idealizing and omnipotent aspects of infantile sexuality.

Freud did not integrate this discussion of autoerotism and overvaluation with the basic model of wish fulfillment, but it is not difficult to do so. The hungry baby who attempts to relieve a physiological tension immediately by visualizing the memory of previous relief (by wishing) is also attempting to bring about relief autoerotically. Both the tension relief of the hallucinated wish and the stimulation of fingers in the mouth are *auto*erotic versions of memories of feeding. Each demonstrates that memory can be used to create the illusion of control via perception in the moment. At various points in *Three Essays* Freud in fact discusses a "drive for mastery" or control that is intrinsic to infantile sexuality as a result of its autoerotism.[1] As the exemplar of autoerotism, fetishism *also* demonstrates that overvaluation implies control and mastery.

Overvaluation, control, and mastery, however, are not primary phenomena. It is quite important, but not always obvious, that both wish fulfillment and autoerotism are never "originary" for Freud. Both are derived from a prior experience of satisfaction that cannot occur without the cooperation of the breast as representative of the external world. Freud is perfectly consistent in this derivation of wishes and infantile sexuality. He always demonstrates how the autoerotic use of mind or body develops out of the self-preservative needs, which are intrinsically object related. In a passage about the original period in which the self-preservative and sexual instincts are indistinguishable, so that the breast exists as an object for the infant, Freud writes: "It is only later that the instinct loses that object. . . . As a rule the sexual instinct then becomes autoerotic" (p. 222).[2] In this schema the overvaluation, control, and mastery implicit to autoerotism—as exemplified by fetishism—are the result of the differentiation of sexuality from self-preservation.

However, there is a possible inconsistency here. The theory of neurosis centers on the repression of infantile sexual wishes. Freud mostly treats the repressed as the fundamental aspect of the greater, unconscious part of the mind. Thus, one finds all the statements about the primacy of wishes and infantile sexual aims as if they were "originary" phenomena, the basic stuff of the mental apparatus. But since wishes and infantile sexuality are always shown to have developed out of another context, one would also expect that context to be given some kind of primary or "originary" status. Autoerotism implies a theory of how one becomes narcissistic, that is, how the infant attempts to use mind and body to fulfill wishes independent of the context out of which they arise. Fetishism, the exemplar of autoerotic overvaluation, then would also have to reflect the derivation of autoerotism. This is not simply a logical inference. The question of the registration of the context out of which autoerotism derives is directly related to the crucial issue of unconscious registration of difference.

Freud's 1911 paper "Formulations on the Two Principles of Mental Functioning" contains ideas essential to this topic. On the whole, the paper's argument reflects the primacy of wishes and drives (the sexual aims). Yet in order to describe how a relation to reality develops out of the apparently original pleasure principle, Freud, perhaps unwittingly, comes to postulate a kind of secondary process intrinsic to the pleasure principle, an unconscious registration of reality.[3] The passage in which he fleetingly envisages this possibility expands the understanding of the context out of which autoerotism is derived.

Freud begins the paper with a typical assertion that psychopathology involves a wishful replacement for an unbearable reality, more globally in psychosis, more partially in neurosis. However, he now feels ready to bring "the psychological significance of the real external world into the structure of our theories" (p. 218). (This reference to the "real external world" should once more be considered in relation to the discussion in "The Psychic Apparatus and the External World" in *Outline*, where the generalization of fetishism was elaborated.) In very condensed fashion, Freud then repeats what we saw in detail in the preceding chapter: the primary process both replaces images of unpleasure with pleasure and withdraws from any registration of undue tension. However, the fact that tension cannot be fully relieved by hallucination compels the registration of it long enough to bring about nonhallucinatory relief: "what was presented in the mind was no longer what was agreeable but what was real, even if it happened to be disagreeable" (p. 219). This is the hypothetical beginning of the reality principle.

Freud supplements what he calls this "schematic account" of the reality principle from the pleasure principle with a celebrated footnote. This note once again refers to the derivation of the pleasure principle itself within a context:

> It will rightly be objected that an organization which was a slave to the pleasure principle and neglected the reality of the external world could not maintain itself alive for the shortest time, so that it could not have come into existence at all. The employment of a fiction like this is, however, justified when one considers that the infant—provided one includes with it the care it receives from its mother—does *almost* realize a psychical system of this kind. It probably hallucinates the fulfillment of its internal needs; it betrays its unpleasure, when there is an increase of stimulus and an absence of satisfaction, by the motor discharge of screaming and beating about with its arms and legs, and it then experiences the satisfaction it has hallucinated. (p. 219, n.4; my emphasis)

Freud's "almost" explicitly solves one problem here but implicitly elides another. He explicitly solves the commonsense objection to the "originary" status of the pleasure principle: if the baby attempted to live by hallucinatory wish fulfillment alone, it would die of starvation. However, since the infant is not conscious of the mother's care, from the infant's point of view tension relief is a product of wishing. After attempting to discharge the tension due to hunger, the infant "*then* experiences the satisfaction it *has hallucinated*." But implicitly, the problem of the context is still elided, for Freud does not say what his theory always implies: there has been some memory of a previous satisfaction, which can be revived with hallucinatory intensity as a wish. Memory implies registration. The elided problem then is the more difficult, and perhaps counterintuitive, one of understanding the registration of the previous satisfaction. This kind of registration readily disappears behind the seeming primacy of the wish. There is no consideration of such registrations in the footnote. We must hold on to their theoretical necessity for a moment, until we reach a pivotal moment in the body of Freud's text.

Freud alludes to a further implicit problem in a passage at the end of the footnote:

> —I shall not regard it as a correction, but as an amplification
> of the schematic picture under discussion, if it is insisted that
> a system living according to the pleasure principle must have
> devices to enable it to withdraw from the stimuli of reality. Such
> devices are merely the correlative of "repression", which treats
> internal unpleasurable stimuli as if they were external—that is
> to say, pushes them into the external world. (ibid.)

Freud is restating the formulation of the pleasure-unpleasure principle from the *Project for a Scientific Psychology* (1895a): primary wish fulfillment always implies primary defense, here called withdrawal from the "stimuli of reality." Unpleasurable, real stimuli potentially raise tension too much. However, to defend against such tension-raising stimuli also implies some registration of them. Freud seems to be saying that during the early phases when the pleasure principle "almost" completely dominates mental functioning, the defense against real stimuli is the correlative of repression. All tension-raising stimuli are treated in the same way. They are ejected from the mental apparatus in an illusory effort to make them disappear somewhere outside the boundaries of the mind. Freud is apparently describing something like projection when he says that unpleasurable stimuli are pushed into the external world. But this is actually, as he says, a description of defense in general, a primal repudiation of unpleasure. The major function of defense, as always in Freud, is to attempt to prevent the mind from being disturbed by unwelcome tension, whether from within or without. But defense is only directed against something registered, however registration is conceived. Thus, Freud is actually describing something like negative hallucination or even primary disavowal: the unconscious repudiation of a registered, tension-raising reality.

This discussion, then, yields another counterintuitive problem. Just as one has to wonder about the status of the memory of previous satisfaction out of which wishes and sexual drives originate, one also has to wonder about the status of the registration of the disagreeable internal or external stimuli, which are defended against in a way correlative to repression.[4] One might think that the registration of such stimuli would have to be fleeting or transitory, but the intensity of the defenses against them says otherwise. Similarly, wishes could not arise out of memories of a previous satisfaction unless these memories were "substantial" enough to be cathected with hallucinatory intensity. We have here a problem already present in the *Project* (pp. 319–21). There Freud emphasized that unconscious memory depends upon the opening of pathways via the overcoming of a resistance. This is why he thought that pain would be particularly responsible for laying down memory traces. At the same time, Freud also postulated that the registration of the experience of satisfaction opened a pathway in unconscious memory that could later be recathected (the wish). In the *Project* then, as well as in this footnote in "Two Principles," the foundations of unconscious memory are the registration of the realities of pain and the experience of satisfaction. It is also clear that there can be primal, unconscious repudiation of such unconscious registrations. The registration of both pain and the experience of satisfaction as memories can be replaced by wish fulfillment.

To return to the body of "Two Principles," after the footnote Freud takes up the topic I am most concerned with, the nature of thought and reality from a psychoanalytic point of view. If the function of the mind governed by the pleasure principle is to wish, then the function of the mind newly, and fragilely, governed by the reality principle is to *think*:

> Restraint upon motor discharge (upon action) . . . was provided
> by means of the process of *thinking*, which was developed from
> the presentation of ideas. Thinking was endowed with character-

istics which made it possible for the mental apparatus to tolerate an increased tension of stimulus while the process of discharge was postponed. . . . For this purpose the conversion of freely displaceable cathexes into "bound" cathexes was necessary, and this was brought about by means of raising the level of the whole cathectic process. *It is probable that thinking was originally unconscious, in so far as it went beyond mere ideational presentations and was directed to the relations between impressions of objects,* and that it did not acquire further qualities, perceptible to consciousness, until it became connected with verbal residues. (p. 221; my emphases)

Freud's originally unconscious thought is a rare conceptualization of unconscious registration of reality. The original reads: "Das Denken war wahrscheinlich ursprünglich unbewußt, insoweit es sich über der blöße Vorstellen erhob und sich den Relationen der Objekteindrücke zuwendete, und erhielt weitere fur das Bewußtsein wahrnehmenbare Qualitäten erst durch die Bindung an die Wortreste" (1911b, pp. 233–34). Strachey's translation of the critical phrase "relations between impressions of objects" is quite accurate. But one must pay careful attention to the words themselves in order to grasp a subtle distinction. Freud is not speaking of unconscious thought as memory of conscious "impressions" of objects. Rather, he is speaking of the relations between the registrations of the object. *Objekteindrücke* has the sense of an "impress" [*ein-drücken*, (to press in)] so that Strachey's "impressions" must be taken literally. One must also note that originally unconscious thinking is carefully distinguished from the "mere presentation of ideas," "*blöße*" also having the sense of bareness. This bareness or mereness of the presentation of ideas is due to their not being bound. They are not part of the process of delaying discharge in order to increase the tension level within the proto-apparatus.

Originally unconscious thought is then a matter of registration ("impression") and not of ideational thinking attached to words. It is also a form of delayed discharge and inherently raises tension. Following Freud's reasoning, originally unconscious thought can act like an unpleasurable stimulus, which can be primally defended against. Since these registrations are originally unconscious, they can be defended against unconsciously. We again have a description of how unconscious registrations of reality that raise tension ("pain") can be defended against through discharge, the major function of wish fulfillment. Sandler (1976) had already elaborated an "unconscious secondary process" intrinsic to wish fulfillment, as discussed in Chapter 1. His idea was that unconsciously registered but conscious dystonic elements of the external world can be defended against via the "centripetal" use of wish fulfillment, the creation of waking illusions. Sandler's conception is readily integrated with Freud's originally unconscious thought: when thinking itself is experienced as an economic threat, it is replaced by "mere presentation of ideas." Such "ideas" serve to defend against the increased tension of unconscious registrations by discharging that tension. Essentially, they are wishes. Like all wishes, as Sandler has already outlined, they can create a reality effect by means of perceptual identity.

Freud's original theory was that tension-raising knowledge of trauma is registered unconsciously but warded off by "primary wish fulfillment and primary defense." The relations between originally unconscious thought and the "mere presentation of ideas" expands this conception. Originally unconscious thinking includes registration of both internally derived tension-raising delay and externally derived "relations between impressions of objects." It synthesizes the two basic facets of unconscious memory from the *Project*: the registration of pain and the registration of the experience of satisfaction. Unpleasurable internal and external stimuli are treated synonymously at this level. Both are unconsciously replaced by matching experience to wish when they inevitably raise tension levels too much. In essence, this is what occurs when, in Freud's account, the hungry baby does not get immediate satisfaction from hallucinatory wish fulfillment. It "betrays its unpleasure . . . by the motor discharge of screaming and beating about with its arms and legs, and it then experiences the satisfaction it has hallucinated." In other words, despite the initial frustration, the baby matches the current experience to a hallucinated satisfaction after it cries and thrashes. By matching satisfaction to hallucination, the baby unconsciously elides the difference between the object related, "real" satisfaction of the instinct of self preservation and the autoerotic satisfaction of hallucinatory wish fulfillment. Simultaneously, pain, the temporal difference of delay, is also elided. Tension-raising unconscious thought, the conjoint registration of pain and the experience of satisfaction, is repudiated when it reaches consciousness as a wish.

According to the model of *Three Essays*, there is originally no distinction between the self-preservative and the sexual instincts. As erotic gratification begins to be sought for its own sake, for example, in infantile thumb-sucking, the self-preservative and sexual instincts "become detached. . . . The sexual instincts behave autoerotically at first; they obtain their satisfaction in the subject's own body and therefore do not find themselves in the situation of frustration which was what necessitated the institution of the reality principle" (p. 222). In other words, it is always possible to fall back upon the intrinsic properties of autoerotism to attempt to eliminate a frustration. Narcissistic overvaluation, control, and mastery are inherent to this autoerotic repudiation of increased tension.

Freud could have integrated this understanding of autoerotism with the concept of originally unconscious thought. The psychic apparatus develops simultaneously in two ways, which can approximately be called non-narcissistic and narcissistic. Non-narcissistically, the experience of satisfaction, the "relations between impressions of objects," and painful stimuli are continually registered, but registered unconsciously, because thinking is originally unconscious and not linked to verbal representation. Narcissistically, the baby attempts not to register the increased tension of the object-oriented self-preservative instincts; it can do so because sexuality can be discharged autoerotically. Via autoerotism the baby produces illusions of control. It (fetishistically) overvalues the "second erotogenic zone" of its own body. Autoerotic infantile sexuality seeking immediate discharge is the economic counterweight to delayed discharge. In this regard Freud writes,

> In the realm of phantasy, repression remains all powerful; it brings about the inhibition of ideas in *statu nascendi* before they can be noticed by consciousness, if their cathexis is likely to occasion a release of unpleasure [undue tension]. This is the weak spot in our psychical organization; and it can be employed to bring back under the dominance of the pleasure principle thought processes which had already become rational. (p. 223)

One regrets that Freud did not refer back to this idea when he spoke of the registration and repudiation of reality in fetishism. The generalization of fetishism led to a paradoxical theory of consciousness dominated by the pleasure principle (primary process) in order to keep registered differentiation unconscious. Wish-fulfilling "mere presentation of ideas," which keeps originally unconscious thought out of consciousness, is the metapsychological explanation of this paradox. Fetishism, like autoerotism then, arises out of the context of unconscious registration of difference. To use the model from "Two Principles," there is a primal, unconscious repudiation of tension-raising internal and external stimuli. Originally unconscious thought is pushed into the external world. Repudiated sexual difference becomes "strange" and "hostile." The "narcissism of minor differences" then wards off this threat consciously. Narcissistic equilibrium is maintained when consciousness is dominated by autoerotism.

In fact, all the clinical examples in Chapter 1 can be understood in this light. A key aspect of the concrete pathology of thought was the use of hallucinatory wish fulfillment in waking life. Grossman (1996), for example, described disavowal as a way of treating dreams as real and perceptions as dreams. Jacobson stressed that concreteness occurs when id fantasies are defensively used in consciousness as "perceptions which lend themselves as *confirmation*" (p. 77). The use of id fantasies as confirming perceptions itself depends upon the "matching" of experience to wish fulfillment. Concrete denial of the analyst's interpretations *en bloc* (Jacobson) evidently depends upon these dynamics. Because concrete patients already have primally disavowed some aspect of differentiating processes, they do the same with the differentiating aspect of the analyst's interpretation. They are then compelled to match external reality to internal wish autoerotically. Their "free associations" are actually tension-reducing mere presentations of ideas, which maintain narcissistic equilibrium. ("I *know* that you're mad at me for being late." "You're a jerk, *just like me*.")

If the analyst does not understand this process, then his or her interventions also become an autoerotic "mere presentation of ideas." As we have already seen, such interventions attempt to make the patient match the picture in the analyst's mind, the picture of a patient who would respond to traditional interpretations of content. Such wish-fulfilling interventions by the analyst not only inevitably lead to power struggles, they also keep the analytic work situated at the level of consciousness. What is unconscious in such situations is the tension of differentiation. The theory of originally unconscious thought deepens the explanation of why the concrete patient treats interpretation as a potential trauma. Registration of effective interpretation opens unconscious pathways, like registration of the experience of satisfaction. But the opening of such pathways always raises tension. Repudiation of interpretation therefore discharges the tension, the potential pain of the analyst's self-preservative function. This is why concrete patients stay in analysis while remaining uninterested in change.

As a general principle, the domination of consciousness by wish fulfillment or autoerotism repeats the process by means of which an originally libidinal–self-preservative drive, with an inherent tie to an object, becomes tension-reducing autoerotism. Freud did not link the registrations of originally unconscious thought to the original libidinal–self-preservative drive from *Three Essays*. However, they are evidently synonymous. The registration of the "experience of satisfaction" can only be conceptualized in terms of the inherent object tie of the original drive. When recathected as wish fulfillments, such registrations do not function as memories, traces of past experience, but as perceptions. (Negative hallucination repudiates the difference between memory and perception.) In other words, there is a registration and repudiation, a primary disavowal, of originally unconscious thought in every wish. In the same way, autoerotism decontextualizes such registrations with illusions of mastery and control. Clinical concreteness is such an autoerotic decontextualization.

Freud's late and early views of fetishism encapsulate this thinking. In the late theory, fetishism is the major example of the substitute formations due to registration and repudiation of reality. In the early theory, fetishism is the major example of autoerotic overvaluation. Autoerotism and concreteness, then, would be the result of the registration and repudiation of originally unconscious thought. They can be reconceptualized as fetishistic substitute formations with an essential narcissistic component.

FERENCZI ON NARCISSISM AND REALITY

Ferenczi took up the problem of the relations between thought and wishes in "Stages in the Development of the Sense of Reality" (1913). The paper was written as a response to, and extension of, Freud's "Two Principles." Ferenczi also postulates an intrinsic link between infantile sexuality and narcissism. In his discussion of wish fulfillment and omnipotence, Ferenczi makes a crucial observation about the infant's experience of having hunger relieved:

> the curious thing is that—pre-supposing normal care—this hallucination is in fact realized. From the subjective standpoint of the child the previously unconditional "omnipotence" [of intrauterine life] has changed merely in so far, that he needs only to seize the wish-aims in a hallucinatory way (to imagine them) and to alter nothing else in the outer world, in order (after satisfying this single condition) really to attain the wish-fulfillment. Since the child certainly has no knowledge of the real concatenation of cause and effect . . . he must feel himself in the possession of a magical capacity that can actually realize all his wishes by simply imagining them. (p. 222)

Freud had already said in "Two Principles" that crying is conflated with the gratification of wishes, because the cry brings the relief first sought through wish fulfillment. He thought that the autoerotism of infantile sexuality produces a permanently narcissistic "weak spot" in the psyche. Ferenczi understands this "weak spot" in terms of the narcissistic fantasies that always mitigate reality. He explicitly links the omnipotence inherent to wish fulfillment to the forms of magical thinking that persist throughout life. This is the point of departure for the tendency to conflate any gratification with autoerotism and wish fulfillment. The match between wish and experience creates a sensation of magical omnipotence. The dream mechanism of negative hallucination is intrinsic to this process, as Ferenczi had already observed:

> the new-born babe seeks to attain a state of satisfaction merely through insistent wishing (imagining), whereby it simply ignores

(represses) the unsatisfying reality, picturing to itself as present, on
the contrary, the wished-for, but lacking satisfaction; it attempts,
therefore, to conceal without effort all its needs by means of
positive and negative hallucinations. (p. 213)

The entire problematic of the preceding chapter is contained in
Ferenczi's use of the word "represses." In "Two Principles" Freud
compared repression to a withdrawal "from the stimuli of reality" by
"push[ing] them into the external world." Ferenczi here is addressing
the same problem—"ignoring" an "unsatisfying reality"—and so cannot literally be describing the repression of a forbidden wish. Rather,
he is describing primary disavowal, which depends upon the negative
hallucination he so carefully mentions. Ferenczi's argument is that just
as the baby's cry also seems to produce a match between wish and experience, so all wishing, due to its intrinsic connection to positive and
negative hallucination, can make apparently realistic efforts to bring
relief conform to the fantasy of omnipotence. Therefore, each phase
of infantile sexuality, with its characteristic wishes, will also lead to
characteristic conflations of reality and fantasy. Wherever there is an
autoerotic, infantile wish there is also a narcissistic reality organization. We find here another important link between (narcissistic) omnipotence and wish fulfillment, a major extension of Freud's idea of
the autoerotism (narcissism) inherent to infantile sexuality.

Ferenczi later makes the point that while the "choice of neurosis"
is determined by libidinal fixation, the "mechanism" of neurosis is determined by "the reality sense that was dominant at the time of fixation" (p. 235). Strictly speaking, this "reality sense" is the form of narcissistic illusion related to the nature of the wishes defended against.
In 1913, the example familiar to all analysts was obsessional neurosis.
Due to the repression of anal sadistic impulses, the obsessive maintains
the magical idea that thinking equals acting; his or her thoughts have
dangerous powers because they are derivatives of the sadistic wishes
always being defended against. But the obsessive also is aware that
thoughts cannot really do harm. Ferenczi therefore takes up the problem of two contradictory states of consciousness, one dominated by
fantasy and the other by reality. This is exactly the problem later investigated by Freud in the work on fetishism:

A part of the mental life, more or less removed from consciousness, thus remains with the obsessional patient . . . and makes
wishing equivalent to acting because—just on account of the
repressions, of the *distraction of attention*—this repressed portion of
the mental life was not able to learn the difference between the
two activities, while the ego itself, which has developed free from
repression and grown wise through education and experience,
can only laugh at this equating of the two. (pp. 216–17)

Ferenczi has described a psyche divided between reality and fantasy, such that the side dominated by fantasy is intrinsically omnipotent or narcissistic. Extending Ferenczi's analysis, one can say that the
side of the ego dominated by narcissism must defend against knowledge of the difference between thinking and acting. Moreover, the
other side of the ego, which "laughs" at the equation of the two, does
not influence the fantasy of the omnipotence of thought. One could
certainly call this defensive effort a "splitting of the ego." When Ferenczi speaks of a part of mental life "more or less removed from consciousness," we can interpret him to have opened the general problematic of defense, the "distraction of attention" from anything that
the ego does not wish to include in its organization, but which has
already been registered unconsciously. Defense, then, necessarily produces an ego split between registration and repudiation of difference.

Ferenczi provides an important insight into the role of narcissism
and repudiation of difference in the dynamics of neurosis. His point
is that wish fulfillment in general produces states of consciousness
dominated by narcissistic control of the difference between fantasy
and reality. Therefore, neurotic symptoms are sustained by narcissistic
reality organizations. One regrets that Freud did not apply this thinking to the later generalization of disavowal.[5] It puts narcissism, registration and repudiation of difference, and the question of reality at
the heart of all pathological substitute formations.

PRIMARY NARCISSISM:
THE CONTEXT OF UNCONSCIOUS THOUGHT

By the time of *On Narcissism: An Introduction* (1914a), Freud had already devoted substantial attention to the topic of narcissism. The pa-

per is less an introduction than a summary and expansion, including a few discussions of primary narcissism. It is not difficult to see why many have chosen not to trouble themselves with this not fully elaborated concept. But when viewed in relation to autoerotism and originally unconscious thought, primary narcissism becomes a necessary correlate of the entire theory. The opening of *On Narcissism*, when read closely, contains both the difficulties and the potential solutions.

The necessity of something like primary narcissism is implicit in Freud's apparently straightforward first paragraph. He says that the term "narcissism" denotes "the attitude of a person who treats his own body in the same way in which the body of a sexual object is ordinarily treated . . . narcissism has the significance of a perversion that has absorbed the whole of the subject's sexual life, and it will consequently exhibit the characteristics which we expect to meet with in the study of all perversions" (p. 73). If Freud wants to study narcissism as a perversion, he of course has to bring it under the rubric of infantile sexuality. But he thereby also inscribes narcissism within the context of derived autoerotism. Further, if the narcissist treats his or her own body as a sexual object, the narcissist can be said to exemplify the infantile sexuality that begins when the infant uses its own body as a "second erotogenic zone." As both a specific perversion related to overvaluation and as an exemplar of perversion, narcissism will become a model condition (like fetishism).

In Freud's second paragraph things become more difficult. He observes that narcissistic attitudes are found in many other disorders—for example, homosexuality—suggesting that investment of libido in the ego might be a regular occurrence in sexual development. He then makes a clinical point: "Difficulties in the psychoanalytic work upon neurotics led to the same supposition, for it seemed as though this kind of narcissistic attitude in them constituted one of the limits of their susceptibility to influence" (ibid.). Until now, neurosis was understood as the disorder most treatable by psychoanalysis. The revival of repressed infantile sexual impulses in the transference could modify defense, hypothetically leading to full object love. However, if analysts regularly come up against narcissistic attitudes in neurotics, it means that neurotics also have invested libido in themselves. They do not only suffer from the repression of infantile sexual wishes.

Theoretically, this narcissistic resistance should come as no sur-

prise. Neurosis by definition concerns defense against perverse infantile sexual wishes. Infantile sexuality itself has an inherently narcissistic component by virtue of autoerotic overvaluation. Thus, the ob-
stacles encountered in the treatment of neurotics are not contingent.
They are intrinsic to infantile sexuality itself. The clinical implication
is that to make infantile wishes conscious may modify the effects of
repression but does not necessarily modify the narcissism built into
all wishes. Thus, there would have to be a stumbling block in a therapy of neurosis conceived only as making such wishes conscious.

Freud's next sentence, purporting to explain the narcissism intrinsic even to neurosis, is somewhat puzzling: "Narcissism in this sense
[that is, as encountered even in neurosis] would not be a perversion,
but the libidinal complement of the egoism of the instinct of self-
preservation, a measure of which may justifiably be attributed to every
living creature" (pp. 73–74). What does he mean—that all patients, including neurotics, will at some point "egoistically" resist analysis in order to protect themselves? If so, one understands why Freud would say
that the narcissism of the instinct of self-preservation is not a perversion: it does not imply a directly sexual relation to oneself. But then
why call it narcissism at all?[6] Or—another way of asking the same
question—what relation would there be between the narcissism that
is the "*libidinal* component of the instinct of self-preservation" and the
narcissism more readily understood in terms of perversion?

To answer such questions, Freud moves from neurosis to psychosis.
He starts the next paragraph by saying that the motivation for "occupying ourselves with the conception of a primary and normal narcissism" arose from the attempt to understand psychosis in terms of libido theory. The neurotic, Freud explains, might break off libidinal
investments to external objects but retains such investments in fantasy:
thus the displacement of such investments onto the analyst. The psychotic, who also breaks off libidinal investments in the external world,
does not unconsciously retain the relation to the object. Rather, the
object-directed libido is reinvested in the ego, producing the characteristic megalomania of psychosis. This megalomania is clearly narcissistic, but it "is no new creation; it is, as we know, a magnification and
plainer manifestation of a condition which had already existed previously" (p. 75). It is not at all clear from the context how we "know"

that the narcissism of megalomania exemplifies a previous condition. Be that as it may, as so often for Freud, an extreme disorder speaks more directly about a general condition of the psyche. He writes: "the narcissism which arises through the drawing in of obect-cathexes [is] a secondary one, superimposed upon a primary narcissism that is obscured by a number of different influences" (ibid.).

The next paragraphs are conceptually easier. Freud justifies the general introduction of the concept of narcissism through the investigations of "omnipotence of thought"—the magical thinking that itself "might be put down to megalomania." By referring back to these familiar ideas, Freud finds a link between primary narcissism, which is putatively conspicuous in psychosis, and the universally narcissistic thought patterns of "children and primitive peoples."[7] Discussing all these forms of omnipotence of thought, he concludes: "Thus we form the idea of there being an original libidinal cathexis of the ego, from which some is later given off to objects, but which fundamentally persists and is related to the object-cathexes much as the body of an amoeba is related to the pseudopodia which it puts out" (ibid.). The inference is that if psychotic megalomania is traceable to primary narcissism, so, too, must be magical thinking. Despite the rather flimsy logic of Freud's conclusion, one should be alert to its implications: the psychic apparatus is primarily narcissistic and thus intrinsically delusional in its omnipotence.

In and of itself this idea is not difficult to understand. The proto-apparatus is almost entirely under the dominance of the pleasure principle and always attempts to substitute hallucinatory wish fulfillment—in other words, a dreamlike, delusional state of consciousness—for the tension of delay and registration of unconscious thought. There is then every reason to conceive of an originally narcissistic state of the psyche. However, Freud from the outset conceives of primary narcissism as the "libidinal component of the instinct of *self-preservation.*" Unfortunately, at this point he does not remind himself of the libidinal–self-preservative drive from *Three Essays*, which was conceived as intrinsically object related. How can one reconcile the "delusional," originally narcissistic—that is, non-object related—state of the psychic apparatus with primary narcissism defined as the libidinal component of an intrinsically object related state?

Freud does not articulate this contradiction but says, as always, that originally there is no difference between sexuality and self-preservation: "as regards the differentiation of psychical energies, we are led to the conclusion that to begin with, during the state of narcissism, they exist together . . . " (p. 76). Although one understands the consistency of Freud's position here and even its relation to what he has begun to call "primary narcissism," he does not attend to the difficult and counterintuitive thrust of his argument. If the instinct of self-preservation is originally tied to an external object, why link such autoerotic formations as megalomania, omnipotence of thought, and magical thinking to primary narcissism? It would be simpler and more consistent to see them in relation to secondary narcissism, which is obviously autoerotic and perverse.

The inconsistency is due to Freud's not reaching an inevitable conclusion: the autoerotic manifestations of secondary narcissism are derived from primary narcissism, just as autoerotic infantile sexuality is derived from the instinct of self-preservation. However, one immediately sees—as Freud does, too—that the logic of this derivation demands an early psychic state in which self-preservation and libido are not yet distinguishable. Within such a state the intrinsic relation to the object would be registered unconsciously. In other words, primary narcissism would designate the theoretically requisite state of registration of "the relations between impressions of objects" (to use the phrase from "Two Principles"). It is a necessary aspect of an unconscious libidinal–self-preservative drive.

To call the inscription of traces within the organization of primary narcissism impressions of an object is misleading in a sense, because object implies representation. It is equally misleading to call this state narcissistic because narcissism always implies reflection and representation. The concepts of object, representation, and reflection demand a relation to perception and consciousness. To link primary narcissism to originally unconscious thought is to show that Freud was fruitfully compelled by his theory to touch upon a functioning of the psychic apparatus that is both unconscious and nonrepresentational but is originally in relation to "reality." Inner subjectivity and outer objectivity are not yet relevant terms here. Thus, reality must not be conflated with the usual objective, reflective, and representational understanding of it. Rather, the memory traces inscribed within primary narcissism can be conceived as the differentiating processes repudiated by primary disavowal. These registrations quickly come to be replaced by hallucinatory wish fulfillments, that is, by representations. Freud did not have a way of thinking about the non-representational processes his theory always implied. Primary narcissism, a somewhat self-contradictory term, is another attempt to grapple with this problem.

The implications of this interpretation of primary narcissism are wide. It can explain why Freud links all forms of omnipotence of thought to both primary and secondary narcissism. The omnipotence of thought revealed in megalomania and infantile belief in magic can be understood as autoerotic forms of consciousness. However, autoerotic states of consciousness are themselves made possible by a prior registration of a reality that is not reflected or represented, but that raises tension levels and "binds." Just as autoerotism itself derives from the registration and repudiation of originally unconscious thought, autoerotic forms of consciousness imply ongoing defense against registered differentiation.

Secondary narcissism, like concreteness, is perceptual in the extreme. It eliminates any alternative to what one does or does not see in the present moment.[8] The self-preservative aspect of originally unconscious thought is thereby repudiated. The image of Narcissus, spellbound by his own reflection while pining away, exactly conveys the point. In the myth, Narcissus is punished for his refusal of all object ties. If we take him to have repudiated the registration of the object and to have substituted for it autoerotic perception in the moment, we can understand how he ignores hunger while gazing at himself. In other words, his autoerotic state of consciousness uses negative hallucination to repudiate the libidinal–self-preservative drive. Narcissus embodies the secondary narcissism derived from primary narcissism. As his own fetish, he is the apotheosis of infantile sexuality.

In the consulting room either the analyst, the patient, or both can be Narcissus. Countertransference enactments are inevitable in the treatment of the concrete patient if patient and analyst share the same narcissistic "sense of reality," to use Ferenczi's phrase. If both have the conviction that "seeing is believing," that perception guarantees real-

ity, both share an autoerotic state of consciousness in which each repudiates the tension created by the other. For the patient, such tension is implicit in the analyst's difference and in the possibility of interpretation. For the analyst, such tension is implicit in the patient's
not matching the picture of a person who will respond to interpretation as usually conceived. Unless the analyst has the flexibility to
think beyond the assumption that perception guarantees reality, he or
she will attempt to do what the concrete patient does: make the
other his or her reflecting image.

The patient who seems to make an analysis into a fetishistic or
narcissistically reflecting experience is constantly repeating the derivation of secondary narcissism from primary narcissism. In other
words, the patient needs to make the analysis into an exclusively autoerotic experience. He or she is too threatened by the unconscious
integration of self-preservation and libido in which differentiation is
originally registered. What I approximately called the nonnarcissistic
and narcissistic development of the psyche is more accurately understood as constant unconscious movement between primary and secondary narcissism. This movement is an unconscious oscillation between reality and fantasy, that is, between unconscious registrations of
differentiating processes and their repudiation by rigid fantasy oppositions (the narcissism of minor differences). Such oppositions generally have the fetishistic structure of relieving presence and threatening absence, maintenance of control and loss of control.

This clinical concept also solves a major theoretical problem. In
the original theory, the unconscious seems to mirror a narcissistically
closed system (as in most of "Two Principles"). When wishes and autoerotism are taken as primary, the theory actually describes the formations of secondary narcissism. However, it is also possible to use
such concepts as originally unconscious thought and primary narcissism to open the theory of unconscious processes. The derivation of
secondary from primary narcissism shows how an unconscious intrinsically open to registration of differentiating processes defensively
comes to represent itself as a closed system. This idea is implicit in the
original conception that the wish is actually the revived memory of
the experience of satisfaction. The unconscious registration of the
experience of satisfaction can only occur in an inherently open or-

ganization. Its revival as a wish, which creates an autoerotic illusion of mastery and control, appears to close that organization.

To the extent that much of Freud's theory does accord primacy to wishes and autoerotism and treats the unconscious registrations of reality as an ephemeral theoretical inference, it tends to operate as a closed system. Neither the libidinal–self-preservative drive, nor originally unconscious thought, nor primary narcissism is given clinical status. For example, when Freud describes narcissistic resistances to analytic "influence" in the opening of *On Narcissism*, he does not consider the clinical-theoretical question of why a patient would maintain himself or herself in a closed, autoerotic position. He does not understand that in the consulting room Narcissus resists analytic influence in order to disavow registration of the analyst's self-preservative, differentiating function. Because the forms of interpretation derived from a repression theory leave the clinician in the lurch in such a situation, it is all too tempting to fall back into an experiential, noninterpretive stance. But neither interpretation as usually conceived nor prolonged experience with a devoted therapist will enable a patient to internalize a process that inherently raises tension or to move from a defensively closed to a more open position. Only the long-term, slowly titrated analysis of the defenses that compel the patient to see the analyst as a reflection of the patient's wishes can produce the necessary shifts in the analytic process.

The move from secondary to primary narcissism is crucial on both sides of the couch. Otherwise, the concrete patient will be compelled to make the analyst match his or her wishes, and the analyst will be compelled to make the patient match his or her interpretations or to match a benign experience. The analyst in fact usually does both, in the hope that his or her experiential impact on the patient will lead to acceptance of interpretations. One of the most difficult aspects of analysis is the crucial transition from illusions of control (for both patient and analyst) to the intense anxieties over the self-preservation and differentiation that cannot be controlled (for both patient and analyst).

A clinical example: A woman who was sexually overstimulated by her grandmother as a little girl has been in analysis with a woman student analyst for many years. The patient is typically concrete, rejecting most of the student's interpretations. When the student attempts to analyze her resistance to interpretation, the patient acts as if the sexual overstimulation were being repeated. She concretely feels that the analyst wants to make her submit to sexual invasion. (Recall, again, Frosch's patient who "knew" that the analyst would lose control of himself if she spoke about her sexual fantasies.) The student has quite devotedly attempted to analyze this resistance with little effect. There is another major problem: the patient consistently leaves treatment a week before the analyst's summer vacation. She steadfastly refuses to consider the issue as anything other than a concrete one of scheduling.

The student analyst has been in the typical countertransference bind. She has felt controlled, impotent, and unable to think about ways to modify the situation. She has been reduced to devotedly sustaining a frustrating process in the hope that something would change over time. Nothing in her training has prepared her to understand that the patient's sexualization of interpretation and control of temporal aspects of the frame are defensive attempts to ensure that the treatment will remain on the level of secondary narcissism. In other words, it was not that the patient really feared sexual invasion at the hands of the analyst; rather, to equate interpretation with sexual overstimulation is insistently to split libido from self-preservation in the transference. The quasi-hallucinatory revival of her memories of overstimulation is a form of wish fulfillment, of "mere presentation of ideas." It gives the patient a moment-to-moment autoerotic control of the differentiating, self-preservative function of interpretation. Her unconscious communication to the analyst is something like this: "Whenever you interpret, I begin to feel traumatized. Trauma for me is equated with sexual overstimulation. By treating your interpretations as sexual overstimulations coming from without, I maintain repudiation of difference and self-preservation coming from within. I must constantly split libido from self-preservation." Similarly, the patient's persistent departure a week early was not a response to separation anxiety. It was instead a power struggle over the temporal aspects of the analytic frame, a struggle over who would control time. In temporal terms, the patient could neither delay her yearly early departure nor even tolerate any delay in the way she spoke about it, so that it might be interpretable. Like the conflation of interpretation with sexual overstimulation, it repudiated unconscious registration of the self-preservative, differentiating function of analytic time.

It took a great deal of time in supervision to help this student understand that the global nature of the patient's defenses also allowed the patient to stay in the treatment. One particular year, the patient had left a week early as usual. In the first session after the break, the patient made no mention of the break. The analyst carefully avoided the content interpretations that she knew would inevitably lead to the patient's concrete response of being sexually invaded. She only remarked that the patient seemed to feel that it was imperative not to talk about the early departure. In the next session, the patient referred back to the analyst's remark of the preceding day—a rare event for her. She said that she could feel herself wanting to respond as if she had been sexually invaded and could feel that she was increasingly unable to talk. In fact, the patient said that the idea of simply talking about the early departure made her want to lose her voice forever. In other words, if she could no longer exert autoerotic control via talking, she would exert autoerotic control by not talking. She did not want to remember what "really" happened in analysis, what the talking was for. But of course she said all this and did not enact the wish not to speak. Her statement that she did not want to remember what really happens in analysis is an instance of attempted primary disavowal: the patient *has* registered the analyst's libidinal–self-preservative function but has attempted to repudiate it via her concreteness. Primary narcissism constantly becomes secondary narcissism.

The analyst's processive intervention has had an immediate effect upon the patient. By avoiding the kind of interpretation that lent itself all too readily to the patient's need to see the analyst as overstimulating her, the analyst has stopped abetting the patient's concrete defenses. By doing so, the analyst is no longer simply reduced to either "mere presentation of ideas" or experiential silence and hope. Consequently, she no longer attempts to control the patient by making the patient match the picture in her mind. By not implicitly insisting that the patient either match her interpretations or reward her for her devotion, the analyst has also moved from secondary to primary narcissism. Analyst and patient are more potentially open to each other. Each has taken the risk of not maintaining autoerotic control of the other.

PRIMARY NARCISSISM, EROS, AND NEUROSIS

The oscillating registration and repudiation of reality in fetishistic formations can be construed, then, as the inevitable oscillation between primary and secondary narcissism. If fetishism is generalizable, this conception would also have to apply to neurosis. Freud certainly began *On Narcissism* by envisaging the narcissistic resistances of neurotics. Where does one find the oscillation between primary and secondary narcissism in neurosis?

Toward the end of *On Narcissism*, Freud returns to the question of neurosis as he introduces the concept of the "ego ideal," famously a forerunner of the "super-ego." Freud now sees the demanding conscience of the ego ideal as a derivative of narcissistic self-love. In his view, one moves from libidinal investment in one's body (the narcissism of infantile sexuality) to investment in an agency that demands perfect conformity with ideal standards. Neurotic repression, Freud says, proceeds from the "self-respect of the ego," in other words, from the ego's wish to meet the demands of its ideal. In an often ignored statement he concludes: "For the ego the formation of an ideal would be the conditioning factor of repression" (p. 94). By undertaking repressions, one shows oneself "not willing to forgo the narcissistic perfection of . . . childhood; and . . . seeks to recover it in the new form of an ego ideal. What [the adult] projects before him as his ideal is the substitute for the lost narcissism of his childhood in which he was *his own ideal*" (ibid.; my emphasis). To paraphrase: if the overt narcissist makes his or her body into an idealized fetish, the neurotic makes the ego-ideal into a fetish. Where Narcissus is enraptured by his own idealized image, the neurotic is enraptured by the image of himself or herself that matches the ego ideal. In either case, the idealization depends upon autoerotism. Neurotic repression, as Freud says, would then have an intrinsic relation to secondary narcissism. But in *On Narcissism* there is no consideration of how the secondary narcissism intrinsic to repression might be derived from primary narcissism.

Freud did begin to examine this problem six years later, in *Beyond the Pleasure Principle* (1920). In Chapter 1 I alluded to his definition of Eros in *Beyond the Pleasure Principle* as the introduction of "vital differences" into the psyche. As a drive, Eros inherently raises tension because it is a principle of differentiation. The "Nirvana" principle, or death instinct, the counterpart of Eros, is actually synonymous with the pleasure principle, the tendency to tension reduction. As Freud eventually says: "The pleasure principle seems actually to serve the death instincts" (p. 63). Freud knows that this reformulation of the basic forces within the psyche causes problems for his original theory of neurosis. Before the concept of narcissism, he reminds us, the ego was known only as a "repressive, censoring agency," always in conflict with the demands of sexuality. The study of both psychopathology and early development, however, compelled the idea that libido is originally invested in the ego before it is invested in objects. According to Freud, "narcissistic libido was of course also a manifestation of the force of the sexual instinct in the analytical sense of those words, and it has necessarily to be identified with the 'self-preservative instincts' whose existence had been recognized from the start. Thus the original opposition between the ego-instincts and the sexual instincts proved to be inadequate" (p. 52).

Once again, as in *Three Essays* and *On Narcissism*, Freud finds himself compelled to posit an original libidinal–self-preservative drive. And once again, he does not integrate his findings on this topic. But it is exactly here that a reconfigured primary narcissism is necessary. The entire analysis of infantile sexuality as derived autoerotism demands a concept of libido invested in both self and other *before* self and other are either differentiated or represented. One can think of primary narcissism in terms of Eros[9]—the registration of nonrepresented traces of libidinal self-preservation, the unconscious thought of "relations between impressions of objects."

If the concept of Eros demonstrates that the opposition of the ego and sexuality derived from neurosis is actually an artifact, then one also has to understand how the repudiation of originally unconscious thought functions in neurosis. Freud says that the old formula that neurosis is based on a conflict between ego instincts and sexual instincts in fact remains valid but not as an intrinsic quality of either the ego or sexuality. Rather, it is a topographical difference, due to repression. Unfortunately, he did not integrate this correction with the idea from *On Narcissism* that the formation of an ideal is the precondition for repression. If so, he could have said that in neurosis the conflict between Eros and the death instinct, between tension raising and tension reduction, is resolved by an oedipal transition from primary to secondary narcissism in two interrelated ways.

First, via repression, the ego creates an idealized image of itself "minus" the drive derivatives that themselves raise tension unduly. In this sense, as Freud says, one does continue to find a conflict between the ego and the sexual instincts in neurosis. However, the conflict is the result of the unconscious need to conform to an ideal and therefore is a narcissistic formation. The extreme super-ego anxiety the neurotic experiences when repressed drive derivatives become conscious can be viewed as the disruption of a closed system: the neurotic is reassured by the idealized picture of himself or herself guaranteed by repression and threatened by the danger of its loss. Further, the idealization of the super-ego in neurosis serves to prevent sexuality from being a function of Eros. In other words, repression also serves to reinforce the autoerotic splitting of libido from self-preservation. The neurotic's rigidly structured secondary narcissism, with its stabilizing, tension-reducing function, becomes more important than consciousness of sexuality in its differentiating form. Clinically, it has long been understood that the neurotic is dominated by unconscious autoerotism and fixation to incestuous object fantasies. It has been less well understood that this autoerotism and incestuous fixation become in themselves a protection against the tension-raising, differentiating aspects of sexuality.[10]

Second, as we saw in Chapter 1, in *Outline* Freud finally says that there is a "fetishistic" formation of two "contrary attitudes" in neurosis, too. One of these attitudes will be repressed, but the other, remaining in consciousness, will cause its own complications. In my revised formulation, in the oedipal phase, as in every phase of development, tension-raising differentiation will be replaced by opposed fantasies. Most typically these are the fantasies of castration and noncastration that replace sexual difference. It is not difficult to integrate this idea with the essential narcissism of the ego-ideal. The repressed attitude will most likely be the one not in conformity with the ego-ideal; however, the non-repressed attitude can remain in consciousness because of its conformity with the ego-ideal. The entire process aims to construct an idealized picture of oneself in conformity with super-ego demands. In addition, to the extent that the neurotic undertakes repressions in order to avoid castration anxiety, strictly speaking the neurotic also conflates reality and fantasy. The neurotic's concrete convictions about the reality of castration as a potential punishment works hand in hand with the creation of an idealized picture of himself or herself. A fairly common version of these dynamics can be found in the neurotic who represses the phallic side of the two fantasies and is all too acutely conscious of the castrated side. In general, then, the neurotic always attempts to match an idealized picture by repressing one of the two contrary attitudes and leaving the other in consciousness.[11]

EROS, TRAUMA, AND UNCONSCIOUS TIME

Beyond the Pleasure Principle famously reconceives trauma as a breaching of the stimulus barrier. Trauma itself has, of course, been a consistent theme in the understanding of concreteness. I began with Freud's early conception of primary wish fulfillment and primary defense as the basic unconscious response to registered trauma. Concrete patients analogously treat differentiation as traumatic disruption and use wish fulfillment as a primary defense, but within consciousness. To use Freud's later terminology, one might say that the concrete patient uses such mechanisms to erect a "stimulus barrier" within the analytic situation. This stimulus barrier is erected against registration of Eros: to disavow the self-preservative, differentiating function of interpretation, the patient uses autoerotism as a global defense.

This comparison of primary disavowal to the stimulus barrier is somewhat inaccurate, however. Freud understands the breaching of the stimulus barrier in terms of undue stimulation from external sources. He says that there really is no such barrier against internal stimulation (p. 29). In concreteness, the analyst's interpretations seem to be treated by the patient as an undue stimulation from an external source. However, the assumption is that this repudiation is based on the prior registrations intrinsic to primary narcissism and Eros. In this context, recall also Freud's statement in "Two Principles" that there has to be a primordial way of withdrawing from unwanted internal or external stimulation. It is very striking that in *Beyond the Pleasure Principle*, after observing that there can be no protective barrier against internal stimuli of the sort that can be directed against external stimuli, Freud does begin to theorize such a barrier as regards time.

Time is a central issue in the dynamics of concreteness or fetishism. The tension-raising, delaying aspect of time is replaced by the temporal immediacy of the dream state in consciousness. In a passage about a stimulus barrier against time, Freud raises the possibility that conscious time itself may be a defense against the tension of unconscious time. This is a very difficult idea, and Freud calls his discussion of it "obscure":

> At this point I shall venture to touch for a moment upon a subject which would merit the most exhaustive treatment. As a result of certain psychoanalytic discoveries, we are today in a position to embark on a discussion of the Kantian theorem that time and space are "necessary forms of thought." We have learnt that unconscious mental processes are in themselves "timeless." This means in the first place that they are not ordered temporally, that time does not change them in any way and that the idea of time cannot be applied to them. These are negative characteristics which can only be clearly understood if a comparison is made with *conscious* [author's emphasis] mental processes. On the other hand, our abstract idea of time seems to be wholly derived from the method of working of the system *Pcpt.-Cs.* and to correspond to a perception on its own part of that method of working. *This mode of functioning may perhaps constitute another way of providing a shield against stimuli* [my emphasis]. I know that these remarks must sound very obscure, but I must limit myself to these hints. (p. 28)

Here Freud is envisioning something like an unconscious time that is not simply the negative of conscious time. The "Kantian theorem" about time and space as "necessary forms of thought" is a theorem about time and space from the point of view of consciousness. This is the objective time of the infinite series of "now" points and the objective space coordinated with it, essentially Newtonian time and space. The familiar idea of the timelessness of the unconscious is a way of saying that an unconscious temporality cannot be the temporality that consciousness learns about by investigating itself (as for Kant). However, there may be another kind of unconscious time, which can be experienced as traumatic stimulation against which protection is needed. In fact, Freud suggests, the way in which the conscious conception of time is taken for granted (Kantian time and space as necessary forms of thought) can be conceived precisely as such a stimulus barrier.

Can one extend Freud's "obscure" remarks? Unconscious time here acts as a quasi-traumatic internal stimulus. Because it is both disruptive and comes from "within," one has to conceive a primal repudiation of it. The conflation of conscious time with time in general serves as this repudiation. It is like a stimulus barrier to the extent that it protects against the impact of unconscious time. Such tension-raising time can appear to be nonexistent once conscious time is conflated with time itself. But this is still a negative definition. More positively, we already know that the temporal form of pain or trauma is delay. Unconscious time, like unconscious thought, can then be conceived in terms of unconscious registration of temporal differentiation, of delay. It would be the time of Eros and primary narcissism —tension-raising, libidinal–self-preservative, *vital* differentiating time. The assumption that conscious time is time itself would be an autoerotic decontextualization of unconscious time. This would be another version of the derivation of secondary from primary narcissism. More precisely, an originally unconscious registration of the reality of delay is repudiated when consciousness is dominated by the immediacy of wish fulfillment. Temporal immediacy as a form of tension reduction protects against the tension-raising time of Eros.

In fetishism or concreteness temporal differentiation is replaced by the conviction that only what one sees "now" is real. Recall the patient who concretely had to leave for vacation before the analyst and who could not tolerate the delay intrinsic to thinking about her early departure. In neurosis, the differentiating function of sexuality is re-

pudiated via the compulsion to see oneself "now" matching an idealized picture, the explanation of the neurotic's narcissistic resistances.
Again, the implication is that in the analysis of neurosis the task is not
merely to make repressed fantasies conscious. This remains essential,
but it is only part of the entire process. The secondary narcissism intrinsic to the idealization of a fantasy that remains in consciousness
and that may be subtly conflated with reality also requires analysis. To
live with one's symptoms, because of a belief in the possible "reality
of castration," repudiates the registration of difference and delay, of
unconscious thought and time, as much as overt concreteness. Ferenczi approached this idea when he spoke of a neurotic ego that is
split between reality and fantasy, but he ignores the difference between them. Thus, in the analysis of every neurotic one will eventually hit upon the use of secondary narcissism to repudiate primary
narcissism, because these dynamics subtend every repression. More
subtly than in overt concreteness, one will also hit upon moments of
resistance to interpretation per se.

An incident from the analysis of a neurotic patient illustrates these
points. A man came to analysis because he had sabotaged his own
performing career. For the first few years of treatment, we had to go
through the painful process of watching him continue to undermine
the opportunities that came his way. Eventually, he was invited to
perform in London, which he regarded as a "make or break" situation for himself and his analysis. In the first session after his week in
London, he rather offhandedly said that the performance had been a
great success; he had already been asked back. He then went on to
talk about his wife, who had been mugged just before he left. She
had not been harmed, and the mugger had to be content with the
piece of cheap costume jewelry she was wearing. The patient had left
for London worried about her and regretful that he had never had
enough money to buy her a proper wedding ring.

After the performance, he said, he had been thinking about me, so
he decided to visit the Freud museum. It was a weekday afternoon,
and he had the place to himself. At first he spent a long time in Freud's
library, where he was overwhelmed by the fantasy of stealing a book.
He did not do so, but the struggle was intense. When he went to the
gift shop, he noticed rings on sale. (I assume that these were copies of

Freud's famous intaglio ring.) Thinking about his wish to give his wife a ring after her mugging, he asked the salesperson, "How much are those wedding rings?" The salesperson replied that she would be happy to sell him a ring, but they were not wedding rings. He insisted that they were, she insisted that they weren't, and finally he stalked out in a rage. "But," he said to me, "I really knew they weren't wedding rings all along."

The patient has produced a fetishistic registration and repudiation of reality: he knows that the rings are not wedding rings but insists that they are. Why? One can infer from his associations that he is identified with the thief who stole his wife's cheap phallic replacement. He would like to give her back the "real thing," a combined expression of concern for his wife and a wish to rephallicize her. We see here his alternation between the two fantasies castrated–not-castrated. His success in London, certainly due to his analysis, is also equated with a theft, the theft of my "phallic" thoughts—thus his conscious fantasy of stealing a book from Freud's library. If he can successfully steal from me, then he can also transform the analysis into a phallic object to be given to his wife: after the fantasy of stealing Freud's book, Freud's ring becomes a wedding ring. He is telling me that he can only see his success in London as the gratification of a transference fantasy of stealing a phallic object from me; hence his offhandedness about this major shift in him. His super-ego demands that he conform to the picture of someone who is "really" castrated and who can only become phallic by a crime. He is conscious of the castrated-thief picture of himself and has repressed the fantasies of his own phallic prowess. (He blamed himself and his sexuality for his mother's death during his early childhood.) The positive transference here reflects a fantasy of myself conflated with Freud as an idealized phallic object to steal from. This is a conflation of fantasy with reality in conformity with super-ego demands, the same super-ego demands that compel him to repress his own phallic fantasies.

However, this entire configuration is derived from the fear of the transference of primary narcissism. His knowledge that the ring is not a wedding ring, while he insists that it is, represents the disavowal of his knowledge that his success in London, after much difficult analytic work, is not "really" a theft from me. However, this knowledge must be disavowed because of his intense anxiety related to the libidinal and self-preservative function of the analysis. (Again, recall the death of his mother.) In fact, he is unconsciously telling me that if, like the sales-person, I insist upon telling him what the analysis "really" is, he will be tempted to stalk out in a rage. In the Freud museum gift shop, in fact, he repudiated the knowledge that would have delayed his wish-fulfilling exit. (Compare the concrete patient who exited a week early every year.) This delay would also have delayed his conviction that his analytic progress was a phallic theft. Tension-raising, unconscious time, linked to the libidinal–self-preservative function of the analyst and to sexual difference, is repudiated in one fell swoop. He stalks out en-raged with the salesperson (the "real," differentiating analyst) who will not accept his conflation of reality and fantasy. One sees here in min-iature the power struggle over the interpretation of reality, the strug-gle that dominates the treatment of the concrete patient.

The patient's material is richly symbolic, with many possibilities of effective, traditional interpretation. However, another option is opened by the integration of primary narcissism with the secondary narcissism of fetishistic structures. This is the option of investigating how threat-ened he is at taking himself and the analysis out of the rigid structure of phallic-castrated fantasies altogether. One can accurately interpret his fantasy of having to maintain himself in the castrated-thief position and the analyst in the idealized phallic position in terms of the repres-sion of his own phallic fantasies. However, neither interpretation would address the more global need to conflate reality and fantasy in order to ward off the self-preservative, differentiating function of the analysis, the primary disavowal of reality enacted with the salesperson. Thus, al-though this neurotic patient did present material in which one sees the conflict between the ego and sexuality as traditionally understood, he also presented a moment of primary disavowal and attempted neg-ative hallucination. We see evidence of both the maintenance and re-vision of the traditional theory of neurosis. There is indeed a conflict between the ego and sexuality here, but there is also an attempt to keep apart the libidinal and self-preservative drives, particularly in the transference.

Certainly there is a significant clinical difference between a patient who disavows the reality of the analysis over the long term and one who does so only at a particularly important moment. However, to the extent that the neurotic creates a transference based upon repressed wishes (here, the analyst in the phallic position), there also has to be a defense against the reality of the analysis, which eventually will be conflated with the transference altogether (the salesperson). The more subtle and transitory nature of such moments in the analysis of the neurotic does not make them any less essential to interpret. On the contrary, the danger is precisely not attending to such moments, which would promote transference cure. When the analyst can accurately use theory to interpret the repressed fantasies of the neurotic, one may find gratification at the "pattern match" between theory and fantasy content. The neurotic may be all too eager to conflate accurate interpretation with the configurations of secondary narcissism in order to disavow the transference of primary narcissism. The analyst may be all too eager to do the same, both for narcissistic reasons of his or her own and because of the intrinsic difficulty of understanding primary disavowal.

At the end of Chapter 1 I asked how one would reconceptualize what the analyst does once mind and psychopathology are rethought in terms of fetishism, disavowal, and ego splitting. The answer derived from the examination of narcissism is that the analyst attempts to modify the secondary narcissism that replaces primary narcissism. This remains an issue of transference analysis. However, it shifts the emphasis to the fetishistic structures in which the transference as a derivative of primary narcissism (the self-preservative pain of a differentiating process) is disavowed. From the analyst's side, difficulty in understanding such configurations may reinforce secondary narcissism and may make him or her fall back upon an autoerotic style of "interpretive hallucination." This will often occur overtly with the concrete patient. But it can occur more covertly with the neurotic, where effective traditional interpretation of repressed content may mask derivatives of primary narcissism. Thus, it is essential to understand that the less global nature of such formations in the neurotic patient are not simply baffling moments that can be passed over.

The strain of analysis for both patient and analyst is that in principle it modifies a closed system of oppositions. Every such system is a "stage in the development of the sense of reality." Such "stages" substitute for the tension-raising unconscious thought and time of primary narcissism. There is an inherent unconscious tendency on both sides of the couch to pull back from increased tension. But if primary narcissism is also the possibility of the conjoint libidinal–self-preservative drive, then of course the general task of any analysis is to engage such tensions. Clinically, this means intervention in the narcissistic reality organization. Without scrutiny of how the analyst uses interpretation and how the patient responds to it and without a grasp of the oscillation between primary and secondary narcissism, analysis risks becoming a form of wish fulfilling, "mere presentation of ideas" for both parties.

CHAPTER 3

A Dialogue with Hans Loewald:
The Two Realities

In a revised metapsychology of fetishism, Eros and primary narcissism account for unconscious registration of differentiation. Freud himself did not see the intrinsic link between Eros and primary narcissism, but Hans Loewald did. Loewald's integration of Eros and primary narcissism is in fact the result of a career-long meditation on the problem of reality in psychoanalysis. He is the most important theoretician of primary narcissism, because he saw it as the key to a more coherent psychoanalytic theory of reality.

So far, I have simply mentioned some of Loewald's ideas as the context demanded. In the discussion of defenses against differentiation in Chapter 1, I cited his understanding of the enactive form of remembering—the global domination of consciousness by dedifferentiating and timeless primary process. At the conclusion of the chapter, I mentioned his conception that internalization of the analyst's different level of organization is the essence of "therapeutic action." In Chapter 2, of course, I referred to the integration of primary narcissism and Eros. Loewald himself, however, never considered registration and repudiation of reality as the central issues of theory and practice. The specific relevance of his investigations of reality and primary narcissism to the generalization of fetishism has to be spelled out. I will also have to take a critical stance toward some of Loewald's thinking in order to integrate it with the revised theory of fetishism.

Loewald is one of the few analysts to maintain Freud's vision that theory and practice pose questions from the "core of nature." To detail the relevance of his thought to the generalization of fetishism is also to deepen the integration of the theories of nature, mind, psychopathology, and treatment. Most particularly, it is to extend the scientificity of psychoanalysis by showing how psychoanalysis itself changes science once the theory of the unconscious modifies the understanding of reality.

THE EARLY LOEWALD: EGO, REALITY, DEFENSE

Loewald's very first paper, "Ego and Reality" (first presented in 1949), sets the stage for all his subsequent work. In it, he focuses on the way in which conceptions of reality influence theory and practice. He begins by questioning the usual idea that the relation between ego and reality is one of adjustment or adaptation, the familiar renunciation of the pleasure principle in favor of the reality principle. This conception, Loewald says, "presupposes a fundamental antagonism that has to be bridged or overcome otherwise in order to make life in this reality possible" (1980, p. 3; all further references are to this volume unless noted). He contends that the main reason for this picture of an inherently hostile relation between psyche and reality is Freud's emphasis on the defensive function of the ego. In Freud's famous phrase, the ego is the "servant of three masters" and always compromises between the demands of the id, super-ego, and external world. Thus, external reality is essentially conceived as hostile and threatening, as is the id, which Freud called the ego's "second external world" (1923, p. 55).

Loewald provocatively notes that Freud's conception of an ego sandwiched between internal and external reality implies that the ego itself is not real. He thinks that this conception is attributable to "certain philosophical preconceptions," which themselves have "far reaching consequences for psychoanalytic theory and practice" (p. 4, n. 1). Although he specifies neither the preconceptions nor the consequences, he does go on to say that as soon as one attends to the development of the ego itself, other ways of thinking become necessary.[1]

Here Loewald broaches the question of primary narcissism. He refers first to *Civilization and Its Discontents*, where Freud, in another of his rare discussions of primary narcissism, again says that the baby does not initially distinguish between internal and external. Rather, there are various stimulations, some of which can be felt at any time (what will eventually be recognized as one's own body) and some of which cannot (the breast). The border between inside and outside is constituted on this basis: bodily sensations are always available, the breast is not. The important implication for Loewald is that this border develops out of a state in which there is no distinction between internal and external. He infers from Freud's idea that the "ego originally contains everything" that psychic development "starts" from a state of "unity with the environment." Only once the border between the location of various kinds of stimulation develops does it make sense to speak of internal and external, of ego and object.

For Loewald, Freud's idea of primary narcissism implies that "the psychological constitution of ego and outer world go hand in hand. Nothing can be an object, something that stands against something else, as long as everything is contained in the unitary feeling of . . . primary, unlimited narcissism" (p. 5). He cites Freud from *On Narcissism*: the "development of the ego consists in a departure from primary narcissism and gives rise to a vigorous attempt to recover that state" (1914, p. 100). Loewald reinterprets this statement as a description of the ego's inherent tendency to integrate with its environment, to "unify" with it.

One could easily object to Loewald's reading of Freud here. When Freud speaks about the attempt to recover the state of primary narcissism, he probably means something like the wish to restore a putatively original omnipotence, independent of an external reality. Even though Loewald is forcing Freud's meaning, he is doing so for an essential reason. He wants to explore the ramifications of the necessary and paradoxical concept of primary narcissism. When Freud speaks about an original state in which internal and external are not distinguished, he (wittingly or not) expands any possible conception of the experience of satisfaction. Although the experience of satisfaction is empirically an object-related event, for Loewald it occurs in a context in which reality or environment cannot be described as either external or objective. Loewald is emphasizing that the formation of a boundary between inside and outside emerges out of the context in which psyche and object are indistinguishable.

Extrapolating further from the state of not-yet-objectified ego-environment unity, Loewald formulates an idea that will dominate his work: "in correspondence to a primary ego, a pre-ego so to speak, of the primary narcissistic stage, we have to conceive of primary objects and primary reality; and further, that this primary reality, and its subsequent stages of development, are very different from 'reality' as a finished product that is related to the 'mature' ego'" (p. 6). The understated tone of Loewald's writing can make it easy to miss his innovative thrust. From the outset he knew that the concept of primary narcissism compels psychoanalysis to think about reality in unusual ways. His specific point is that once one conceives of something like primary narcissism, the usual view of a "hard," finished external reality, to whose objectivity the ego must reluctantly adapt, becomes questionable. Not that this is not a certain view of reality. Rather, psychoanalysis contains a theory that can explain how objective, external reality develops out of another, more primary kind of reality. Moreover, the primary reality of primary narcissism is not simply a primitive state to be replaced by the more familiar view of objectivity: it continues to develop.

The primary objects of primary narcissism exist before one can properly speak of an external, "objectified" object. Loewald does not refer here (or anywhere else) to Freud's own understanding that primary narcissism is the complement of an intrinsically object-related instinct of libidinal self-preservation. But his sense that primary narcissism is a state of ego-environment integration expands the idea. The "object" intrinsic to the libidinal–self-preservative drive would be a nonobjectified primary object of primary reality. Freud's "originally unconscious thought" (*Objekteindruckung*, the registration or "impression" of the object) also takes place within the organization of primary narcissism. Primary reality itself would be a question of such unconscious registrations, for example, the memory of the experience of satisfaction. It would have to be taken into account in any theory of the relations between ego and reality, because external reality itself develops out of the registrations of primary reality.[2] These ideas may seem abstract, but they have immediate relevance to fetishism and concreteness. As compromise formations, fetishism and concreteness always lead to the inference of unconscious registration of reality. In Loewald's conception of primary narcissism there is an intrinsic bond between the unconscious and reality—the same departure from the usual conception implied by the revised theory of fetishism.

Loewald construes the ongoing development of primary reality in terms of libidinal tension. His idea is that as the border, or "membrane," between internal and external, ego and object, is constituted, so are the forces between them:

> As the mother becomes outside, and hand in hand with this, the child an inside, there arises a tension system between the two . . . libidinal forces arise between infant and mother. As infant (mouth) and mother (breast) are not identical, or better, not one whole, any longer, a libidinal flow between infant and mother originates, in an urge towards re-establishing the original unity. It is this process in which consists the beginning constitution of a libidinal object. (p. 6)

When Loewald speaks of "original unity" here, he means original ego-environment integration. As the border develops between inside and outside, the baby feels the tension of the unavailable breast. The urge to maintain the state of integration can then retrospectively be called an urge to restore unity. Given that the border between inside and outside functions more as a "membrane," Loewald wants us to think of a permeable division. In fact, the continued possibility of permeable divisions between inside and outside *is* primary reality. Freud's *Objekteindruckung*, as a way of thinking registration and primary narcissism together, ramifies Loewald's point. Registration within a psychic organization that does not yet oppose inside and outside presupposes permeable divisions between psyche and environment. This is how an unconscious continuously capable of forming traces of primary reality functions.

According to Loewald, the co-constitution of ego and object, as libidinal tension develops between mother and child, means that "libidinal tension" describes the impulse toward integration with the en-

vironment. Freud's original libidinal–self-preservative drive is an analogous idea and in a sense more consistent. For Loewald, libidinal tension seems to develop out of a tensionless state. For Freud, the original drive has its original tensions: "originally unconscious thought"
raises "cathectic levels" in the psyche. Freud does not do much with
this idea, but without some conception of tensions within primary
narcissism, Loewald runs the risk of seeing this state as having no dynamics. If the energy that flows through the "membrane" is understood as the tension-raising libidinal–self-preservative drive, then tension is there from the beginning.

Certainly, Freud's view of libido almost entirely traces the development of erotic pleasure progressively less integrated with environment. Once libido and self-preservation are split, the infant becomes
autoerotically internal, and reality becomes external. The internal
world of fantasy and wish fulfillment seems more detached from external reality and the "unconscious" more exclusively dominated by
the pleasure principle. The more internal and external are opposed to
each other, the less permeable the border between them. The separation of aim and object develops under the increasing dominance of a
pleasure principle and secondary narcissism for which there is opposition between internal wish and external demand.

Loewald himself, however, does not say much about autoerotic infantile sexuality. He sometimes gives the impression that he replaces
the theory of infantile sexuality with his concept of original ego-
environment integration. Although he continually stresses the role of
such traditional entities as the Oedipus complex, the castration complex, and the super-ego and is always attentive to bodily passion, the
secondary narcissism of infantile sexuality is not often mentioned in
his work. Summarizing the major differences between his own views
and Freud's, Loewald writes:

> If we understand the Oedipus conflict and the castration threat as
> the prototype of the demands of reality, it should be clear how
> strongly for Freud the concept of reality is bound up with the
> father . . . who as an alien, hostile, jealous force interferes with
> the intimate ties between mother and child. . . . The threat of
> the hostile reality is met by unavoidable . . . submission to its

demands. . . . The significant point . . . is that reality is seen as an outside force, for Freud most typically and decisively represented by the paternal figure, which actively interferes with the development of the child in such a way that the ego essentially is on the defensive, and in fact becomes the defensive agency within the psychic apparatus. . . . On the other hand, we know from considering the development of the ego as a development away from primary narcissism, that to start with reality is not outside, but is contained in the pre-ego of primary narcissism, and becomes, as Freud says, detached from the ego. So that reality, understood genetically, is not primarily outside and hostile, alien to the ego, but intimately connected with and originally not even distinguished from it. I believe that in Freud's thinking *these two concepts of reality have never come to terms with each other.* (pp. 7–8; my emphasis)

That the hostile, defensive relation to reality is a result of oedipal submission to the father accurately describes much of Freud's thinking. However, this passage can leave one with the impression that, for psychoanalysis in general, the hostile, defensive relation to reality *should* be construed as the "paternal" version of reality. Perhaps this is the result of Loewald's conception of a "tensionless" primary narcissism. Primary reality may not be "outside and hostile, alien to the ego," but there *is* tension in primary narcissism, the tension of unconscious registration of reality. Wish fulfillment serves to discharge this tension, from the oral phase on. The defensive relation to reality is intrinsic to the autoerotic separation of aim and object and thus coexists with primary narcissism. Loewald's point that Freud's two views of reality have never come to terms with each other is extremely well taken. But the two views of reality are more consistently integrated if they are understood as the necessary unconscious oscillation between primary and secondary narcissism in all phases of development.

Loewald's second essay, "The Problem of Defense and the Neurotic Interpretation of Reality," sharpens the analysis of "Ego and Reality." He speaks of the "special efforts [that] have to be made by the environment, and over a prolonged period of time, to create approximately appropriate psychological conditions for . . . development" (p. 22). The essence of environmental provision is the "regressive movement" that minimizes the "discrepancy" between infant and environment so that the infant can remain in "integrative interaction" with it (ibid.). There is a threat of a "difference between the integrative level of the individual and the integrative level of the environment. To the extent to which this difference is being bridged by the regressive supportive channeling of the environment, development can proceed" (p. 23).[3] Defense in general is an "attempt to come to terms with experiences that cannot be integrated on the level of development reached by the ego in other areas of its integration with reality" (p. 24). Defense then "substitutes" a more primitive, restricted level of "adjustment" for an aspect of reality that represents the threat of too great a difference between "ego" and "environment" (ibid.).

Although Loewald does not put it in quite these terms, his general conception of defense is one in which the threat of differentiation compels the creation of a less differentiated reality, be it internal or external. Thus, defense implies not only a regression of the ego but also a regression in the organization of reality itself. He comments: "The clinical and theoretical importance of this fact has not been recognized, to my knowledge, by psychoanalysis, even though the clinical evidence of it . . . is overwhelming" (p. 26). Of course, Loewald could have cited Ferenczi's "Stages in the Development of the Sense of Reality" on precisely this point. In Chapter 2 I cited the passages in which Ferenczi said that the "mechanism" of neurosis is determined by the "reality sense dominant at the time of fixation." Because all symptoms perpetuate a narcissistic reality organization, while development continues in other areas, Ferenczi, too, spoke of an ego "split" between two different organizations of reality.

Loewald's more general aim here, however, is not to rethink defense clinically but theoretically. He wants to demonstrate how defense is enmeshed in a theory that itself is organized "regressively." Returning to the themes of ego and reality, he reasserts that, from its inception, psychoanalytic theory has tended to view the organization of the psychic apparatus in terms of defense against a basically hostile reality. He now goes one step further and reminds us that the general definition of drive portrays it as a force hostile to the psyche, because it creates a disturbance, a tension that has to be reduced.[4] Loewald integrates this basic understanding of drive with the basic understanding of defense: "just as instincts have been seen as opposed to external stimulation imposed upon the organism and the nervous system, so the individual has been understood as essentially opposed to and imposed upon by the external world" (p. 28).

Loewald's linkage of drive and defense in terms of tension reduction is akin to Freud's early definition of primary process in terms of wish fulfillment and defense. The discharge function of positive hallucination (wish fulfillment) and the denying function of negative hallucination (defense) both serve to eliminate undue tension. There is not much room in this construction for anything other than a hostile relation to environment. (Although Freud includes the experience of satisfaction in this analysis, he does not specifically examine its relation to the principle of tension reduction.) As Loewald says, this "whole conception is neither in accord with modern biological thinking, nor with Freud's own insights concerning the differentiation of ego and external reality out of an original identity in the early stage of primary narcissism" (ibid.).

Loewald goes on to make a sweeping argument about why psychoanalysis developed a theory of an essentially hostile relation between ego and reality, due to the original conception of drive. He maintains that this conception itself grew out of a view of culture as a hostile imposition, which in turn demanded "fear and suppression" of "nondefensive regression" (p. 29). This general cultural climate is also "the climate in which neurosis grows. . . . The hostile, submissive-rebellious manipulation of the environment and the repressive-reactive manipulation of inner needs . . . is the domain of neurotic development. It is the above-described discrepancy situation, repeated and re-enacted on a different level" (ibid.). Loewald means that his basic concept of defense as the result of too great discrepancy between ego and environment is not only something that occurs first within the individual. Rather, it grows out of the general environment in which there is traumatic difference between the individual and "culture." However, and this is the crucial point, the conjoint development of defense on both the cultural and individual levels is also what made psychoanalysis possible:

This historical experience is perhaps the main reason for the
overextension of the concept of defense in dynamic psychology
—as well as for the rise of dynamic psychology itself. The
discrepancy between the integrative capacity of the individual
and the level on which the cultural environment and development has to be integrated by the individual . . . has constantly
increased. But it is discrepancy, tension, and conflict that make
us aware of dynamics, of the interplay of forces that otherwise
remains hidden. And we may understand psychoanalysis and
psychoanalytic treatment itself as an expression and utilization
of the need to rediscover and reactivate the submerged communication channels leading from the origins of our lives to . . .
neurotic symptom formations, and defense systems and
operations. . . . (pp. 29–30)

For Loewald, Freud developed a view of reality that is actually a
manifestation of defense, and he did so in tandem with his views of
drive as disturbance and "culture" as imposition. If Loewald is correct
that the dominant psychoanalytic understanding of reality is itself defensive, then one must ask about what disturbance to itself psychoanalysis might be defending against. Loewald states the problem co-
gently, in terms of his own understanding of the relation between
defense and environment:

On three levels, then, the biological, psychological and cultural,
psychoanalysis has taken for granted the neurotically distorted
experience of reality. It has taken for granted the concept of a
reality as it is experienced in a predominantly defensive integration of it. Stimulus, external world, and culture, all three, on
different levels of scientific approach, representative of what is
called reality, have been understood unquestioningly as they are
thought, felt, experienced within the framework of a hostile-
defensive (that is regressive-reactive) ego–reality integration. It
is a concept of reality as it is most typically encountered in
the obsessive character neurosis. . . . Psychoanalysis has most
searchingly analyzed and shown us the neurotic structure and the
defensive function of obsessive symptoms and of the obsessional

character formation. But it has not recognized, in its dominant current, that psychoanalytic theory has unwittingly taken over much of the obsessive neurotic's experience and conception of reality and has taken it for granted as "the objective reality." (p. 30)

What is the view of reality that psychoanalysis has unwittingly taken over from obsessional character neurosis? Precisely that "reality" is the "hard" objectivity to which a "soft" subjectivity must unwillingly adapt, because the pleasure principle always makes "internal" fantasy preferable to "external" reality:

The conception of organism-environment, ego-reality, as an antagonistically related pair of opposites or isolated systems, lets the reality principle appear as a defensive-adaptive principle by virtue of which the pleasure principle becomes repressively modified, and fantasy becomes an isolated remnant of this earlier principle. In the process of reality testing and the establishment of the reality principle, fantasy is seen as split off. . . . To the extent to which fantasy is split off, ego and reality in their mutual integration become restricted and impoverished, as can be seen in hysterical and obsessional symptom formation and in the corresponding character disorders. Projective-introjective processes, which are elements of the still rather obscure complex of integrative activities we call fantasy, continue in more highly differentiated forms to operate in the development and elaboration of reality during man's lifetime. Otherwise reality would be static (as indeed it has been conceived as being in psychoanalytic theory). It becomes static and hostile, visible in each individual patient, to the extent to which his life has become merely a defensive-reactive struggle. *It is this neurotically impoverished reality, a form of reality that is exercising its great destructive power on all of us, in whose image the psychoanalytic concept of reality has been formed* [my emphasis]. The psychoanalytic investigation and understanding of ego development and ego structure, as it progresses, will also lay the foundations for an understanding of the *dynamic* [author's emphasis] nature of reality. The clearer the distinction

between integration as such and defensive types of integration
becomes, the more apparent also will be the difference between
the idea of an alien, hostile reality (a finished product imposed on
the unsuspecting infant, from there on and forever after) and the
integrated dynamic reality (forever unfinished) on the elaboration and organization of which we spend our lives. (pp. 31–32)

When Loewald refers to organism-environment or ego-reality as
"antagonistically related" pairs "of opposites" or "isolated systems," we
can refer back to the clinical-theoretical problem of concreteness. Fetishistic compromise formations substitute fantasies of opposition for
an unconsciously registered and repudiated differentiating process.
What Loewald calls here a "forever unfinished" "dynamic reality" is
precisely what I called the processive aspects of reality. Loewald's idea
that this dynamic reality is the reality of ego-environment integration
makes it another way of conceiving primary reality and primary narcissism. It becomes static and hostile to the extent that defense has to
substitute a view of reality derived from secondary narcissism for the
dynamic reality of primary narcissism. In other words, the permeable
border between internal and external becomes a rigid opposition.
This is the general implication of Loewald's idea that defense itself
leads to a regressive organization of reality. In specifically sexual terms,
for example, the fetishist attempts to substitute a static, finished thing
for the sexual difference that overwhelms him or her. The opposition
castrated–not-castrated dominates consciousness. In more general
terms, the concrete patient substitutes an "objective" perception of the
analyst for the dynamic reality of the analyst's interpretive function.
The opposition between the analyst's concretely relieving or threatening function then dominates the transference. The fetishist, or the
concrete patient, is perhaps a more inclusive model than Loewald's
obsessive character for a view of a static reality in which internal and
external are closed systems opposed to each other.[5]

An exclusive theory of an internal, fantasy-driven subjectivity opposed to an external objectivity would itself be fetishistic or concrete.
It conflates two fantasies, "inner" and "outer" or "subjective" and
"objective," for a dynamic, constantly differentiating process of ego-
environment integration. On the whole, this is the view of reality

that psychoanalytic theory frequently defends against.[6] A permeable border is intrinsically threatening in that one can always become what one differentiates from. Rigid opposition provides the illusion of control of what is inside and what is outside, at the cost of a hostile relation between the two. Whether one chooses the obsessive character, the fetishist, or the concrete patient as the model for the construction of a defensive view of reality, the point remains the same: reality itself is recast as something exclusively external and objectifiable in order to gain control of it.

When psychoanalytic theory unquestioningly conflates its view of reality with this defensive structure it creates the clinical possibility that analyst and patient will just as unquestioningly share the same view of reality. Moreover, the theory of the psychic apparatus itself as a closed system is part and parcel of this view of reality. Tension reduction is the primary function of such a closed system, which is threatened by any conception of itself as intrinsically open and non-static. What Loewald calls the "destructive power" of this view of reality is vividly evident in the destructive narcissism of small differences dominant in the analysis of the concrete patient. Loewald's warning that psychoanalysis itself has unquestioningly adopted the obsessive character's view of reality can be applied to any attempt to "destroy" the derivatives of primary reality, whether in the consulting room or in the construction of theory.

INTERNALIZATION, IDENTIFICATION, AND ANXIETY

"Internalization," the concept that first appeared in a 1962 paper, "Superego and Time," has become synonymous with Loewald. Loewald is discussing the relations between primary narcissism and hallucinatory wish fulfillment. In this context he proposes to understand the ideal ego as a

> recapturing of the original primary-narcissistic, omnipotent
> perfection of the child by a primitive identification with the
> omnipotent parental figures. It is an identification representing
> the re-establishment of an original identity or unity with the
> environment and would seem to have connotations akin to

hallucinatory wish fulfillment. (Just as the early deprivations and disillusionments are undifferentiated antecedents of the later separations and relinquishments, so the early wish-hallucinations are antecedents of the later internalizations and so-called "restitutions of the object in the ego.") This ideal ego represents a return to an original state of perfection, not to be reached in the future but fantasied in the present. This state of perfection of the ego— perhaps the ideal undifferentiated phase where neither id nor ego nor environment are differentiated from one another—gradually becomes something to be wished and reached for. (pp. 46–47)

Loewald is adding an important element to the ontogenesis of the wish. Primary narcissism denotes a state of "unity" with the environment in which internal and external are not distinguished. Once they do become separate, there is an urge to reunify them (the libidinal tension system), which takes on the connotation of omnipotent perfection. Reunification and omnipotence are then implicit to every wish fulfillment. But Loewald would have been more consistent here if he had characterized omnipotent reunification as the essence of secondary narcissism. (I made the same point about Freud's confusing attribution of omnipotence to primary narcissism in Chapter 2.) The organization of primary narcissism is neither omnipotent nor non-omnipotent, since aim and object are not yet separated within it. But this also means that wish fulfillments contain within them the trace of ego-environment integration. This is why Loewald also says that "wish-hallucinations are antecedents of the later internalizations." Internalization will become the concept that describes how an ego-environment integration lost to defense can be restored. It is the complement of primary narcissism, that is, the push toward a non-omnipotent, differentiated ego-environment integration.

Crucially, Loewald makes these points in the context of a discussion of time. Identification and wish fulfillment are atemporal in that they attempt to perpetuate an eternal present. Temporality, Loewald writes, is the possibility of a future reintegration with the environment which does not magically and exclusively attempt to make good a loss in the present, as happens in every dream. As a relation to what is not immediately present, time is intrinsic to internalization.

This temporal process consists of "internalizations of interactions and not of objects. . . . The process of internalization or introjection involves a change in the internal organization of elements; this, while hard to conceptualize is of the utmost importance" (pp. 49, 51). In identification, time itself is static: it only exists in the present tense, as wish fulfillment. In internalization, time becomes the possibility of an integration with environment that is never "perfect" or "omnipotent," always open to the future. Moreover, the very possibility of change in an internal organization implies that the organization is itself intrinsically temporal, that is, intrinsically open to greater differentiation.

Loewald's conception of time can be integrated with Freud's "obscure" thought from *Beyond the Pleasure Principle* about unconscious time. Unconscious time, like unconscious thought, is a derivative of primary narcissism. It is a time of differentiation and delay, the temporality of the "not now." It implies the possibility of change of internal elements, because it is intrinsically open. Conscious time, said Freud, functions as a "stimulus barrier" against unconscious time. It defensively substitutes the temporal immediacy of wish fulfillment, the "now" of tension reduction, for unconscious time. Unconscious time would then be the time of internalization, the time of an opening to the future. Differentiation itself is a temporal taking in of a process, an interaction. When Loewald says that it is hard to conceptualize the internalization of interactions that change inner organization, he implies that it is easier to conceptualize the present, dedifferentiating identification of subject and object in wish fulfillment.

Loewald's "On Internalization" (1973) pursues these lines of thought. The paper is central to his construction of a theory of treatment that does not replicate a defensive organization of reality. He begins by contrasting two possible views of internalization. From the standpoint of immediate gratification, of the drives as tensions to be reduced, he notes that "internalization" appears to be a defensive flight born of "frustration, disappointment and fear" (69). It connotes an insubstantial inner world of substitutes for necessarily lost objects —defensive identifications. This picture of the psychic apparatus is always one in which internal and external reality, "drive" and "culture," are disturbances. Loewald then goes on to hypothesize that there are other ways to think of the relations between drive, object, and psychic structure. If drives and object ties themselves structure the psyche through interaction with environment, then internalization may be conceived as "the basic way of functioning of the psyche, not [simply] one of its functions" (p. 71). It is easy to anticipate that Loewald will use internalization to describe the ongoing primary narcissistic integration with environment.

After contrasting the two possible views of internalization, each depending upon the basic conception of the relation between psyche and reality, Loewald writes that his basic thrust is to respect "an oscillation between such various standpoints, as perhaps in their juxtaposition and combination lies the secret of success in understanding more about the conflicted and ambiguous creatures that we are. The richness and imprecision of psychoanalytic psychology are, to an extent, due to such oscillations, implicit as they have for the most part remained" (p. 70). Here, then, Loewald is allowing for an intrinsic oscillation between the two views of reality, the one in which drive is essentially a disturbance and the other in which drive is essentially the integrating force of the "libidinal tension system." If internalization is a concept relevant to both views, then it would have to have an internally divided structure. It would necessarily oscillate between primary and secondary narcissism, between dynamic primary reality and static objective reality.

Loewald asks a question about clinical process in relation to the divided structure of internalization. The theory of neurosis states that unsuccessfully repressed material returns in distorted form, because it is still unacceptable to the ego that repressed it in the first place. In the course of analysis, one hopes that the distorted material will be reintegrated into the ego organization. Loewald therefore asks, What then is the basic function of the ego—to defend against disturbances to its organizations or to accept and integrate them? Loewald says that the answer again depends upon the point of view from which the question is asked. From the standpoint of the pleasure or constancy principle, the integration of previously warded off material is a complication, a "delay on the return road to the state of rest." However, from the standpoint of the ego itself, when acceptance replaces repression there is a "gain in its organization and functioning" (p. 74). Loewald clarifies the two points of view: "One might indeed maintain that repression, to the extent to which it is successful, deadens and restricts psychic life, thus being a more direct route to the state of rest and preferable from this standpoint. With further and higher ego organization, far from getting closer to a state of rest, there is more life" (ibid.). When Loewald links repression to the "state of rest," in essence he echoes Freud's early view of primary defense as the force of psychic inertia.

To expand Loewald's thought, one can say that psychoanalysis itself comes about for two reasons. Loewald has already mentioned the first reason: the ego does carry out defenses, demanding a theory and practice that explains repression in relation to tension reduction. The second and less obvious reason is that the ego does more than repress. If it could not reintegrate repressed material, there would be no possibility of psychoanalytic treatment. Thus, the ego cannot be driven only by the need to reduce tension, as conspicuous as this force is in any defensive operation. If it were not also driven to integrate what it has warded off, if there were not a push toward what Loewald calls "more life," then analytic interpretation of repressed material would be pointless. Repression, taken as the generic for defense, is the way in which the ego protects its current organization by closing itself to whatever disturbs it. Internalization connotes the "loosening" or "opening" of that organization (p. 75).

Loewald, then, is describing an ego inherently split between primary and secondary narcissism, between an opening that creates change through disturbing current structure and a closing that prevents change by eliminating disturbances to current structure. In temporal terms, the opening of primary narcissism implies the possibility of a relation to the "not now," while the closure of secondary narcissism implies the maintenance of an eternal "now." Psychoanalysis, then, is a product of both. However, its theory has tended to stress only the latter, as when Freud emphasizes that dreams exist only in the present. This is why Loewald writes that

> it is of the utmost importance, both theoretically and clinically, to distinguish much more sharply and consistently than Freud ever did between processes of repression and processes of internalization. . . . While in defensive organization (repression) object

cathexis is maintained on an infantile level, internalization implies a transformation of object cathexis into narcissistic cathexis,
that is, more complex ego organization. . . . I use narcissistic
here in a metapsychological, not in a clinical-descriptive sense.
(pp. 76–77)

This contrast between repression and internalization is crucial to
any theory of analytic therapy conceived as a modification of defense
against differentiating processes. When Loewald speaks of transforming an object cathexis into a narcissistic cathexis from a metapsychological point of view, he is describing the move from secondary to
primary narcissism: something previously split off from the ego is integrated within it, raising tension levels. In this context, Loewald
himself has begun to use the vocabulary of splitting, which is inevitable in any basic discussion of defense:

What is internalized, in the sense in which I use the term, is not
split off from the coherent ego but becomes or has become an
integral part of the coherent ego. While what is internalized, and
what is repressed are both unconscious (in the dynamic sense),
the former is a structural element of the coherent ego, the latter,
the repressed, is not. . . . *We may ask whether repression, under given
circumstances, could be a way-station on the road to internalization. It is
conceivable that repressed material may ultimately be dealt with by the
coherent ego, not by "making the unconscious conscious," but by unconscious ego processes which undo the splitting off.* But insofar and as
long as repression is an active process, characterized by the
ego's defensive activity of protecting its current organization
against disruptive influences, repression is in opposition to
internalization and prevents it, as much as it prevents or inhibits
adequate interaction with the external world. (pp. 78–79; my
emphasis)

Repression as a "way-station on the road to internalization" essentially describes primary disavowal, a process that registers and repudiates "disruptive influences" unconsciously. This is why Loewald
has introduced the vocabulary of "splitting"—Freud's "splitting of the

ego in the process of defense"—to describe the effect of repression. His idea that "unconscious ego processes" may undo splitting is not only an abstract possibility, it is exactly what must occur when traditional forms of interpretation, which depend upon "making the unconscious conscious," cannot address concrete or fetishistic compromise formations.

However, Loewald's thought here is somewhat constrained by the equation of repression with defense. Freud found himself moving toward splitting and disavowal in order to conceptualize that anything defended against also has to have been registered. The difficult implication is that what is apparently external to the ego is also internal to it—the basic structure of primary narcissism. A primary defense has to account as much for the intrinsic tie between the ego and what disturbs it (registration) as for the severing of that tie (repudiation). Repression is no longer the most general concept of defense within this problematic. It does not account for the tie to whatever is defended against, and it assumes defense against objectified contents.[7] Primary disavowal, then, is the registration and repudiation of Loewald's dynamic primary reality.

Loewald enters into a discussion of the life and death drives at just this point. He summarizes his view that the death instinct is really "nothing new" in Freud's theory but rather another way of speaking about the intrinsic tendency to return to a state of rest, to diminish tension. For Loewald, what

> *is* new in Freud's last instinct theory is the life instinct as a force or tendency *sui generis*, not reducible to the old pleasure-unpleasure principle. . . . This change of viewpoint is, at least in part, due to Freud's finally capitulating before the fact that stimulus tension is, in and of itself, not necessarily unpleasurable and a state that tends to be avoided, no matter how much the constancy principle demands this conclusion. Tension is no longer seen exclusively from the standpoint of inanimate matter as a disturbance . . . a force must be assumed to operate in mental processes that favors the tensions of mental life, works in opposition to as well as in fusion with the motivating power of the death instinct. (pp. 79–80)

Given this argument, Loewald takes the next step of integrating re-pression—again as the generic for defense—with the death instinct. Defense attempts to maintain the ego organization in a less disturbed, more inert state, on what Loewald calls a "lower organizational level." Internalization is basically "under the sway of Eros," since it promotes reintegration of "disruptive influences" (p. 80). Like Freud, Loewald thinks that the life and death drives work in fusion and in opposition with each other. The same would have to hold for defense and internalization:

> Such a formulation allows for a share of the other polar force in both processes. This is necessary in order not to do violence to the fact that repression-defense has a protective function, and that internalization, if unchecked by the lure of objects external to the psyche's own structures, and if these structures are un-protected against overload by defensive barriers, leads to inner sterility and diffusion. (p. 80)

The same point can be made even more sharply in terms of primary disavowal. If it both registers the tensions of differentiating processes and repudiates them, it can be said to show the workings of life and death, differentiation and change, dedifferentiation and inertia. The oscillating structure Loewald always notes—the division of internalization between the dynamic and static views of reality—is the basic structure of primary disavowal. Freud, of course, initially noted the oscillating structure of disavowal and splitting in his discussion of fetishism. Had he been aware of the contradiction in his own analysis of fetishism—castration as the disavowed reality—he might have been able to see that the construction of the fetish is more than a "monument to the horror of castration," which it certainly is on a secondary level (the fantasied making good of an equally fantasied loss in the present). It is also the defensive "monument" to the dynamic reality of sexual difference. The fetish, again, oscillates on two levels. It primarily oscillates between a registered, uncontrollable differentiating process and its repudiation, and secondarily between castration and noncastration as an attempt to gain omnipotent control of sexual difference. Freud could have viewed this primary oscillation as

an example of what Loewald calls the life and death instincts working in fusion and in opposition to each other. Loewald in turn, had he
given more attention to disavowal, ego splitting, and secondary narcissism, could have extended Freud's view of the fetish as a model for
symptom formation. As a compromise formation, the fetish exemplifies the fusion and opposition of the dynamic and static views of reality, of integration with environment and defensive attempts to gain
control of it.

Loewald moves in this direction when he again takes up the concept of identification. I have already discussed his earlier distinction
between identification and internalization, that is, taking in an object
versus taking in an interaction. He now expands this idea in terms of
difference:

> Identification as such leads to an identity of subject and object
> or of parts or aspects of them. Insofar as, in identification, they
> become identical, one and the same, there is a merging or
> confusion of subject and object. Identification tends to erase a
> difference. . . . Identification is a way-station to internalization,
> but in internalization, if carried to completion, a redifferentiation
> has taken place by which both subject and object have been
> reconstituted. . . . To the extent—always limited in the vicis-
> situdes of human life—to which internalization comes to
> completion, the individual is enriched by the relationship he
> has had with the beloved object, not burdened by identification
> and fantasy relations with the object. (p. 83)

As in the discussion of repression, dedifferentiating identification is a
"way-station to internalization." The theory of the "way-station" always answers to the demand for a conjoint moment of registration
and repudiation. One cannot describe such a process in other than
oscillating terms:

> By internalization, then, the . . . identity of subject and object,
> are given up, destroyed, and separate "identities" are formed. . . .
> In this sense, identity does not mean identity between subject
> and object, but self-sameness, individuality. . . . *Mental life is so*

constituted that it oscillates between the two poles: internal identity, which makes object relations in the true sense possible, and identification that dissolves the differences between subject and object. . . . Therapeutic analysis, of course, represents or should represent such an internalizing phase in life. (pp. 83–84; my emphasis)

When Loewald says that analysis should represent an "internalizing phase in life" there is an implicit caveat. If internalization differenti- ates, then one has to be particularly attentive to any tendency toward identification in analysis. In the extreme, the fetishistic or concrete patient demands that the analyst identify with whatever fantasy the patient imposes. The patient then "knows" that the analyst is "just like" him or her. Even to begin to interpret the transference is to ini- tiate the differentiating, or in Loewald's sense internalizing, process that the patient has to defend against. While this problem is conspic- uous in the analysis of the concrete patient, it occurs more subtly in every analysis. The example of the neurotic patient at the end of Chapter 2 illustrates this point. The patient defensively had to elimi- nate awareness of his progress in analysis. He did so by identifying the analyst with the phallic position and himself with the castrated posi- tion, such that he could "steal" a "fetishized" thing—a book, a ring— from the analysis. In Loewald's terms, instead of internalizing the in- teraction with the analytic process, the patient defensively wished to identify with an object. In training analyses, in particular, there is an inherent tendency to identify with the analyst rather than to inter- nalize an interaction.[8] The dedifferentiating secondary narcissism of such identification with the training analyst may then be enacted in the future analyst's own therapeutic work and institutional activities. The fear of what Loewald calls "individuality," in other words, of self- sameness as a manifestation of difference, can then dominate the ana- lyst's professional life.

Metapsychologically, analytic therapy involves a shift in drive or- ganization. The transference moves from what Loewald calls "object cathexis," based on dedifferentiating identification, to "narcissistic" internalization of a redifferentiated analyst-patient relation. The ana- lytic process itself becomes an environmental force. This is the force of *Objekteindruckung*, the differentiating "impress" of the relation to the analyst. The individuality of Loewald's thought is that, like Freud, he is always interested in unconscious dynamics. He maintains the drive or "energic" point of view, where so many of those who emphasize ego-environment integration seem to abandon it. Overall, he defines "instincts" as the most primitive "intrapsychic motivational forces"—which sounds like Freud. The difference is that he sees such forces developing out of a psychic matrix or field constituted essentially by the mother-child unit.

> Instincts are . . . forces that *ab initio* manifest themselves within and between what gradually differentiates into individual and environment. . . . Instincts remain relational phenomena, rather than being considered energies within a closed system, to be 'discharged' somewhere. The differentiation, within the original matrix, of individual and environment involves the differentiation of narcissistic and object cathexis. (pp. 152–53)

By "narcissistic" Loewald again means not the libidinal cathexis of the ego as object but the primary narcissistic action of forces within the ego that raise its organizational level. "Object cathexis" itself refers to "instinctual currents between individual and environment (or objects)."

Although Loewald always maintains a drive perspective, as mentioned, he sometimes simply seems to substitute his conception of primary narcissism, in which drives are "relational phenomena," for the tension-reducing function of the psyche as closed system. In the passage just cited Loewald seems to disqualify the notion of drives as energies to be "'discharged' somewhere." Here we re-encounter a fundamental problem in his work. Because he presumes that primary narcissism is a tensionless state, he does not consider the potentially traumatizing aspect of raising tension levels, what one might call the "trauma of Eros." Raised tension can always border on the traumatic and therefore can always potentially produce a need for discharge. By not giving due attention to this possibility, Loewald can seem to dispense with the tendency to tension reduction.[9] However, one can extend his idea that in identification a differentiation is erased to include the concept of differentiation as trauma. Whenever differentiation becomes overwhelming, the "instinctual" relation to the environment becomes one of tension reduction, and the psyche's picture of itself as a closed system becomes a defensive necessity. This is the "moment" of autoerotism or of secondary narcissism, an organization as intrinsic to drive experience as the integrative, relational organization.

These energic concepts are crucial for a general conception of clinical process. From the standpoint of identification, of taking in the analyst as object, analyst and patient function as closed systems. When the analytic process is effective, "unconscious ego processes" begin to transform this tension-reducing opposition into integrating differentiation. But the transition from a defensively closed to a more open organization does not occur without anxiety—a possibility Loewald does not envisage. Following his argument, however, one can conceptualize "internalization anxiety." It is the tension aroused when unconscious splitting off of primary reality is modified. In general, internalization anxiety is always provoked by the move from a more closed to a more open system. For example, the student analyst's patient in Chapter 1 spoke of "trees flying through the air" as she began to register the difference between herself and the analyst.

The treatment of the concrete patient who consistently left a week early for vacation provides another example: As the analyst grew more skilled at making processive interventions, she could note more carefully the patient's movement away from the analytic process. At one particular moment, when the patient again responded to an intervention as if the analyst were sexually overstimulating her, the analyst simply said, "Right now you and I are not on the same page about this," a fine way to capture splitting and disavowal in the moment. The patient snapped back: "If you and I were on the same page, my world would fall apart." In other words, when the analyst disturbs the patient's concrete defenses, integration with the analytic process is intolerable. The patient's visceral response captures quite well the intense anxiety related to internalization of repudiated differentiation. This is a question left in abeyance by Loewald. The clinical danger of having no conception of internalization anxiety is that the analyst may assume that an intrinsic drive toward integration will take care of itself. Loewald does seem to make this assumption.

PERCEPTION, MEMORY, AND PRIMARY NARCISSISM

Internalization anxiety clarifies the role of anxiety in fetishistic or concrete compromise formations. It is the result of a three-phase process. Registration of difference itself always raises tension levels. For each individual, at some point this tension feels intolerable. Difference and tension are repudiated via the conflation of dedifferentiating wish fulfillment with reality. The result is a displacement of tension onto exaggerated signal anxiety organized in terms of threatening absence and relieving presence. Any destabilization of this structure, any possible re-encounter with repudiated difference, revives the tension—internalization anxiety.

In terms of defense, internalization anxiety is closely tied to the basic mechanism of concreteness, the elimination of the difference between memory and perception via negative hallucination. Loewald also refers to this problem in a remarkable passage in "Perspectives on Memory" (1980). He explains that he intends to reexamine the basic Freudian assumption that memory is an unconscious, internal registration and perception a conscious, external registration. This view evidently leaves out a conception of perception in the organization of primary narcissism in which inside and outside have not yet differentiated from each other:

> The act of perception is an interaction, and what is registered would be that interaction. The mental activity involved in perceiving, its modification in the interaction with the perceptual stimulus, is reproduced, or rather . . . is continued in the registering act. This is an act that, seen from the standpoint of an outside observer, reproduces or continues internally a process that has occurred between the subject and an object or stimulating agent. Perceiving, in the beginning of mental life, is an instinctual activity, and the stimulus perceived is by that very fact an instinctual stimulus. The internal reproduction of that instinctual interaction is equally an instinctual activity. Indeed, from the standpoint of that bundle of instincts which is the primitive infantile psyche, interaction with something outside and internal interaction are indistinguishable; nor does the infantile psyche differentiate a

perceptual act (having occurred) from a memorial act (occurring now). Memory, as registration or recording, and perception are identical for the infant. (pp. 154–55)

The original Freudian distinction between perception and memory was elaborated within an unquestioned subject-object, internal-external opposition. Loewald's point here is that as soon as one begins to think of internalizing processes derived from "original" ego-environment integration, the "original" registrations cannot simply be described as the internal storage of something external. Just as ego and environment differentiate from each other, so do memory and perception. Within the later, more "objective" opposition of memory and perception resides the possibility that "a memorial act occurring now" can be experienced as a perceptual act or that a perceptual act can be experienced as an "instinctual" (drive) stimulation.

Loewald reminds us that the experience of satisfaction is precisely one in which perception equals memory. For the infant "there is no difference between the actual event of satisfaction and its reproduction" (p. 155), that is, no difference between perception and memory. It is important to proceed very carefully here. When Loewald says that for the infant there is no difference between the experience of satisfaction and its reproduction, he is describing the infant's conscious experience. This is like Ferenczi's idea from "Stages in the Development of the Sense of Reality" that "from the subjective standpoint of the child . . . he needs only to seize the wish-aims in a hallucinatory way (to imagine them) and to alter nothing else in the outer world, in order (after satisfying this single condition) really to attain the wish-fulfillment" (p. 222). Ferenczi was clear that elimination of the difference between the experience of satisfaction and its reproduction was a manifestation of omnipotence—secondary narcissism. The equivalence of memory and perception in terms of primary narcissism is not the same as the equivalence of memory and perception in terms of secondary narcissism. According to Loewald, the first would be an example of internalization, the second of identification. Within primary narcissism the equivalence of memory and perception is the essence of the differentiating registration of the experience of satisfaction. The autoerotism of secondary narcissism repudiates that registration, creating illusions of control and omnipotence. Wish can then match experience. Certainly secondary narcissism arises out of primary narcissism; internalization and identification always oscillate, as Loewald says. But he does not consistently distinguish the oscillating positions.

There is actually a persistent confusion within Loewald's conception of primary narcissism. This confusion is significant because it characterizes the entire psychoanalytic conception of "reality." For Loewald, primary narcissism indicates both the possibility of a dynamic, primary, "other" reality, intrinsically temporal and open to change, *and* the "original unity of instinctual and cognitive mental processes [that] would accord with the conception of an undifferentiated phase out of which id and ego develop . . . at the level of that phase there also is no differentiation of subject and object or inside and outside or of temporal modes" (p. 164). This description makes primary narcissism sound like hallucinatory wish fulfillment itself: "In primitive hallucinatory wish fulfillment, i.e. in the recathexis of the registration of an experience of satisfaction, there would be no distinction between the past or present state of being or between external and internal reality" (p. 159). Of course the entire thrust of Loewald's theory is that primary narcissism contains both possibilities, but that is not the same thing as construing it as an originally "undifferentiated phase."

The difficult problem that Loewald comes up against, but does not engage, is to conceive an originally differentiated stage, in which differentiation itself is not understood in internal-external, subject-object, memory-perception terms. On the one hand, it is clear why he would call this an "undifferentiated phase out of which id and ego develop." If id designates the source of internal stimulation and ego the system that receives external stimulation, then Loewald is quite justified in calling this phase undifferentiated: the sources of stimulation themselves have not been differentiated. As he says, perceptual and drive stimulation are the same activity in this phase. On the other hand, if primary narcissism is the state in which the experience of satisfaction is registered but in which subject and object are not yet differentiated, there is an "internalization of interaction," a "registration of trace," not organized in subject-object terms. Thus, it is tempting but inaccurate to call primary narcissism an undifferentiated state because subject and object are not differentiated within it.

Loewald himself therefore repeats certain "neurotically distorted" views of reality when he takes subject and object as the indices of differentiation and when he refers to an originally undifferentiated state.[10] He makes primary narcissism look like a primitive state exclusively dominated by the mechanisms of wish fulfillment. This state can only be one that has to be surpassed in progressive development, according to the usual conception that Loewald does so much to counter. His other conception of primary narcissism—the dynamic, primary reality that continues to develop—makes it the possibility of nondefensive integration with differentiating tensions throughout life. Internalization of environment can always become defensive identification. Integration itself is the registration of a differentiating process. When such registrations provoke undue tension they are split off—the repudiation of primary reality. An unconscious inherently open to registration of differentiating process becomes a tension-reducing closed system. Any reopening of the closed system provokes internalization anxiety.

ENACTIVE REMEMBERING: THE FRAME

It is essential to have a grasp of the preceding argument as we approach Loewald's formulation of the enactive form of remembering. This concept is directly related to concreteness. Loewald proposes to "go beyond Freud's formulation" of memory versus action by distinguishing between "enactive and representational remembering" (p. 164). He says that enactive remembering includes "not only acting out and transference repetitions, but also identificatory reproductions." "Identificatory reproductions" are those in which "the individual is not aware that he is reproducing something from the past," that is, in which the distinction between perception and memory is suspended.

Loewald's problem here is the same as Freud's when he described the paradoxical state of dream consciousness that suspends reality testing. Loewald puts the problem in terms of differentiation:

> [enactive] remembering is unconscious in [the] deeper, dynamic
> sense, inasmuch as it shares the timelessness and lack of differenti-
> ation of the unconscious and of the primary process . . . there is
> no past as distinguished from present. From the point of view of
> representational memory, which is our ordinary yardstick, we
> would say that the patient, instead of *having* a past, *is* his past, he
> does not distinguish himself as rememberer from the content of
> his memory. In representational remembering, the mind presents
> something to itself as its own past experience, distinguishing
> past from present and himself as the experiencer from what he
> experienced. (p. 165)

Enactive remembering, then, is the clinical manifestation of the original equivalence of memory and perception. Loewald recapitulates
his analysis of registrations within primary narcissism:

> we discussed *original registrations as reproductive continuations of inter-
> actional experiences* and said that in its primitive beginnings there
> is no differentiation of an internal process ("memory") from an
> interplay of primitive psyche and environment ("perception"),
> and no distinction between present (the moment of reproducing)
> and past (the time when what is reproduced occurred). This, of
> course, also means that there is as yet no difference between the
> agent and the product of his activity, *between registering and its
> content.* (p. 166; my emphases)

Enactive remembering is a persistent use of dedifferentiating perceptual identity—or as Loewald says, "identificatory reproduction."
However, he does not explain the clearly defensive function of enactive remembering. Rather, he seems to understand it as a derivative
of primary narcissism, but again of primary narcissism understood
only as an undifferentiated state. This apparently undifferentiated
state is made possible by registrations of interactions in which there
is "no difference . . . between registering and its content." Loewald
does not grasp his own description of differentiation within primary
narcissism. Wherever there is "registration" there has to be differentiation, even if there is no differentiation between memory (registra-

tion) and perception (content), that is, between inner and outer, subject and object. Enactive remembering, then, is not simply an avatar of an originally undifferentiated state. Rather, it defensively eliminates integrative, differentiating registrations of environment.

Finally, Loewald will not even consider a defensive function of enactive remembering. He does make a topographical distinction that both enriches his analysis and causes more problems: "The distinction between enactive and representational memory resolves itself into that between unconscious and preconscious memory. Unconscious memory follows the laws of primary process, whereas preconscious memory is determined by secondary process" (p. 166). Loewald does not only mean here that primary process is more primitive and comes first, while secondary process is more developed and comes later. Rather:

> Mental and memorial processes are primary if and insofar as they are *unitary*, single-minded, as it were, undifferentiated and non-differentiating, unhampered, as Freud has described it, by laws of contradiction, causality, and by the differentiation of past, present, and future and of subject and object, i.e. by the differentiation of temporal and spatial relations. Condensation and displacement, considered as indications of the influence of primary on secondary process, are regressive influences in the direction of an original density where all our distinctions and dichotomies do not hold sway. Mental processes are primary to the extent to which they are nonsplitting, to the extent to which they do not manifest or establish duality or multiplicity. . . . It is clear that into this category fall what we call magical thinking, omnipotence of thought and movements and gestures, as well as identification, coenesthetic reception, and many other phenomena of so-called primitive mentality. . . . The secondary process is secondary insofar as in it *duality* becomes established, insofar as it differentiates; among these differentiations is the distinction between the perceiver and the perceived. . . . Mental processes, in the development from primary to secondary process, undergo a splitting of themselves by which an inner encounter arises, which leads to all the distinctions and dichotomies characteristic

for secondary process. . . . The term preconscious indicates something about the character of secondary process. The essential characteristic of preconscious mental processes is not that they lack conscious awareness, but that they involve that internal splitting by which what I would call an inner *conscire* [literally, knowing-together] arises in mental life. We are most familiar with this *conscire*, with this splitting into different psychic elements which thereby may encounter and know each other, from consciousness. But it is not conscious awareness of such things that establishes that knowing. . . . In primary memorial activity, such inner splitting and *conscire* is lacking. (pp. 167–69)

Loewald's important concept of *conscire* as a preconscious, secondary process, differentiating activity answers the need for a nonconscious relation to reality.[11] Loewald knows that "conscious awareness, and verbal expression of dynamically unconscious, primary process mentation is possible" (p. 199), as evidenced by the dream, by psychosis, and by the enactive form of remembering itself. As he puts it, the "unconscious mental processes may be known to the ego, although the inner, preconscious *conscire* is absent" (ibid.). When the distinction between memory and perception is eliminated within consciousness, when a patient "is" his or her past rather than "having" a past, then *conscire*, the integrative differentiation of memory and perception, has been eliminated from consciousness. But Loewald does not explain how and why such an elimination of *conscire* occurs. He seems to be content with a topographical distinction between unconscious and preconscious, as if situating primary and secondary processes within the two "systems" explains the function of enactive remembering.

Such a description does not provide sufficient dynamic understanding. In Chapter 1, I examined Sandler's understanding of how waking illusions are sustained by the dream mechanism of perceptual identity. Sandler's illusions are akin to enactive remembering. However, there is a contradiction between Loewald's and Sandler's theories of how primary process can come to dominate consciousness. This contradiction clearly illustrates the nondynamic nature of Loewald's understanding of enactive remembering. Sandler situated the

conflict between "reality" and "fantasy" within the same nonconscious system. When he described the way in which perceptual identity works to create illusions in waking life, he was compelled to
speak of "*unconscious* secondary process" in order to account for how
the ego protects itself from disturbances it has to have registered.
Sandler did not emphasize differentiation in the way Loewald so
valuably does. However, he understood that in waking life, as in the
dream, primary process can dominate the ego in order to keep registered realities unconscious.

It might seem like splitting hairs to contest Loewald's assignment
of nonconscious differentiation to the preconscious instead of to the
unconscious. However, the point is to expand the conception of unconscious processes in order to conceive the dynamics and treatment
of the enactive form of remembering. If, as Loewald says, primary
memorial activity has the attributes of wish fulfillment and if secondary process is automatically eliminated from it, then one must
conceive an unconscious process in which integrative differentiation
(*conscire*) is globally defended against. Loewald does not envision that
conscire is linked to the registrations of interactions within the organization of primary narcissism. To assign *conscire* to the preconscious is
to beg the question of unconscious registration and repudiation of
primary reality.

In fetishism, for example, sexual differentiation is the trace of an interaction. Because every such registration can provoke internalization
anxiety, as it becomes preconscious it can be turned into the fantasy
structure phallic-castrated, which itself may become entirely conscious. But the defensive, fetishistic oscillation between two fantasies
in consciousness would not occur if there had not been unconscious
registration of sexual difference and unconscious repudiation of it. In
other words, the unconscious can specifically be understood as the
form of mental functioning in which nonperceptual traces of registered tension can be handled either through internalization or identification. The great change in this conception of the unconscious is
that it "thinks" in nonrepresentational terms (increases tension), as well
as wishes (reduces tension). The preconscious would be the area in
which traces already registered move toward consciousness. However,
such traces do not move toward consciousness as mental contents but

as differentiating processes. If such processes have been repudiated unconsciously, internalization anxiety motivates the global substitution of primary process wish and defense for *conscire*. The fantasy content of the wish then becomes conscious, as a defensive substitute for *conscire*. This content is then subject to secondary disavowal. It is split into opposed fantasies, which can be conflated with reality through timeless and dedifferentiating enactive remembering.

Because enactive remembering dedifferentiates, it would have to produce resistance to interpretation. Patients who globally resist interpretation also tend to want to control the actual analytic environment in order to ward off the loss of control implicit to internalization anxiety. There will be problems around time, money, and almost any other "concrete" aspect of the environment, from the magazines in the waiting room to the light in the office, the position of the furniture, the placement of pictures on the wall. Control of the frame is a form of enactive remembering. This is why interpretations do not become effective until there is some progress around internalization of the frame. Therefore, the analyst will have to understand how vital it is both to tolerate and then to address the frame violations. The clinical aim is to address the behavior as something that sustains the patient's illusions of safety and danger. As such illusions are analyzed, the patient will experience distress at not being able to control the frame in the service of warding off the trauma of Eros—integration with a differentiating environment. As internalization anxiety itself is analyzed, the differentiating function of the frame can become conscious without immediate repudiation. This process can eventually make transference interpretation therapeutically viable.[12] In Loewald's sense, internalization of the frame helps to register the trace of the interaction with the analyst. In my sense, internalization of the frame is vital to the modification of primary disavowal. The frame's differentiating function makes it a manifestation of primary reality.

How does Loewald conceptualize analysis as an "internalizing phase of life"? In "Perspectives on Memory" there are two related answers to the question of therapeutic process, but both are problematic in that they do not address the question of the frame.

First, throughout early childhood, Loewald contends, the transition from primary to secondary process, from unity to duality, takes place through the mediation of interaction with the parents. While such a statement can appear to be banality itself, Loewald has something quite specific in mind. His idea is that the move from unity to duality means that representation becomes possible, so that the ego, "as agency of the secondary process presents something to itself, whether this is material from the outer or the inner world" (p. 168). In other words, a division within mental processes occurs: perceiver is not perceived, memory is not perception, representation maintains the division of past and present. This division does not come about consciously; it is another manifestation of preconscious *conscire*, the "knowing together" of elements that remain distinct.

Loewald contends that representation as a function of *conscire* is made possible by reflective interactions between parent and child. These interactions contain the possibility that the child might become other than what he or she already is. The "otherness" necessary for representation, the difference between oneself and one's image, is brought to the child by the parents:

> dichotomous reflexion—I am not speaking here of conscious reflection—is set in motion or made possible by the fact that the parents actively reflect the child to the child by their responsive encounters with him, encounters that become elements in the child's eventual inner reflexiveness. It is this mirroring of the child on the part of the parents, a mirroring that inevitably, because of the parents' higher mental development, reflects "more" than the child presents, which leads to the development of secondary process. Words provided by the environment are one prominent example of this mirroring "hypercathexis," which, according to Freud, makes it possible for the primary process to be succeeded by the secondary process. *The interpretations given to the patient in analysis, especially, in our context, when enactive remembering is interpreted in terms of representational memory, are a highly developed form of such hypercathecting reflection, which the patient may then make his own.* (pp. 168–69; my emphasis)

Loewald's point in this passage is that the difference in mental organization between parent and child is an environmental factor whose trace can be registered. He distinguishes between "dichotomous reflexion" and conscious reflection in order to describe nonconscious internalization of differentiation. In analysis itself, this would be the process that makes self-observation, or the observing ego, possible. For Loewald, the analyst's words, as verbal interactions between patient and analyst, must be gauged to promote internalization. If the difference in organization between analyst and patient is too great, the result is traumatic impingement. If the difference is too small, unifying identification is promoted.

All of this makes good therapeutic sense. However, there is a problem in Loewald's description of the effects of interpretation upon enactive remembering. When enactive remembering is interpreted representationally, he says, the patient "may then make his own" the different level of the analyst's organization. Clinically, we have consistently seen that when the analyst interprets "representationally," that is, symbolically, to the enacting or concrete patient, the "difference in organizational levels" between analyst and patient is too great, leading the patient to attempt to eliminate it altogether. The patient then hears the interpretation enactively. It becomes for the patient a manifestation of the analyst's enactment, an invitation to a power struggle over whose view of reality will prevail.

What Loewald consistently does not take into account is that the frame element of the analyst's different level of organization can in and of itself be experienced as traumatic. To analyze the enactive form of remembering, the analyst most often has to find ways of intervening which are calibrated to a non-traumatizing degree of difference between himself or herself and the patient. Such interventions can be compared to good parenting in their sensitivity to possible impingement. However, they require a sophistication of dynamic understanding, translated into a simplicity of intervention, that cannot—and should not—be expected of even the best parents. Parents do not have to think about the difference between enactive and representational intervention. The model here is that it does not, and should not, matter to the mother that in nursing the baby she promotes the illusion that the experience of satisfaction matches wish fulfillment. The analyst, on the other hand, has the extremely difficult therapeutic task of meeting the patient at the level where enactive re-

membering operates defensively, where it is on the cusp of representational memory. It is the analyst's task to bring internalization anxiety into the session. Without this understanding, the analyst can fall
into the trap of believing that the patient should make representational interpretations his or her own. If the patient cannot do so, the
analyst may feel like an inadequate parent who is not providing the
right experience for the patient. It is all too easy then to enter into a
parental power struggle with the patient. Even without the power
struggle, it is possible to lapse into hoping that experience with a
consistently benevolent analyst will have a therapeutic effect.

Loewald's second answer to the question of therapeutic process in
relation to enactive remembering is more dynamic. For the analyst-
observer, he says, the "unitary, enactive memorial process-structure
. . . corresponds to a dual, secondary memorial structure that is isolated from the former and readily available only to the analyst as
agent of secondary-process mentation" (p. 169). As an outside observer, the analyst can understand the duality embedded in the patient's passionately unitary ideas in enactive remembering. However,
the relation to the analyst itself embodies the unitary structure: the
transference is real. The clinical problem is the defense against interpretation where it counts most, as concerns the transference.

How can one move from an enactive to a representational transference? Here is Loewald's dynamic formulation of how interpretation leads to representation:

> The unconscious structure, in and through the act of interpre-
> tation as a hypercathectic act again becomes, in the case of
> de-repression, an "idea," i.e. a secondary process structure.
> Becoming an idea means that the unconscious structure loses
> its unitary, instinctual, "single-minded" character and becomes
> reinserted into a context of meaning, i.e. into a context of
> mutually reflecting and related mental elements. The linking
> is no longer merely one of reproductive action; it is one of
> representational connection. (p. 169)

This is an excellent description of therapeutic *aims* in the treatment of
enactive remembering. However, Loewald seems to maintain a naïve

faith in the hypercathecting capacity of traditional interpretation as "de-repression." The question is whether traditional interpretation can accomplish Loewald's aim: the transformation of reproductive action into representational connection. To trust in the hypercathexis implicit to interpretation does not address defenses against the frame function of interpretation. Equally, to think in terms of "de-repression" is not to address the interplay of primary and secondary disavowal that sustains enactive remembering.

Loewald does not address such issues, but he does provide a compelling explanation for the persistence of enactive remembering:

> The loss involved in the transformation of the unitary, single-minded character of primary memorial activity is, I believe, the cause for what Freud has called the resistance of the id. This loss is fended off by the "compulsion to repeat," which forever remains an active source of conflict between id and ego . . . the sadness and grief of mourning perhaps also concerns that loss, that giving up of the unitary single-mindedness of instinctual life that tends to preserve in some way the primary narcissistic oneness from which we have to take leave in the development of . . . secondary process mentation. That development involves being split from the embeddedness in an embracing totality, as well as that internal split in which we come to reflect and confront ourselves. (pp. 170–71)

Loewald's reference to "loss" has to be understood on several levels. When enactive remembering dominates consciousness, the fantasy of union remains unquestioned. The dedifferentiating drive toward union derives its force from the id. Thus, the drives can always operate in the service of preventing loss of union. Loewald profoundly ascribes the id's compulsion to repeat to the possibility of using wishes to prevent differentiation or internalization.

For the patients themselves, however, mourning of the loss of union usually occurs only at the end of a very long analysis. Such therapeutic progress does not come about only by interpreting defense against loss. In enactive remembering, the patient can seem to fear separation and loss, because loss is concretely identified with loss of the idealized, relieving object. On the primary level, such loss is preferable to the tension of traumatic differentiation. To oversimplify, one can outline at least five forms of secondary fantasies of loss that regulate primary internalization anxiety: the loss of the relieving object, the loss of protection against undue tension, the loss of the "certain knowledge" contained in oppositional structures, the loss of control of differentiating processes, and finally the loss of the illusion of embeddedness in an embracing totality. To interpret the fear or pain of such losses, without interpreting how they fend off internalization anxiety, would be like interpreting the "reality of castration" as the essential problem in fetishism.

In enactive remembering, what the patient primarily defends against is not loss but contact. Again, this is the kind of contact Loewald calls "differentiating integration" with environment, or *conscire*. It is contact with the analytic frame as a manifestation of primary reality. In drive terms, it is a manifestation of Eros—binding and tension raising. Such contact can also be understood in terms of the libidinal–self-preservative drive, which both registers satisfaction and overcomes a resistance. Either possibility implies a certain degree of pain, the pain of differentiation. To understand defenses against *conscire* in these terms is to understand why internalization of the frame is essential to the modification of enactive remembering. To the extent that a patient controls the frame, the patient is engaged in a defensive power struggle against internalization. But internalization of the frame is a complex, long-term therapeutic task, demanding processive intervention into primary disavowal. It calls for both tolerance and rigor on the part of the analyst. The tolerance comes from understanding the internalization anxiety warded off by control of the frame; the rigor comes from understanding the necessity of analyzing disavowal of primary reality. Both are essential to the modification of enactive remembering.

THERAPEUTIC ACTION AND SCIENCE

Loewald's best-known paper, "On the Therapeutic Action of Psychoanalysis" (1960), is not directly concerned with enactive remembering. Its aim is to elucidate the concepts of interaction and environment in psychoanalytic treatment generally. Loewald wants to demonstrate that effective analysis depends upon internalization and interaction, even in the standard treatment of the classical neuroses. Further, he takes up two fundamental issues. How does a basic conception of unconscious processes determine the understanding of treatment? What are the implicit views of reality and science in a given conception of unconscious processes?

Loewald's basic goal is to provide "deeper insight into the psychoanalytic process" as it produces structural change via "interaction with environment" (p. 221). He immediately introduces what is probably his most famous idea: structural change is mediated by the relationship to the analyst as a "new object" (ibid.). In general, the idea of the analyst as a "new object" has been oversimplified. It has been used to support the most naïvely "experiential" view of analysis, that is, that therapeutic progress comes about through an "object relationship" with someone who promotes development instead of hindering it. Loewald himself contributes to this distortion in his comparisons of analysis to parenting. But he is clear that he is not advocating any changes in classical technique, for example, a more "relational" approach to treatment (p. 222). "Environment" has to be understood metapsychologically in order to grasp what he means by "new object."

The heart of the matter is the "view of the psychic apparatus as a closed system" (p. 223). From within the assumption of a closed system, the analyst's neutrality is supposed to guarantee scientific objectivity and clinical efficacy. The analyst is to remain outside the patient's dynamics in order to allow their full projection and interpretation in the transference. This familiar classical conception of analysis does not consider the functions of objectivity and neutrality in the total therapeutic setting. The neutrality of the analyst does promote the controlled regression of the transference, according to the usual understanding. But the purpose of the regression is to allow intervention into the processes that have prevented "integration and differentiation" (*conscire*). There is nothing "new" in the transference regression: the relation to the analyst repeats the difficulties of integration and differentiation. By interpreting what is "old," however, the analyst also makes himself or herself available for a "new way of relating to objects

as well as of being and relating to oneself." Every time the analyst interprets the "old," in fact, he or she "implies aspects of undistorted reality which the patient begins to grasp step-by-step as transferences are
interpreted" (p. 225). Neutrality and objectivity therefore also have to
include revived differentiation and integration.

Inclusion of the new object relation within analytic neutrality is
for Loewald another meaning of positive transference. His basic definition of "newness" in terms of integration and differentiation also
implies the raising of tension levels within the psychic apparatus. The
"old" is the closed system of drive discharge. The "undistorted reality" represented by the analyst is the opening to the registrations repudiated by the closed system. To rethink positive transference in
terms of the relation to the "new object" is to conceptualize analytic
therapy as the movement from a closed to an open system, from static
to dynamic reality.

The problem, for Loewald, is that analytic neutrality has only been
conceptualized in terms of the closed system. It has been conflated
with the "neutrality" of the scientist toward the subject under study.
The specific conditions of psychoanalysis, however, change the basic
setup of traditional neutrality: the "subject" itself is active in relation to
the observer, and the observer actively attempts to modify the subject:

> While the relationship between analyst and patient does not
> possess the structure, scientist-scientific subject, and is not charac-
> terized by neutrality in that sense on the part of the analyst, the
> analyst may become a scientific observer to the extent to which
> he is able to observe objectively the patient and himself in
> interaction. The interaction itself, however, cannot be adequately
> represented by the model of scientific neutrality. It is unscientific,
> based on faulty observation, to use this model. . . . What I am
> attempting to do is to disentangle the justified and necessary
> requirement of objectivity and neutrality from a model of
> neutrality which has its origin in propositions which I believe
> to be untenable. (pp. 226–27)

The key idea is that the analyst may become objective if he or she
examines himself or herself and the patient in interaction. The inter-

action itself, however, cannot be conceived in conventionally neutral terms. Integration and differentiation depend upon the interaction between analyst and patient, while in conventional science there is (supposedly) no such interaction. The necessity of this interaction is precisely what Loewald calls "environment": "in the analytic process this environmental element, as happens in the original development, becomes increasingly internalized as what we call the observing ego of the patient" (p. 228).

In the light of Loewald's early work, environment as "undistorted reality" cannot mean the objectivist view of reality that psychoanalysis has unwittingly taken over from obsessional character neurosis. In the light of his later work, internalization of interaction does not mean identification with an object. Environment then means real differentiating processes that cannot be objectified, the kind of primary object relation intrinsic to dynamic primary reality. Time is generally the best analogy for such processes. In Loewald's initial discussions of internalization, time was rethought as an opening to a future that does not attempt to make good a loss in a static present. As a differentiating interaction, interpretation is temporal. When Loewald says that environment becomes internalized as "what we call the observing ego of the patient," he means approximately what he will mean later when he speaks of how enactive memory becomes representational memory. Timeless and dedifferentiating primary process is opened to the "not now." The observing ego develops out of this internalization: there is division within immediate perception.

The focus on internalization of environment makes more conspicuous a process that always occurs in analytic treatment:

> "Classical" analysis with "classical" cases easily leaves unrecognized essential elements of the analytic process, not because they are not present but because they are as difficult to see in such cases as it was difficult to discover "classical" psychodynamics in normal people. Cases with obvious ego defects magnify what also occurs in the typical analysis of the neuroses, just as in neurotics we see magnified the psychodynamics of human beings in general. (p. 231)

If psychoanalysis in general depends upon internalization of a differentiating interaction, then any scientific view of it must be able to theorize such a process. Loewald's idea is that the objectivist view of the psychic apparatus as a closed system simply cannot do so. We know from his earliest work that he attributed the closed-system understanding of the psyche to the tension–reduction model of the drives. However, he always maintains that drives, or psychic energy, are essential to a scientific understanding of psychoanalysis. Thus, he inevitably returns to the problem of psychic energy in terms of the open system.

This is the point at which all the previous conceptions of Eros and primary narcissism are integrated, one of the most critical moments in Loewald's work. The introduction of Eros in *Beyond the Pleasure Principle* is for Loewald the major instance of Freud's progress in this respect. Loewald importantly notes that at the end of his life Freud explicitly said in *An Outline of Psychoanalysis* that, while the definition of the drive as a return to a previous state fits the death instinct quite well, this definition simply does not apply to Eros. The old concept of tension reduction is recast as the death instinct. The aim of Eros is not to abolish tension but to raise it by "binding together." Loewald concludes that in rethinking the drives Freud

> does not take as his starting point and model the reflex arc
> scheme of a self-contained, closed system . . . it is by no means
> the ego alone to which he assigns the function of synthesis, of
> binding together. Eros, one of the two basic instincts, is itself an
> integrating force. This is in accordance with his concept of
> primary narcissism as first formulated in *On Narcissism*, and
> further elaborated in his later writings, notably in *Civilization
> and Its Discontents*, where objects, reality, far from being originally
> not connected with libido, are seen as becoming gradually differentiated from a primary narcissistic identity of inner and outer
> world (see my paper on "Ego and Reality," 1951). (pp. 234–35)

Primary narcissism is as much a modification of the theory of the drives as it is of the ego. Freud did not quite grasp how productive it would be to synthesize the concept of Eros with primary narcissism, perhaps because of his difficulty with moving outside a conventional subject-object, closed-system scientificity.[13] Nonetheless, Freud offers the elements for a theory of the psychic apparatus as both open and closed, intrinsically tied to environment (Eros) and split off from it (the death instinct). Because ego and id differentiate from each other out of primary narcissism, according to Loewald the concept of Eros "moves away from an opposition between instinctual drives and ego. . . . The concept Eros encompasses in one term one of the two basic tendencies or 'purposes' of the psychic apparatus as manifested on both levels of organization" (p. 235). Ego and id, then, will function according to both tendencies. From the point of view of the death instinct and tension reduction, the id presses for immediate discharge and the ego engages in defensive operations. From the point of view of Eros, the id raises tension levels and the ego expands by integrating these tensions.[14] Eros itself expresses the originally conjoint status of the instinct of self preservation and libido (*Three Essays*). In *Beyond the Pleasure Principle*, Freud says that the opposition between the instinct of self-preservation and the sexual instincts is inadequate from the point of view of Eros—a confirmation of Loewald's point of view. As the force of integration with the environment, Eros registers the "traces" of drive activity in which self-preservation and libido are not split from each other. In Loewald's terms, this would be the way in which "instinctual drives organize environment and are organized by it no less than is true for the ego and its reality. It is the mutuality of organization, in the sense of organizing each other, which constitutes the inextricable inter-relatedness of 'inner and outer world'" (ibid.).

In its traditional sense, Loewald says, interpretation uncovers the regressive material within compromise formations. Here one would also want specifically to include the "narcissistic" reality organization that always accompanies defense, as discussed by Ferenczi. In a less traditional sense, as Loewald states, the very fact that the analyst interprets creates the possibility for "freer interplay between the unconscious and preconscious systems" (p. 240). The interaction between analyst and patient has to contain the possibility of the differential that will help to create the freer interplay within the patient's mind: "This process may be seen as the internalized version of the overcoming of a differential in the interaction process. . . . Internalization itself is dependent on interaction and is made possible again in the analytic process" (pp. 240–41). In environmental terms, then, interpretation as interaction promotes greater contact with the primary reality of the analytic frame and simultaneously greater contact with split-off parts of oneself.

But one cannot assume, as Loewald seems to, that environment is internalized without conflict. On the contrary, because it implies differentiation and raised tension levels, environment can unconsciously be treated as trauma linked to internalization anxiety. Prolonged resistance to interpretation speaks dramatically to defense against the differentiation implicit to the observing ego. Loewald also says very little about the self-directed aggression that Freud derives from the death drive. Sexuality itself can become a (self) destructive force when primary disavowal splits self-preservation from libido. Analogously, active defense against the self-preservative function of analysis produces a transference dominated by autoerotism. Thought is then used as tension reduction, implying the narcissistic attack on difference. Loewald's lack of focus on the self-destruction that Freud derives from the death instinct is of a piece with his failure to address the defensive function of enactive remembering. Dedifferentiation is always linked to a balance in favor of blind narcissistic aggression, that is, an aggression that cannot observe itself in action.[15]

A comprehensive understanding of the role of environment in the analytic process would evidently have to encompass both its registration and its repudiation. The processive aspect of interpretation would be most visible in the interventions that address primary disavowal, since primary disavowal itself registers and repudiates environmental differentiation. However, Loewald's lesson is that processive interpretation is implicit even in the most traditional interpretation of repressed content: there is no interpretation that does not imply the analyst-patient differential. A scientific conception of analytic therapy would have to be very vigilant about not falling back into the naïve pseudo-scientificity that disavows primary reality —non-perceptual, differentiating energic processes. It would equally have to take into account the inevitability of the "neurotically distorted" view of reality, the replacement of primary reality with closed oppositional systems.

SCIENCE, ENERGY, REALITY

Loewald's commitments to science, to concepts of psychic energy, and to a rethinking of reality led him to consider the relations between psychoanalysis and the great revolution in twentieth-century physics. In "The Waning of the Oedipus Complex," a relatively late paper (1976), he again takes up the theme of reality organizations in which there is no distinction between subject and object. He speaks of the "ambivalent search for primary narcissistic unity and individuation" as a "psychotic core" that is as universal as the Oedipus complex. Given that psychic life starts from primary narcissism, all the implications of its reality organization have to be included within psychoanalytic theory—and here the analogy to physics:

> Our hitherto normal form of organizing reality, aiming at a strict
> distinction and separation between an internal, subjective, and
> an external, objective world, is in question. Our psychotic core,
> as it comes increasingly into view, prevents us from being as
> much at home and at ease with this solution as our scientific
> forefathers were. I believe that our quest for individuation and
> individuality, and for an objective world view, is being modulated
> by insights we are gaining from the "psychic reality" of pre-
> oedipal life stages. We even need to re-examine Freud's distinc-
> tion between psychic reality and factual, objective reality, not
> that this distinction might be invalid. But its validity appears to
> be more circumscribed and limited than we assumed, analogous
> to Newtonian physics: the new theories and discoveries of
> modern physics do not invalidate Newtonian physics, but they
> limit their applicability. (pp. 403–4)[16]

There is a vast topic implied in this analogy. Loewald is basically saying that classical physics developed within a worldview in which a sharp subject-object opposition represented a scientific advance. The point has often been made that the modern subject and the modern concept of objectivity (mathematization of physical processes) emerged together in the work of Descartes. The revolution in physics in the late nineteenth and early twentieth centuries did not invalidate classical physics, as Loewald says, but showed its limitations. In psychoanalysis, the closed system–tension reduction conception of the psyche was a product of applying the classical view of science to unconscious processes. In and of itself, this, too, was a significant advance. However, the compelling force of other ways of conceiving energic processes and of other forms of reality organization also showed the classical psychoanalytic conception to have limitations. I have been making a similar argument about repression and primary disavowal: repression as the model of defense belongs to the classical conception of the psychic apparatus, while Freud's late shift to disavowal as the model of defense can be integrated with his conceptions of Eros and primary narcissism. Psychoanalysis itself, in Loewald's view, is as much in a position to contribute to a rethinking of science as is physics and in fact has to do so if it is to develop a coherent theory of therapeutic action. By analogy then, Loewald is asking us to consider that, just as the unsuspected reality of the subatomic world contributed to changing science's conception of itself, so the reality of environmental processes must lead psychoanalysis to change its own conception of itself as both scientific and therapeutic.

In "Psychoanalysis in Search of Nature: Thoughts on Metapsychology, 'Metaphysics,' Projection" (1988a), Loewald offers his final words on this very large topic. The paper is only five pages long but bears prolonged commentary from many points of view.[17] I will approach it as a final synthesis of Loewald's integrative view of science, nature, and psychoanalysis. He begins with a typically quiet challenge to received notions of reality: "With the psychoanalytic conception of the unconscious and of psychic reality psychoanalysis is stepping outside the bounds of nineteenth-century natural science and its interpretation (a hermeneutic construction) of nature as objective material reality" (p. 49). His point is that the equation of nature with objectivity is itself a subjective, that is, hermeneutic, interpretation. This thought is difficult for those who still wish to accredit the received opposition between *Geisteswissenschaften* and *Naturwissenschaften*, between subjective, interpretive disciplines and objective, quantifiable ones. Even if Freud consciously wished to make psychoanalysis a *Naturwissenschaft*, the scientific-therapeutic necessity of interpretation itself upsets the traditional opposition: interpretation supposedly belongs to the subjective disciplines. Thus, psychoanalysis is in a position to demonstrate how objectivity itself is a subjective construction, an interpretation of nature. We again hear an echo of the idea that without such critical reflection, psychoanalysis tends to take over a "neurotically distorted" view of objectivity.

Loewald then takes a more radical step. He says that although clinical psychoanalysis is certainly concerned with the "detailed exploration of the human microcosm," the fact that it is based on a theory of unconscious processes also means that it "must not lose its moorings in a theory of nature" (ibid.). He alleges that Freud's "speculations" on the forces of life and death in nature as well as in the mind are the outcome of a theory of unconscious processes that does not fit the traditional divisions into subjective and objective disciplines. Going a step further than the early Freud who found defense a question from the core of nature, Loewald contends that psychoanalysis itself compels a revised view of nature. One can begin to think about nature in the way psychoanalysis has taught us to think about mind, in other words, as not organized the way our consciousness tells us it is:

> The traditional theory of nature is changing, and with that change the theory of knowledge of nature is changing. Nature is no longer simply an object of observation and domination by a human conscious mind, a subject, but an all-embracing activity of which man, and the human mind in its unconscious and sometimes conscious aspects, is one element or configuration. . . . It may indeed be claimed that in traditional natural science too, the objectivity achieved in human consciousness was *projected* onto the universe and to what we call, then, physical material reality, and that this nature, so structured by us was now perceived as ultimate reality. . . . (p. 50)

When Loewald says that nature "is no longer simply an object of observation and domination by a human conscious mind, a subject" he is taking the Freudian idea that conscious subjectivity cannot directly perceive psychic reality and extending it to "material reality."[18] His early discussion of the objectivity of the obsessive character takes on an added dimension. If the aim of the obsessive character is to exercise defensive control over a dynamic reality by rendering it static, then traditional objectivity itself is another version of this dominating project. It is then justifiable to construe traditional objectivity as the projection of a defensively controlling subjectivity.

Freud's late generalization of the dynamics of fetishism can be extended even farther in this way. If fetishism reveals the way in which mind substitutes static objects for differentiating processes and creates perceptual certainty about oppositional structures, then the relation between the subject and his or her fetish also reflects traditional objectivity. In *Three Essays* Freud intuited that infantile sexual wishes always imply mastery and domination, because they create autoerotic illusions of control. This makes the wish itself the possibility of projecting subjectivity via perceptual identity and then taking the projection as perceived fact—precisely the problem of the fetishistic or concrete patient. Certainty about perception shows us how a certain kind of objectivity is a form of wish fulfillment. But wishes, in Freudian theory, are themselves made possible by the trace of the experience of satisfaction. A coherent theory of unconscious processes therefore has to understand that the wish itself contains the trace of primary, dynamic reality, just as the fetish contains the disavowed trace of sexual difference. This is the prerequisite for not making the wish into the ultimate internal reality and for not confusing reality with static objectivity.

Interpretation then is not essentially the objective perception of unconscious content but, as Loewald says, a differentiating interaction. One cannot emphasize too much that when interpretation is taken only as the objective perception of unconscious content, the analyst is in the position of sharing the same view of reality as the concrete patient. Enactive remembering then meets enactive interpretation. However, as a defensive response to the trauma of differentiation, enactive remembering is inevitable. So is enactive interpretation, if the analyst responds defensively to the patient's repudiation of the interpretive function. As we begin to understand the inevitability of defense against differentiating interaction from both sides of the couch, we also begin to understand the difficulty of moving beyond traditional objectivism—and all its subjectivistic counterparts. This approach to unconscious process and therapy then makes psychoanalysis into a powerful theory of the intersection of mind and nature. It can explain how we come to have one view of nature in order to defend against another: static, objective reality is the substitute for differentiating primary reality.

In "Psychoanalysis in Search of Nature" Loewald specifies that he wishes to revive the old idea of "*natura naturans* (nature as active process)," in preference to "*natura naturata* (nature as the assembly of created objective entities" (ibid.). He is well aware that the theology one often finds in many older philosophies of nature is no accident. He understands the link between nature and divinity as an attempt to project the structure of consciousness over nature, such that unconscious processes remain unknown: "Older philosophies . . . struggled with similar problems but were still able, in the last resort, to appeal to God as universal consciousness being the origin and model of human consciousness" (ibid.). In this single sentence Loewald has again covered a vast territory. Nietzsche, for example, consistently tried to demonstrate that the privileging of consciousness, and the model of objectivity that derives from it, is always a theological undertaking. Even purportedly "godless" science can be obliviously consonant with the metaphysics of religion. Analogously, the way in which a fetishistic object can be idealized and given theological status shows how a certain objectivism and religion can co-exist. If science is to free itself of metaphysical constraints, it has to free itself of the model of objectivity intrinsic to the privileging of consciousness. For interpretation to be scientific, the analyst cannot have a fetishistically objectivizing, or unquestioningly theological, understanding of its function.

As the specific discipline of the unconscious, psychoanalysis as both theory and therapy is actually in a position to rethink science. This is why Loewald contrasts the unacknowledged theology of traditional objectivity with what he calls postmodern science. Loewald is using "postmodern" in a specific sense, that is, in the sense in which the modern era of objective science and internal subjectivity originated in the work of Descartes. This worldview began to change dramatically in the late nineteenth century, philosophically with Nietzsche, psychologically with Freud, and scientifically with the revolution in physics. He writes: "Postmodern science appears to convey a new insight: we understand something about nature and reality, know something about them, by being open to their workings in us and the rest of nature as unconscious life, the openness being what we call consciousness. This insight—also very ancient—transcends, subsumes into itself the antagonism of 'ego' and 'reality' which ultimately derives from the equation of psyche and consciousness" (ibid.).

Postmodernity, then, is with no exaggeration the age of psychoanalysis, the age in which the usual objectivity of science becomes questionable as it is shown to be a defensively projected picture of subjectivity, of consciousness. This is why Loewald's aim is not to do away with the idea of objectivity but rather to make it more consistent. If psychoanalysis has conclusively demonstrated the workings of the unconscious, then the way in which it compels us to rethink mind compels us to rethink nature and how we gain knowledge of it. Loewald's point is that psychoanalysis has pushed consciousness into a new kind of openness—an openness to what is within it yet not available to it. When he speaks of "nature as unconscious life" he means that we will understand more about nature if we become open to the limitations of our conscious understanding of it. Returning to his earliest theme, the "antagonism of 'ego' and 'reality,'" he can now say that the traditional subject-object opposition is intrinsic to a prepsychoanalytic conception of mind and therefore of science. If psychoanalysis maintains the static, "neurotically distorted" view of objectivity, it is not consistent with itself. One finds this contradiction throughout Freud's work, and in Loewald's as well, as when he takes the subject-object opposition as the condition for differentiation.

Loewald understands the progressive investigation of the preoedipal as the specific psychoanalytic reason for moving out of defensive objectivity. Here again "instinct" as originally "environmental" is the crucial concept. The conjoint origin of internal and external out of primary narcissism makes the assumption of an individual, internal psyche questionable:

> We must further briefly consider the emergence of individuation and the interpretation of "psychical" as *endopsychic*. Equating the two takes its cue from consciousness, which is individualistic. Unconscious and instincts assume decidedly individual features, as the human id, in the rise of consciousness, and this is the main

concern of psychoanalysis. The origin of individual psychic life,
however, is a transindividual field, represented by the mother/
infant matrix, not an individual unconscious and instincts
residing in an individual. The objectivity of traditional modern
science is an outcome of the gradual differentiation of this
field culminating in individual consciousness. Yet it disregards
(represses) the transindividual matrix which continues to actively
originate . . . the various *transformative internalizations* of individual psychic life, i.e. endopsychic life. In other words, an earlier
form of "infantile amnesia" is at work in traditional natural
science. (pp. 50–51; my emphases)

If we take the mother/infant matrix as the representative but not exclusive manifestation of primary narcissism, then we can view the
emergence of an "individual unconscious" as the first manifestation
of secondary narcissism: the conjoint self-preservative libidinal drive
becomes the autoerotic infantile sexuality apparently not intrinsically
tied to an object. When Loewald links Eros to primary narcissism and
to "integrative differentiation," he provides another description of the
"transformative internalizations of individual psychic life." In other
words, the differentiation that "binds" individual and environment is
always operative, but it can always lead to defensive splitting from environment. The idea that there is an "earlier form of 'infantile amnesia'" operative in natural science means that psychoanalysis itself,
should it assume a purely individual unconscious, continues to "repress" what makes it possible. "Disavow" is by far the better word here
for many reasons. What I have described as primary disavowal captures the specifically psychoanalytic idea that the registration of primary, nonobjectified reality will always be repudiated to some extent.
It describes the constant (and not exclusively oral) transition from
primary to secondary narcissism.

When read closely, Freud's theories themselves enact their own
form of primary disavowal. From the experience of satisfaction, to
originally unconscious thought and time, to primary narcissism, and
to Eros as the binding introduction of "vital differences" not regulated by tension reduction, Freud's theory always hints at unconscious
processes that are not exclusively individual. But it mainly tends to

present wish and fantasy as the original psychic content. Wish and fantasy then function as objective psychic reality. In and of itself, as Loewald states, this was a scientific advance, but it carried along with it a certain view of science—while actually transforming it. The theory itself then seems to perform the primary disavowal that registers differentiating processes and repudiates them via opposed fantasies taken as concrete reality. But wherever primary disavowal operates, the traces of the split-off primary reality have been registered. In Freud's theory, these traces become discernible in those moments that take him beyond the closed-system view of the psyche.

Clinically, the enactive form of interpretation would perpetuate the primary disavowal contained in the "traditional natural science" view. For the attentive analyst, however, the push toward enactive interpretation, like enactive remembering, would indicate the precise places where interventions addressed to defensive objectivism are necessary on both sides of the couch. The idea that defense against differentiating processes is inevitable for both analyst and patient means that objectivizing power struggles are inherent in the analytic process. It remains the analyst's responsibility to understand such power struggles and to be able to analyze his or her own role in them. Such countertransference analysis then becomes a way to understand how to intervene in the patient's compelling need to maintain such a struggle.

What Loewald says about the transformation of natural science as the view of nature itself changes holds entirely for psychoanalysis as therapy:

> What is needed is a natural science that realizes that the interpretation of nature in terms of (individualistic) consciousness limits our view, granted that it has pragmatical validity for human conscious thought and action and appears to enhance man's domination of the world. But a deeper understanding of nature will widen the horizons of a science of nature and increase, one may hope, its power of mastery, a mastery that involves yielding no less than dominion. Such deeper understanding subordinates the traditional view to a more comprehensive perspective on nature as unconscious activity (*natura naturans*). Psychoanalytic theory is on that path, and so are the physical sciences themselves

(Freud remarked on the parallels). Indeed, "classical" psychoanalysis fights a rearguard action against such a wider framework,
a battle in which theoretical physics is no longer immobilized.
(p. 51)

Loewald's concept of the analyst as "new object" and of analysis as
"internalization of an interaction" speaks exactly to the revised view
of analytic therapy. Defenses against the transference as a derivative of
primary narcissism call for the kinds of intervention in which the analyst cannot assume domination based on objective knowledge of
unconscious fantasy content. Such a stance does "widen the horizon"
of the theory of unconscious processes but also calls for a "yielding"
to the uncontrollability of dynamic, primary reality. The treatment of
the concrete patient is conspicuously concerned with all the environmental frame aspects of analysis, including the possibility of interpretation itself, because such patients actively repudiate the primary
reality they also register. This is also why maintenance of the usual
framework of classical analysis is so important. The classical framework—such as the frequent sessions of regular duration, the use of
the couch, the analyst's neutrality—provide the maximal interaction
with the analyst's differentiating function, including maximal defense
against it. Effective treatment depends upon the analyst's not using
the frame as a form of domination. The analyst may have to yield to
the concrete patient's various defensive objectivizations of it, including the "real" transference, in order eventually to help the patient yield
—not submit—to the analytic environment. This is the largest implication of Loewald's concept of internalization: differentiated integration with the analytic framework is necessary for structural change.
Further, because the analyst cannot escape the tendency toward enactive, objectivist interpretation, in yielding to it, and then understanding it, he or she gains a better grasp of internalization anxiety. In
this way the analyst can achieve a more truly neutral stance toward
the complicated resistances to therapeutic differentiation. This non-
objectivist approach to psychodynamics is implicit in what Loewald
calls "objective observation of the analyst and patient in interaction"
(1980, p. 227).

The analogy to physics is appealing because progress in atomic physics seems so consistently to have implied the questioning of the most apparently objective view of reality. Implicit in Loewald's thinking—as seen in the citation from "The Waning of the Oedipus Complex"—is that the psychotic "core" of preoedipal dynamics opens psychoanalysis on a psychological level to the kind of subatomic world that was opened up for physics.[19] As Loewald says, this is a world in which the opposition of psychic and "material reality" is "superseded in a fully developed conception of the unconscious" (p. 51). He claims that Descartes' distinction between *res cogitans* (mind) and *res extensa* (nature) was the "germ" of the opposition between psychic and material reality, which is his oldest theme. Looking back to "Ego and Reality," it is now possible to see that from the beginning of his work, Loewald was attempting to demonstrate the unspoken Cartesianism of Freud's basic theories in order to show why a scientific view of analytic therapy had to bring to light and modify such presuppositions.[20] The theory of the life and death instincts is so important because it also supersedes the idea of a fundamental antagonism between conscious and unconscious, ego and id. These psychoanalytic oppositions, again, are derived from the opposition of *res cogitans* and *res extensa* (ibid.). Each time one makes such a statement, it must be borne in mind that like nature, a "material reality" not antagonistically opposed to psychic reality is a transformed materiality. It is the materiality of environment, of differentiating processes as "real" but as inconceivable according to typical modes of consciousness, as subatomic particles. Clinically, it is the materiality of all the environmental or frame elements of the analyst-patient differential.

The second part of "Psychoanalysis in Search of Nature" contains a major discussion of the relations between metapsychology and metaphysics in terms of the theory of projection. Analysis of it would take us too far astray here. Loewald concludes the paper with a programmatic statement: "the connections of the contemporary shift in interest and emphasis to preoedipal issues with the foregoing theoretical considerations, need to be articulated: the changing views on nature and the instincts turn to a more 'archaic' core of being, and so does present-day clinical work" (pp. 53–54). Certainly one understands what Loewald means and implies here. Just as attention to the preoedipal demands that psychoanalysis revise both its theoretical underpinnings and clinical practice, so attention to subatomic processes produced a revolution in the epistemology of science and scientific practice. For psychoanalysis especially, however, it is somewhat misleading to think of such changes only in terms of the archaic or the preoedipal. As Loewald emphasized from the beginning, primary reality develops. It does not stop at the beginning of the Oedipus complex.[21] The generalizability of fetishistic structures means that all psychopathology implies some version of a substitution of classical oppositions for a differentiating process. The two views of reality, the static and the dynamic, the oppositional and the differentiating, are basic properties of the unconscious. Thus, they are intrinsic to all psychopathology and to the everyday practice of psychoanalysis.

CHAPTER 4

The Part Object, Depressive Anxiety, and the Environment

Loewald has provided a compelling account of the "two realities," the dynamic and the static, the environmental and the objectivist. His theory of enactive remembering—the replacement of dedifferentiating primary process for differentiating integration with environment—adds a crucial dimension to the generalization of fetishism. However, Loewald did not account for the potentially traumatizing aspects of primary reality or for the anxiety that motivates defense against registration of it. He did begin to envisage the task of addressing unconscious ego processes that maintain splitting, but he did not seem to grasp that the splitting off of primary reality is very difficult to reverse. Karl Abraham, Melanie Klein, and D. W. Winnicott all elaborated concepts that can supplement the understanding of enactive remembering. In reading Abraham, Klein, and Winnicott, I will be tracing first the emergence of the concept of the part object, then how the concept led to Klein's idea of depressive anxiety, and finally why Winnicott modified the concept of depressive anxiety. Because all these ideas directly relate to the clinical problem of concreteness, they also provide more insight into fetishistic structures.

Abraham introduced the idea of the part object in his final paper, published in 1924. Strikingly, Abraham eventually compared the part object to what he knew of Freud's work on fetishism. (He died before Freud's late return to the topic.) Abraham sensed that part object dynamics also produce a conflation of reality and fantasy: he il-

lustrated part object transferences with examples of concreteness. In
fact, even before introducing the part object, in 1919 he had already
written about the apparently analyzable patient who resists interpretation and therapeutic change. Abraham's early clinical description of
such patients is unflinching and accurate. Unfortunately, he did not
integrate this earlier work with his later work on the part object. Nor
did he notice some major contradictions in his later theory. An examination of all these questions has its own merits and will deepen
the understanding of Klein.

Klein herself always stressed that the origins of her theory lie in
Abraham's work. She introduced the concept of depressive anxiety in
order to account for the transition from part to whole object relations,
from the paranoid-schizoid to the depressive position. For Klein, this
is the transition from splitting to integration, from relative dominance
of aggressive fantasy to libidinal engagement with reality. Klein had her
own version of the basic conflict between death and life, emphasizing
the internal destructiveness Freud attributed to the death instinct. In
the first phase of her work this destructiveness is tied to splitting, idealization, and difficulties in symbol formation—all aspects of concreteness. In Klein's thinking, the overcoming of splitting can produce an
anxiety as great as the anxieties intrinsic to part object relations. Regression from depressive position integration to paranoid-schizoid
splitting is motivated by this anxiety, which she labels "depressive anxiety." In her later work, the addition of projective identification to the
defenses of the paranoid-schizoid position explains the conflation of
reality and fantasy—the "real" transference. Projective identification
has to be given due weight in any dynamic account of concreteness.[1]

Winnicott began as a Kleinian and considered depressive anxiety
an essential contribution to psychoanalysis. His understanding of it
also emphasizes the conflation of reality and fantasy, past and present.
However, Winnicott effected a fundamental change in Klein's formulations. He found depressive anxiety more compelling when reconceptualized in terms of environment—Loewald's central concern.
Splitting, for Winnicott, is the splitting of environment from instinct.
This introduction of environmental thinking into the theory of splitting allows a synthesis of depressive anxiety with internalization anxiety. Like Loewald, Winnicott thought that psychoanalysis needs a

conception of reality other than the usual objective or subjective ones. For him, this is famously a question of transitional phenomena. Winnicott in fact contrasts transitional phenomena to fetishism in his account of depressive anxiety. The interplay of depressive anxiety and transitional phenomena will expand the understanding of the registration and repudiation of primary reality and the theory of enactive remembering.

ABRAHAM

In a prescient paper, "A Particular Form of Neurotic Resistance Against the Psychoanalytic Method" (1919), Abraham seems to have been the first analyst willing to write about his experience with patients in analysis who resist interpretation per se. Given the paper's early date and the centrality of interpretation to the entire enterprise, Abraham's forthright description is admirable. His theoretical vocabulary suffers from the inevitable restrictions of its time, but his clinical rigor leads him to anticipate some major issues.

Abraham contrasts the expectable intermittent resistances found in all neurotic patients to the resistances of another group of patients. This other group manifests resistances that are kept up "without interruption during the whole of their treatment" (pp. 303–4). Abraham notes that this significant problem had received almost no consideration in the psychoanalytic literature to date, and we can say that it has taken almost eighty years for due attention to be paid to it.

Here is Abraham's clinical description of the problem:

> The patients of whom we are speaking hardly ever say of their
> own accord that "nothing occurs" to them [the typical form of
> intermittent neurotic resistance]. They rather tend to speak in a
> continuous and unbroken manner, and some of them refuse to
> be interrupted by a single remark on the part of the physician.
> But they do not give themselves up to free associations. They
> speak as though according to programme, and do not bring
> forward their material freely. Contrary to the fundamental rule
> of analysis they arrange what they say according to certain lines
> of thought and subject it to extensive criticism and modification

on the part of the ego. The physician's admonition to keep
strictly to the method has in itself no influence on their conduct.
(p. 304)

Abraham understands quite well that the non-stop speech of a patient
who seems uninterested in anything the analyst has to say cannot be
considered free association. Rather, the patient is using speech to
ensure that the entire experience of analysis conforms to projected
wishes. This resistance can cover the whole of the treatment, despite
the patient's "extraordinarily eager, never-wearying readiness to be
psychoanalyzed" (ibid.). Both Jacobson and Loewald, in our day,
speak of the global nature of concreteness or enactive remembering.
One also hears in this description the worrying possibility of pseudo-
analysis or endless analysis that many of the authors cited in Chapter 1
discussed.

Abraham notes that the patients who manifest this particular form
of resistance can present symptoms that are the traditional indications
for analysis. However, "in their attitude towards psychoanalysis and the
physician they all produce a certain number of characteristics with as-
tonishing regularity" (ibid.). It does not occur to him that the "regularity" of this process, which covers the whole of analysis, might be
due to defenses larger than those that produce the various neuroses.
Abraham at no point will begin to think that he might be dealing
with a general, rather than a particular, form of resistance. For him,
this form of resistance is exceptional because it does not conform to
transference-resistance as conceptualized within the repression model.
Abraham was facing what could only have been an anomaly for him.

His first stab at an explanation is conventional. He speaks of the
unconscious defiance of the father that motivates these seemingly
compliant patients. He then moves on to narcissism, control of the
analytic process, and tension reduction—that is, the pleasure principle in both its defensive and discharge functions:

They only say things which are "ego-syntonic." These patients
are particularly sensitive to anything which injures their self-love.
They are inclined to feel "humiliated" by every fact that is
established in their psychoanalysis, and they are continually on

their guard against suffering such humiliations. They furnish any
number of dreams, but they adhere to the manifest content and
understand how to glean from the dream analysis only what they
already know. And they not only persistently avoid every painful
impression, but at the same time endeavour to get the greatest
possible amount of positive pleasure out of their analysis. This
tendency to bring the analysis under the control of the pleasure
principle is particularly evident in these patients and is, in common with a number of peculiarities, a clear expression of their
narcissism. . . . The tendency to regard a curative measure merely
as an opportunity for obtaining pleasure and to neglect its real
purpose must be regarded as a thoroughly childish characteristic.
(p. 305)

Did Abraham engage in countertransferential power struggles with
these "thoroughly childish" patients? He puts his finger right on the
problem—the tendency to neglect the "real purpose" of the analysis
—but seems to consider it an infantilism, metapsychologically speaking, of course. He aptly describes the patients' need to avoid narcissistic humiliation. Dynamically, he understands this narcissism in terms
of the conjoint push to avoid anything painful (primary defense) and
to use the analysis to gain pleasure (wish fulfillment). As he says, the
manifest narcissism of such patients equals the tendency to bring the
analysis under the control of the pleasure principle. When he calls
such behavior childish, he is probably echoing Freud's description of
the baby putatively under the exclusive dominance of the pleasure
principle.

There is no reason to reproach Abraham for not attending either
to the subtleties of Freud's analysis of the "fiction" of exclusive dominance by the pleasure principle from the "Two Principles" paper or
to the related problem of "originally unconscious thought." However,
both concepts produce a different metapsychology, as does the barely
developed concept of primary narcissism. Abraham wants to fit a dynamic description of these patients into the more generally known
version of Freudian theory. He seems unaware that this description
reflects the theory so well that he is left without therapeutic leverage.
For example, he connects the defense against "every painful impres-

sion" to the disregard of the "real purpose" of the analysis only in terms of defiance (and eventually envy). He cannot really conceive its overall defensive function. To do so, he would have needed to think about why the "reality" of analysis provokes such global defense. In other words, he would have needed to think about defense directed against the differentiating function of interpretation.

Abraham seems to have total confidence in a metapsychology which leads only to an apt description of his difficult patients. This problem is particularly apparent in his description of the transferences of these patients:

> The narcissistic attitude such patients adopt toward the method of treatment also characterizes their relations to the analyst himself. Their transference on to him is an imperfect one. They grudge him the role of father. If signs of transference do appear, the wishes directed on to the physician will be of a particularly exacting nature; thus they will be very easily disappointed precisely in those wishes, and they will then quickly react with a complete withdrawal of their libido. They are constantly on the look-out for signs of personal interest on the part of the physician, and want to feel that he is treating them with affection. Since the physician cannot satisfy the claims of their narcissistic need for love, a true positive transference does not take place. In place of making a transference the patients tend to identify themselves with the physician. . . . In this way they abandon the position of patient and lose sight of the purpose of their analysis. . . . It is exceedingly difficult to get them away from preconceived ideas which subserve their narcissism. They are given to contradicting everything, and they know how to turn the psychoanalysis into a discussion with the physician as to who is "in the right." (pp. 306–7)

When the patient globally identifies with the analyst and engages in power struggles over who is in the right, the transference is "imperfect." By "imperfect," Abraham means that, consistent with ignoring the real purpose of the analysis, the transference itself cannot be interpreted. This is the clinical observation made by all the authors I have cited: when the transference is "real," for the patient it is only a question of "who is right."

Abraham's clinical example here is entirely a propos. He speaks of a patient who claimed to understand analysis better than he did. The patient was afraid that he might say something unfamiliar to himself, but familiar to the analyst, who would then be the "cleverer" of the two. "The same patient," Abraham writes, "who was much interested in philosophical matters, expected nothing less from his psychoanalysis than that science should gain from it the 'ultimate truth'" (p. 307). The patient, then, has a defensive need to make his analysis a guarantor of objectivity. Should the analyst believe himself or herself to be in possession of some ultimate, objective truth, he or she would be employing a metapsychology that mirrors this philosophy. An interpretive technique that lays bare these truths, using psychodynamic descriptions, will gratify the patient in that it inevitably misfires. There cannot be two "ultimate truths," and only one party can "be in the right." Abraham's example illustrates the point that global defenses provide the patient with a (fetishistic) conviction of being in possession of the standard of objectivity. The analyst's metapsychology must be able to account for this problem without replicating it.

Intriguingly, Abraham introduces the idea of envy at just this point. After saying that his patient expected that "science" should gain "'ultimate truth'" from his analysis, Abraham states: "The presence of an element of *envy* is unmistakable in all this" (p. 307). This envy is manifest in the patients' wishes "to do everything all by themselves." The result is often a pursuit of analysis at home, of "'auto-analysis,'" as a way of depreciating "the physician's powers" (ibid.). This envious depreciation of the analyst, Abraham asserts, is both a revolt against the father and an unrestrained masturbatory equivalent.[2] "'Auto-analysis' is . . . a form of day-dreaming, a substitute for masturbation, free from reproach . . . " (p. 308).

Certainly Abraham is right that the patients' autoanalytic activity is a form of autoerotism, and certainly it may represent a revolt against any interfering parental power. However, the globally defensive nature of this autoerotic activity is more fruitfully understood as a manifestation of infantile sexuality per se, the splitting of self-preservation from libido. Thus, the particularly resistant patient compulsively repeats the derivation of autoerotism at every moment of the analysis. The patient's resistance, as Abraham says, is globally narcissistic. But Abraham cannot conceive that this is a global repudiation of a registered but unbearable libidinal–self-preservative tie to the analyst.

Envy and depreciation are essential components of autoerotic fantasies conflated with reality. The analyst's power is as much a creation of fantasy as the patient's need to counter it. One would therefore have to be very careful about interpretation of envy. If the analyst assumes that he or she does have some kind of power of objectivity that the patient envies, then the analyst remains with the patient on the fantasy level. Translated into the logic of fetishism, the analyst would unconsciously believe in the "reality of non-castration" as the antidote to the "reality of castration." One can only wonder how Abraham addressed the envy he discerned in his patients' autoanalysis if he saw it as defiance of "the father."

Envy also leads to sadism, one of the most important links between Abraham and Klein. Abraham addresses sadism by way of anality, which will become his great topic. Here he claims always to find elements of obsessional thinking in his "particularly resistant" patients: "In view of the more recent results of psychoanalysis we shall not be surprised to find pronounced sadistic-anal traits in all the cases. Their hostile and negative attitude towards the physician has already been mentioned; and anal-erotic motives explain the rest of their behavior" (p. 308).[3] Abraham isolates a specific anal fixation in his difficult patients. In general, he says, their unconscious aggression is a repetition of anal power struggles:

> talking in the analysis, by means of which psychic material is discharged, is compared to emptying the bowels. . . . They are persons who have only with difficulty been taught in childhood to control their sphincters and to have a regular action of the bowels. . . . The neurotics under discussion continue this tradition of infantile behavior. They pride themselves as it were, upon being able to decide whether, when, or how much they will give out from their unconscious psychic material. Their tendency to bring perfectly arranged material to the analytic hour shows not

only an anal-erotic pleasure in systematizing and cataloguing
everything but exhibits yet another interesting feature. Freud has
recently drawn attention to the unconscious identification of
excrement and gifts. Narcissistic neurotics with a strong anal
disposition such as we are dealing with here have a tendency
to give presents instead of love. Their transference on to the
physician is incomplete. They are not able to expend themselves
unconstrainedly in free associations. As a substitute they offer
their physician gifts; and these gifts consist of their contributions
to psychoanalysis which they have prepared at home and which
are subject to the same narcissistic over-estimation as the
products of the body. (p. 309)[4]

Abraham raises many important issues here. First, the implicit tie of
envy to sadism can take over the entire function of speaking to the
analyst. Speech then takes on a pure discharge function, as a sadistic
exertion of control. This autoerotic, sadistic exertion of control can be
compared to Freud's idea (in *Three Essays*) that infantile sexuality contains an intrinsic component of cruelty and control. In this sense, anality typifies narcissistic aggression. But if control is intrinsic to infantile
sexuality, anality does not have to serve as a specific fixation point. The
problem with linking such resistances to anality alone is that one
would not think of oral and oedipal versions of them as well.

Second, Abraham's description of such thoughts as presents given
to the analyst provides another way of thinking about fetishistic compromise formations. The patient concretely expects the analyst to accept an idealized, objectified thought in order to forestall interpretation. What Freud in "Two Principles" called the "mere presentation
of ideas," which replace "originally unconscious thought," then becomes the imposed offer of a present. The treatment itself is equated
with a fetishistic exchange, in which the patient expects the analyst
to accept the "gift" of his "ultimate truths." The "thought-gift" is a
defense against the possibility that the analyst might think of something not included in the patient's opposed fantasies. Although Abraham has opened an extremely important topic here, he again seems
able only to describe this as infantile behavior. The fetishistic exchange
that the patient wishes to impose upon the analysis is not understood

as a primary defense against the possibility of interpretation itself. That the patient may have crucial reasons to defend against the positive transference does not occur to him at all.

Abraham ends on a note of clinical pessimism. He observes the generally protracted nature of these analyses but sees the patients' willingness to spend time and money on the repetition of power struggles as their unconscious aim: "The patients are making a sacrifice to their narcissism. They are all too apt to lose sight of the fact that the object of the treatment is to cure their neurosis . . . it might be said that nothing is too dear for their narcissism" (p. 310). If the patient loses sight of cure, then, as with Narcissus himself, even his or her self-preservation is not too dear for his or her narcissism. One would have to think then not only about the sadism directed against the analyst but the sadism directed against oneself. This is the self-destruction implicit in the splitting of self-preservation from libido. More sophisticated dynamic understanding does not give the analyst any omnipotent power to effect change in these patients. They remain as difficult today as Abraham found them in 1919. However, it is not possible to help them at all if one does not understand the self-destruction implicit in their narcissistic resistances.

Despite his doubts about these patients, Abraham also says that if "it is possible to overcome their narcissistic reserve, and, what amounts to the same thing, to bring about a positive transference, they will one day unexpectedly produce free associations, even in the presence of the physician" (ibid.). In other words, a positive transference is essential if free association is not to have a purely autoerotic discharge function—if it is to become interpretable. Do the father complex, secondary narcissism, and anality explain why this is so? Why is the positive transference so rigidly defended against? The answers to such questions require a theory impossible to conceive in 1919. Whatever the shortcomings of Abraham's theory, however, his description of these globally resistant patients—which is the same as that encountered today—did not have much impact on his contemporaries. The idea that there are patients in analysis who resist interpretation per se should not have been seen as a minor dilemma, the subject of an obscure paper. It should have led to a major reconsideration of the metapsychology of interpretation. But it did not.

Abraham's great last paper, "A Short Study of the Development of the Libido, Viewed in the Light of Mental Disorders" (1924), is devoted to the question of what makes "full" object love possible. The answers to this question will lead to the concept of the part object and will provide the bases for the theory of the depressive position. Although I will take a somewhat critical approach, emphasizing some of the paper's contradictions, it is a highly original contribution to Freudian theory.

The long road to the explanation of full object love starts with a clinical problem. Abraham examines the psychodynamics of depression and obsession in order to account for both their similarity and difference. Following Freud, he understands depression as an unconscious reaction to object loss, with subsequent reincorporation of the lost object. But he adds a new dimension to the dynamics of obsessional neurosis. For Abraham, the obsessive is threatened by the same kind of object loss as the depressive but does not unconsciously experience the loss. Where the depressive has to compensate for loss via reincorporation, the obsessive has some other way to stave it off. What is it?

To answer this question, Abraham asks another one. He assumes that depression and obsession share an anal fixation point because of the unconscious dominance of sadism in both conditions. But he wonders whether there is really an adequate explanation of the close ties of anality and sadism. He takes it as given that a sadistic or destructive attitude toward the object begins with oral cannibalistic fantasies. A "complete capacity for love is only achieved when the libido has reached its genital stage," that is, in the eventual move out of autoerotic infantile sexuality in adolescence. If so, then the sadism of the anal phase must contain some kind of transition from oral cannibalistic fantasies in the direction of the Oedipus complex and finally full object love. The obsessive's "holding on to" the object would illustrate this transition.

To establish more clearly the linkage of anality and sadism, and to explain how the obsessive holds on to the object, Abraham asserts that anal erotism contains "two opposite pleasurable tendencies"—expulsion and retention. Sadism also contains "two opposite tendencies"—destruction and control (pp. 425–28). The specific nature of anal phase object relations explains the workings of these opposed tendencies:

> in the middle stage of his libidinal development the individual regards the person who is the object of his desire as something over which he exercises ownership and . . . he consequently treats that person in the same way as he does his earliest piece of private property, i.e. the contents of his body, his feces. Whereas on the genital [N.B., not phallic] level "love" means the transference of his positive feeling on to the object and involves a psycho-sexual adaptation to that object, on the level below it means that he treats his object as though it belonged to him. And since the ambivalence of feelings still exists in full force on this inferior level, he expresses his positive attitude towards his object in the form of retaining his property, and his negative attitude in the form of rejecting it. Thus when the obsessional neurotic is threatened with the loss of his object, and the melan-choliac actually does lose his, it signifies to the unconscious mind of each an expulsion of that object in the sense of a physical expulsion of feces. (pp. 425–26)

Abraham operates on two levels here. First, on the level of the theory of anality, he has specified two different aims within the same phase. These different aims can create different fixation points and thus account for the difference between depression and obsession. Second, on the general level of the theory of infantile sexuality, he has deepened the understanding of autoerotism. Within the fantasies that always accompany autoerotic stimulation, the object, too, is treated as if it were part of oneself. Thus, the object in such fantasies is as much under one's control as is one's own body or, more precisely, is equated with a part of one's body. Anal objects in particular are property that one has the right to destroy or retain. Clinically, the depressive regresses to the rejecting half of the anal phase. He or she gets rid of the hated object and then reincorporates the property he or she always has the right to repossess. The obsessive regresses to the dominating half of the anal phase. When threatened with object loss, he or she retains the object as property inside himself or herself. The obsessive has the right to dominate and even to torture this object-as-property. His or her neurosis is essentially comprised of defenses against these impulses.

In 1924 this was a novel way to rethink depression and obsession. Despite the continued viability of this theory, however, it is based on a narrow version of infantile sexuality. Abraham's "baby" is exclusively autoerotic. Nowhere will Abraham take into account Freud's idea that autoerotism is derived from an intrinsically object-related libidinal–self-preservative drive. The anal phase then gains in importance. Within it there is a transition from expelling and destroying the object to retaining and torturing it. Abraham's conclusion is that "the tendency to spare the object and to preserve it has grown out of the more primitive, destructive tendency *by a process of repression*" (p. 428; my emphasis).

With these modest words Abraham introduces a new idea into psychoanalysis. Once the theory of infantile sexuality is taken in Abraham's codified way, it is obliged to account for how and why the child moves beyond autoerotism.[5] Using the "motor" of an inherent sequence of psychosexual phases, Abraham takes the transition from the first to the second anal phase as the beginning of a tendency to retain the object. This is essentially the same question that will preoccupy Klein and Winnicott: how does one envisage the beginning of concern for an object? Abraham's answer is that the initial concern is for the object as part of oneself; in other words, it is still narcissistic. Concern is first expressed as anal retention, a form of omnipotent control. If the transition from the first to the second anal phase takes place by way of repression, it is critical to understand exactly what Abraham means. What makes it possible to make an object part of one's system of control, and then what makes it possible to move beyond such control?

Abraham's answers to these questions are consistent with his basic presumption of an exclusively autoerotic baby. Any psychoanalytic theory that does not question this presumption also has to hypothesize an originally undifferentiated state, as does Abraham here. His reasoning is at first clinical and on its own terms illuminating. After concentrating on obsessional neurosis, he returns to depression. He contends that the depressive's fixation point is in the first anal phase, before any tendency to conserve the object. The object, then, is always expelled, creating the countertendency to reincorporate it. Oral reincorporation is cannibalistic, so in depression there is conflict over wishes to devour and swallow. But beneath the guilt-provoking cannibalistic fantasies, one always finds a wish for pleasurable sucking, which is not cannibalistic. It is the original condition of being at one with the object:

> We are thus obliged to assume that there is a differentiation within the oral phase of the libido, just as there is within the anal-sadistic phase. On the primary level of that phase the libido of the infant is attached to the act of sucking. This act is one of incorporation, but one which does not put an end to the existence of the object. The child is not yet able to distinguish between its own self and the external object. Ego and object are concepts which are incompatible with that level of development. There is as yet *no differentiation made* between the sucking child and the suckling breast. Moreover, the child has as yet neither feelings of hatred nor of love. Its mental state is consequently free from all manifestations of ambivalence in this stage. The secondary level of this phase differs from the first in that the child exchanges its sucking activity for a biting one. . . . In the biting stage of the oral phase the individual incorporates the object in himself and in so doing destroys it. . . . This is the stage in which cannibalistic impulses predominate. . . . It is in this stage that the ambivalent attitude of the ego to its object begins to grow up. We may say, therefore, that in the child's libidinal development the second stage of the oral-sadistic phase marks the beginning of its ambivalence conflict; whereas the first (sucking) stage should still be regarded as pre-ambivalent. (pp. 450–51; my emphasis)

In other words, before the oral cannibalistic stage, there is no object because there is no ego. Ego and object come into existence with the possibility of a hostile relation between them. Before a hostile relation to the object is possible, there is an undifferentiated, pre-ambivalent stage. Abraham has actually taken the "closed system" view of the psychic apparatus to an extreme. That the "unconscious" must be intrinsically open, or there would not even be a closed system, is something he cannot conceive. He can only think about ambivalence in terms of love and hate. He cannot think of an intrinsic conflict between Eros and death, that is, between registration of differentiating processes in an open system and their repudiation via tension-reducing wish fulfillment, creating the closed system. This is the irreducible ambivalence between the opening of the space for representation and the defensive attempt to close that space with objectifying representations, the basis of fetishistic structures.

The absence of any possibility of this kind of thinking is apparent in one of Abraham's clinical examples. The context is his discussion of the pure pleasure in sucking, the model of the undifferentiated, preambivalent state. It is the case of a depressed man who

> would employ all sorts of devices to create in himself the illusion
> that he had a woman's breasts, and would take special pleasure in
> the phantasy that he was suckling an infant. Although he played
> the part of the mother in this phantasy, he would sometimes
> exchange his role for that of the child at her breast. . . . Thus,
> for instance, he used to behave in a very curious way with the
> cushion on the sofa during analysis. Instead of leaving it where
> it was and laying his head on it, he used to take it up and put
> it over his face. His associations showed that the cushion repre-
> sented the breast being brought close to his head from above.
> (p. 449)

We have here the entire clinical problem of concreteness, illusion, fetishism, and primary and secondary disavowal. Abraham does not quite understand that his patient fetishistically conflates reality with the two fantasies of "being" the breast and "having" the breast. When the patient actually picks up the cushion during his session, he concretely transforms something from the analytic environment into a "fetish," which objectifies his oscillating fantasies. One has to think that he is telling the analyst that he expects the analytic process, and the analyst himself, to conform to this fantasy.

Did this patient also display the "particular form of neurotic re-

sistance against the psychoanalytic method"? Abraham does not say,
but my theory would predict that he did. The moment at which the
patient puts the cushion over his face in the session is one in which
any direct interpretation of his wish for the analyst to give him the
breast would be an objectifying power struggle. The patient would
concretely experience the analyst as trying to regain control of an
"objective possession." (It is *his* couch and *his* cushion.) The analytic
task is rather to intervene in order to address defenses against the
maintenance of the minimum space for looking at oneself. But the
analyst cannot even begin to conceive of such a process if, like Abraham here, he or she understands the patient to have regressed to a
preambivalent phase. The analyst could name this wish, and the patient could respond, "Yes I want that, and that's why I'm putting the
cushion on my face." At this point, the analyst would be in the position of simply telling the patient that he is being infantile. The
counterpart to this kind of power struggle would be a naïvely experiential one. The analyst might presume that the patient needs the
freedom to regress to an undifferentiated phase in order to form a
positive transference. Here, too, the assumption of an originally undifferentiated phase would lead to a kind of therapeutic nihilism.
The analyst would hope for the best in tolerating the regression,
with various theoretical justifications. But he or she would have no
conception of the compromise formation expressed through enactive remembering.

Abraham's undifferentiated, preambivalent phase takes on even
more importance when he makes it the point of departure in a cir-
cular journey toward full object love:

> Within the first—the oral—period, the child exchanges its
> pre-ambivalent libidinal attitude, which is free from conflict, for
> one which is ambivalent and preponderantly hostile towards
> its object. Within the second—the anal-sadistic—period, the
> transition from the earlier to the later stage means that the
> individual has begun to spare his object from destruction. Finally,
> within the third—the genital—period, he overcomes his ambiva-
> lent attitude and his libido attains to its full capacity both from
> a sexual and a social point of view. (p. 453)

Development starts from a preambivalent phase, takes a long detour through ambivalence, and finishes at a postambivalent phase that is a return to its origin. Unambivalent genitality replaces the original unambivalent love of the breast. This theory is not as naïve as it sounds. Abraham's stress on the origin and vicissitudes of ambivalence led him to pay more attention than anyone previously to sadistic fantasies. We owe to Abraham the best initial synthesis of biting, devouring, expelling, torturing, and eventually robbing (in the phallic phase) impulses with infantile sexuality. Anyone who knows Klein can immediately see why she always acknowledged her debt to Abraham.

However, the idea of preambivalence and postambivalence makes no sense at all in terms of an unconscious always split between differentiation and dedifferentiation, between internalization and identification. From this point of view any differentiating process raises tension, including genital difference. Abraham treats genital difference as what Loewald called a static reality, an objective fact to which one can unambivalently adapt if one is sufficiently healthy. The possibility of this unambivalent adaptation resides in the "objective fact" of the preambivalent, nondifferentiated phase. This is a kind of theology of development. There is an original state of grace from which one is exiled with the first "bite" but to which there is always hope of return. In Abraham's account, as in the biblical one, "knowledge" is equated with a hostile relation to reality. This is the basic assumption about reality that became the focus of Loewald's critique.

Freud's unwitting encounter with this problem is encapsulated in his insistence on castration as the reality disavowed in fetishism. Freud did not notice his equation of fantasy with reality because he, too, could not envisage unconscious registration and repudiation of sexual difference. Abraham has his own version of this difficulty. Like Freud, he winds up with a two-fantasy structure (like castration and non-castration), because he cannot envision unconscious registration of difference. Crucially, for Abraham this structure informs the entire conception of the part object. He begins to introduce the part object in his discussion of the oral dynamics of depression. He speaks of withdrawal of the breast as a primal castration, leading the future depressive to want to revenge himself on his mother for this by castrating her in his turn, either taking away her breasts or her imaginary penis. In his imagination he always chooses biting as the means of doing it. . . . I should like once more to lay stress on the ambivalent character of those phantasies. They involve on the one hand a total or partial incorporation of the mother, that is, an act of positive desire; and on the other, her castration or death, that is, a negative desire tending to her destruction. (p. 463)

The mother's imaginary penis is, of course, the familiar prototype of the fetish. Equation of the breast with the imaginary penis makes perfect sense in terms of the logic of castration. Once the breast can be lost and reappropriated in the same way as the mother's imaginary penis, the breast itself is a fantasy object, in a sense the first fetish. (Abraham's patient who put the cushion over his head during sessions concretely creates a breast fetish during his sessions.) As an act of desire, the reappropriation of the lost object leads to "total or partial incorporation," and as an act of revenge it is equivalent to the mother's "castration or death." How is it possible for the same act to be "total *or* partial," "castration *or* death"?

From within the framework of secondary narcissism, the fantasy of loss of an idealized part of the body equals complete devaluation. To lose the idealized part is to lose the whole of the narcissistic structure it supports. To reappropriate it is to redress the narcissistic balance; thus the logic of "total or partial" incorporation, of "castration or death." However, "partial" and "total" are as much fantasy formations as castrated and non-castrated. The fantasy of the part object would inevitably imply a fantasy of an ideally intact whole object.

For example, Abraham describes a woman kleptomaniac whose unconscious fantasy was to reappropriate from the father the penis that had been stolen from her. Her aim was to rob the father of "his envied possession so as to have it herself or to identify herself with it" (p. 484; recall the patient discussed at the end of Chapter 2 who had the fantasy of stealing a book from Freud's library). Abraham understands the patient's thievery to mean: "'I do possess that desired part of the body, and so I am equal to my father'" (ibid.). We see here precisely what he meant when he spoke of "total or partial incorporation." To identify with the father, to become his equal, the patient had to have the illusion of reappropriating the idealized, lost (part) object. As soon as one is concretely identified with the reappropriated part object, one wholly attempts to eliminate the difference between oneself and the object. "Partial" equals "total" as soon as the "object incorporated" has a structural relation to the fantasy of the "mother's imaginary penis," that is, the fetish.

Abraham discusses another patient who showed the oral, anal, and phallic versions of this dynamic. For this patient, "the mother also was represented by only one part of her body, namely her breasts. They had obviously been identified in the child's mind with the supposed penis of the female. She was alternatively represented by her buttocks, which in their turn stood for her breasts" (pp. 485–86). Abraham's clinical acumen leads him to understand that something like the fantasy of the mother's penis may be operative in oral, anal, or phallic terms. Because the relation to the object is a fantasy—in other words, an autoerotic creation—Abraham says that such structures indicate regression to a stage

> somewhere between narcissism and object-love. Another fact . . .
> pointed in the same direction. This was that the libido was in an
> unmistakable state of ambivalence towards its object and showed
> a strong tendency to inflict injuries on it. Nevertheless, that
> destructive tendency had already been subjected to limitations.
> At this stage the sexual aim of the individual must have been
> to deprive the object of a part of its body, i.e. to attack its
> integrity without destroying its existence. We are put in mind
> of a child which catches a fly and, having pulled off a leg, lets
> it go again. We must once more emphasize the fact that the
> pleasure in biting is very markedly associated with this form
> of object-relation which had hitherto escaped our notice.
> (pp. 486–87)

Abraham contends that he is saying something new here: a phase of object relations between narcissism and object-love had been previously unremarked. He asserts that in this phase libido is "ambivalent," because the "destructive tendency had already been subjected to limitations." Abraham does not notice that he is describing the possibility that he had previously attributed to the second anal phase. This was the fixation point for obsessional neurosis. The obsessive allegedly showed the first possibility of holding on to an object when threatened with its loss. Now Abraham is saying that once the breast can function as the homologue of the mother's imaginary penis, the partial-total incorporation of the object is possible. There is an as yet unexplained limitation of this process, so that the object also survives—like the fly whose leg has been pulled off. This limitation is operative from the oral phase on.

Abraham had originally said that the transition from the first to the second anal phase was made possible by a repression to be explained. In fact, he never offers such an explanation, because he cannot if this process exists at every phase of infantile sexuality. Abraham needs a theory that explains what he has unwittingly described: fantasies of total destruction always coexist with a limitation of destruction. Neither repression nor a "motor" of inevitable progression from preambivalence through ambivalence to postambivalence can explain these dynamics.

The inadequacy of his theory in these clinical situations is immediately apparent when Abraham broaches the problem of concreteness. He speaks of a patient who "used to play with the idea of biting off his father's finger. And once, *when he believed that I was not going to continue his analysis, he all of a sudden had the same thought about me*" (p. 487; my emphasis). This transferential moment is for Abraham a clear illustration of an ambivalent, sexual-destructive wish that also implies the "desire to spare the existence of the object except for one part, and the desire to keep that part his own property forever. We may thus speak of an impulse of *partial incorporation* of the object" (ibid.). In the context of a possible forced termination, the patient expresses the need to find a way to stay with the analyst forever. The condition for this endless presence of the analyst is a "partial incorporation" of a part of the analyst's body—the analyst's finger. This partial-total identification with the analyst also implies his survival, at very least like the fly whose leg has been pulled off.[6] Again, the oral part object relation is already ambivalent in the way first ascribed to the second anal phase.

Here my theory would predict primary disavowal of differentiation and a concrete or "real" transference. This is exactly what Abraham goes on to describe:

> the following incident will show how greatly occupied his mind
> was in this stage of his analysis [that is, when he was reacting to
> the possibility of the analysis' not being continued] with the idea
> of biting off things. On one occasion he was speaking about a
> man under whom he was working who represented both his
> father and his mother in his unconscious and towards whom
> he had an extremely ambivalent attitude. As often happened
> with him his free associations flowed over into phantasies of a
> markedly concrete kind, which would at times be interrupted
> by an affective "blocking." A "blocking" of this nature occurred
> as he was speaking about his superior. In accounting for that
> stoppage in his associations he said, "Now [in the fantasized
> situation] I must first tear out his beard with my teeth; I can't
> get any further till I've done that." The patient was thus himself
> saying that there was no possible way of avoiding the intrusion
> of those phantasies which belonged unmistakably to the class of
> partial cannibalism. (pp. 487–88)

Abraham apparently did not see the connection between this description and his description of the "particular form of neurotic resistance." He does speak of an "intrusion" of fantasy that blocks free association and does use the word "concrete." In the face of a fantasy of forced termination, the patient attempts to exert autoerotic control, as Abraham had previously described. What is new here is that part-object fantasies are intrinsic to control and concreteness. But the contradiction in Abraham's argument is critical: because total control or destruction equals incorporation of a part object, it somehow coexists with concern. This concern implies registration of the object.

Abraham describes just this process in his next paragraph, although without knowing that he does so. This miscomprehension of his own accurate description probably explains why Abraham fails to see that he attributes to the oral phase what he had previously attributed to the second anal phase:

Complete and unrestricted cannibalism is only possible on the basis of unrestricted narcissism. On such a level all that the individual considers is his own desire for pleasure. He pays no attention whatever to the interests of his object, and destroys that object without the least hesitation. On the level of partial cannibalism we can still detect the signs of its descent from total cannibalism, yet nevertheless the distinction between the two is sharply marked. On that later level the individual shows the first signs of having some *care* for his object. We may also regard such a *care, incomplete as it is, as the first beginnings of object-love in a stricter sense, since it implies that the individual has begun to conquer his narcissism.* But we must add that on this level of development *the individual is far from recognizing the existence of another individual as such* and from "loving" him in his entirety, whether in a physical or a mental way. His desire is still directed towards removing a part of the body of his object and incorporating it. This, on the other hand, implies that he has resigned the purely narcissistic aim of practicing complete cannibalism. (p. 488; my emphases)

The complications and inconsistencies of this passage take us back to the problems of Freud's concept of primary narcissism. Abraham first describes an unfettered pleasure principle: "total cannibalism" is equivalent to the hypothetical stage of pure tension reduction. The object is exclusively a function of the push toward immediate discharge. But more intuitively than not, Abraham knows that something else has to be going on: the part object relation, as he has continually insisted, also implies something other than unfettered destructiveness, some "care" for the ongoing existence of the object. He sees this "care" as the first manifestation of possible object love, in other words, the first manifestation of what will eventually become genitality. Thus, it embodies the first overcoming of narcissism. However, it is also necessary to postulate that this first possibility of object love, of "care" for the object's existence, occurs in a manner so that one does not recognize "the existence of another individual as such." Abraham does not understand the implications of a necessary postulation of the coexistence of partial (total) cannibalism with care for a nonrecognized object. Without knowing it, he has described a conjoint libidinal–self-preservative drive—"care" as protogenitality, as differentiation within primary narcissism, which oscillates with the fiction of exclusive dominance by the pleasure principle, the autoerotism of secondary narcissism. This is the oscillation between nonrepresentational registration of the "trace" of the object, such that "care" for the object equals "care" for oneself, and the repudiation of that registration, such that "care" is split from sexuality.

Abraham's patient becomes concrete when the tension generated by his care for the analyst equaling his care for himself becomes too great: he is afraid that the analysis will stop. As in the article on the "particular form of neurotic resistance," the patient blocks registration of the "real" purpose of the analysis. He says that he must concretely gratify his impossible fantasy of tearing out the beard of his "superior" (idealized) mother-father with his teeth. The space of linking-differentiating *conscire* is eliminated, and the patient's material cannot be interpreted symbolically. Further, Abraham has anticipated the structure of depressive anxiety: the part object fantasy, with its connotations of total destruction, meets concern for the ongoing existence of the object. The twin inconsistencies of Abraham's argument can be integrated. The protogenitality of the oral phase is a consequence of registered and repudiated "care." The part object itself embodies the two fantasies of partial and total destruction as a repudiation of differentiating care. The part object has a fetishistic structure not only because it functions like the maternal phallus but also because it serves to repudiate registered difference.

Abraham does in fact articulate the link between the part object and the fetish. It is a tribute to his clinical rigor that when he does so, he also senses that he is describing a generalizable process:

> If we suppose that there is such a stage of "partial love" as has
> been depicted in the development of object-love, further facts
> are opened to us and we begin to understand a certain peculiarity of sexual perversions [of infantile sexuality per se] . . . I refer
> to the pervert's concentration of interest on certain bodily parts
> of his object, the choice of which often seems very curious to
> us. This peculiarity is most strikingly exhibited in the fetishist.
> To him the whole person is often only an accidental appendage

to one particular part of his body which alone exercises an irresistible attraction over him. . . . In the light of our present knowledge this psychological process, by means of which the greater part of the object is reduced to insignificance and excessive value is attached to the remaining part, is seen to be the consequence of a regression of the libido to this supposed stage of "partial love"; and it *ceases to be an isolated event found in a certain kind of illness, and falls into place among a large number of allied psychological phenomena.* It is not the intention of this study to go more deeply into the symptoms of fetishism. But it may be useful to point out that those parts of the body on which the fetishist tends to concentrate his inclinations are the same as those we meet with as the objects of "partial love." (p. 491; my emphasis)

The devaluation of the "greater part of the object" and the accompanying idealization of "the remaining part" again expresses the two fantasies of total and partial destruction that begin in the oral phase. These fantasies coexist with the "care" for the nonrecognized other. This "care" can justifiably be included within (Loewald's) primary reality, because it is not objectifiable. The part object then is the fetishistic construction which repudiates the tension of these registrations throughout development.

Abraham intuits that the link of the part object to the fetish says something about perversion—or infantile sexuality—in general. Wherever it is a question of perversion, of infantile sexuality and the basic properties of wishes, it will be a question of the part object. For psychoanalysis, this means everywhere: Abraham knows that the part object is not "an isolated event found in a certain kind of illness" but is rather intrinsic to "a large number of allied psychological phenomena." Abraham seems to have been unaware of the depth of his observation. Freud, too, began to generalize fetishism in his very last writings—with no reference to Abraham's earlier anticipation of his idea.

KLEIN

The theory and technique elaborated by Klein are offshoots of the concept of the part object, of early sadistic fantasies, and of a particular interpretation of the death drive. For Klein, the baby is from the very start faced with the problem of a self-destructive impulse. Following Freud, she saw the projection of this self-destruction as both a necessary defense and as the origin of aggression and counteraggression. In fact, Klein argues that the part object is made sadistic by projection of the death drive. It is then inevitably reintrojected. The basic problem of the "Kleinian baby" is to find a way out of such vicious cycles. The solution is the depressive position.

Klein's strong and original theories are burdened by an extreme version of objectivism. For her, the death drive is an impulse like any impulse. Because sadistic part object relations are operative as soon as the death drive is projected, the early ego finds itself in a situation it can barely cope with—thus Klein's picture of the rather desperate, global, and inadequate projective-introjective defenses of this phase. Thus, too, the literal existence inside the infant of persecutory part objects. Like Abraham, Klein is untroubled by Freud's formulation of a conjoint libidinal–self-preservative drive. Eros is not an issue for her at all. Because she has no doubt about the death drive as a drive, she has no doubt about the early fantasy derivatives of it. This last criticism of Klein is hardly new. Whether in the doctrinal debates within the British Psychoanalytic Society or in subsequent friendly or unfriendly accounts, Klein is often reproached for her reification of the concept of internal objects. She takes part object fantasies as internal, objective realities, with no reflection on the concept of reality that would have to define psychoanalysis as science.

When a psychoanalytic theory takes reality and fantasy as givens, there is almost inevitably a disavowal of primary reality within the theory itself. This means that there are places within the theory that become inconsistent because they require a rethinking of reality that does not occur. As concerns Klein, this is a vital issue for at least three interrelated reasons. First, Klein consistently expanded the understanding of unconscious processes beyond the repression model. Repression is the defense that dominates the more objectivist conception of psychic reality. Why then do Klein's groundbreaking attempts to expand the concept of primary defenses finally lead to an even more extreme objectivism? This question is particularly relevant to Klein's concept of projective identification. In her own terms, projective identification determines the relations of psyche and reality. Since a basic conception of defense always informs the basic conception of reality in a given theory, projective identification has to be looked at from this point of view. Second, Klein's introduction of the two "positions"—the paranoid-schizoid and the depressive—describes the possibility of oscillation between two realities throughout development. For Klein, these are the realities of part and whole object relations. As with Abraham, it will become quite important to understand the concept of reality implied by the oscillation between part and whole and whether it replicates a naïve conception of external reality. Third, Klein is justly celebrated for her understanding of depressive anxiety. Depressive anxiety motivates oscillation between the two positions, between splitting (part object relations) and integration (whole object relations). It explains why integration of what has been split can cause regression and a return to increased splitting. Again as in Abraham, the move from part to whole object relations is the move from fantasy to reality. Depressive anxiety explains why the move from fantasy to reality, from splitting to integration, can be threatening. It is another important index of how Klein conceives reality. We will have to ask whether the reality that Klein opposes to fantasy is the reflecting opposite of the part object and thus actually a conflation of reality and fantasy.

In her 1930 paper "The Importance of Symbol Formation in the Development of the Ego" (1976) Klein already sets in place both a very valuable and very inconsistent theory of symbolism. She does so, naturally, from her particular vantage point of expanding Abraham's theory of sadistic part object fantasies. To state baldly her well-known thesis: in the oral phase the cannibalistic desire to "devour the mother's breast (or the mother herself)" provokes fantasies whose aim is to gain possession "of the contents of the mother's body and to destroy her by means of every weapon which sadism can command" (p. 96). Klein's eternally controversial idea that oral cannibalistic fantasies initiate a primordial Oedipus complex and early super-ego formation is purposely left aside here. What is essential for my discussion is Klein's answer to the same question Abraham put to himself: If infantile sexuality is dominantly sadistic, how does object love become possible?

Klein believes that this question is also one of understanding how the infantile ego copes with extreme anxieties. The infant's sadism, she contends, is a source of danger both to the baby itself and the object it attacks. This inherent sadism therefore prematurely confronts the ego with a situation it can barely master. The defenses initiated in such a "primitive" organization are equally primitive. Klein cites Freud's view from *Inhibition, Symptom, and Anxiety* (1926) that in early life defenses other than repression dominate. She could also have referred to "Instincts and Their Vicissitudes" (1915a), one of her favorite Freud texts and often cited by her elsewhere.[7] There Freud also discussed modes of defense that precede repression, emphasizing projection, and spoke of the earliest relation to an external object in terms of hate. In any event, in order to conceptualize the ego's response to the danger represented by its own sadism, Klein says that one must envision a defense which equals early anxiety in its primitive violence, a defense that "differs fundamentally from repression" (p. 97). She gives an account of identification that goes straight to the problem of reality.

Klein reminds her readers that in the theory of libidinal development identification is "the forerunner of symbolism." The baby first comes to take pleasurable interest in anything outside itself through identification. Whatever is outside is equated with the baby's own mode of functioning. She calls this process "symbolic equation" (p. 97). "Equation" denotes the identification and "symbolic" its status as a forerunner of later sublimations:

> side by side with the libidinal interest, it is the anxiety arising in the phase [of sadism] . . . which sets going the mechanism of identification. Since the child desires to destroy the organs (penis, vagina, breast) which stand for the objects, he conceives a dread of the latter. This anxiety contributes to make him equate the organs in question with other things; owing to this equation these in their turn become objects of anxiety, and so he is impelled constantly to make other and new equations, which form the basis of his interest in the new objects and of symbolism. (p. 97)

Klein is describing a defense as voracious as the impulse it defends against. Every identification of an external object with the child's own sadism only makes things worse. Anxiety is increased every time a new part object—the organ that stands for the person as external object—is equated with the child's sadism. Thus, there is a constant search for new objects to equate with those created in the child's own image.

It is not difficult to interpret this conception as an even more extreme version of the "reality at first bite" that we saw in Abraham. Loewald, of course, could view this theory as the apogee of the equation of objectivity with a hostile relation to reality. Klein takes it as given that the infant increasingly turns to the outer world only in order to find new objects to equate with its sadism. By implication, what Klein calls "symbolic equivalence" would be the origin of destructive narcissism: outer reality increasingly conforms to one's own destructiveness as a defense against it. The reality that one comes to "know" via identification or symbolic equivalence is then dedifferentiated in the extreme. It exists only as a reflection of one's own aggression.

Klein herself does not directly engage the question of a dedifferentiated reality organization. The closest she comes to it is in her description of "wanting to know"—epistemophilia. Because "symbolic equivalence" is the necessary forerunner of symbolism per se, Klein contends that

> upon it is built up the subject's relation to the outside world and to reality in general. . . . [T]he object of sadism at its zenith, and of the epistemophilic impulse arising and coexisting with sadism, is the mother's body with its phantasied contents. The sadistic phantasies directed against the inside of her body constitute the first and basic relation to the outside world and to reality. Upon the degree of success with which the subject passes through this phase will depend the extent to which he can subsequently acquire an external world corresponding to reality. We see then that the child's earliest reality is wholly phantastic; he is surrounded with objects of anxiety, and in this respect excrement, organs, objects, things animate and inanimate are to begin with equivalent to one another. As the ego develops a true relation to reality is gradually established out of this unreal reality.

Thus, the development of the ego and the relation to reality
depend on the degree of the ego's capacity at a very early period
to tolerate the pressure of the earliest anxiety situations. And, as
usual, it is a question of a certain optimum amount of the factors
concerned. A sufficient quantity of anxiety is the necessary basis
for an abundance of symbol formation and of phantasy; an
adequate capacity on the part of the ego to tolerate anxiety is
necessary if it is to be satisfactorily worked over and if the basic
phase is to have a favourable issue and the development of the
ego to be successful. (p. 98)

This passage leaves one in the dark about how the infant finally arrives
at a "true relation to reality." Nonetheless, it is possible to read this passage as a compelling account of the origin of concreteness. What
Klein calls "unreal reality," in a richly contradictory phrase, describes
the galloping conflation of fantasy and reality. Part objects are absorbed
into a sadistic universe due to a defensive process as violent as what it
defends against. Since Klein is describing fantasies of total destructiveness, she has also explained why the creation of an "unreal reality" has
to be a global process. The concreteness of symbolic equivalence is a
globally dedifferentiating sadistic defense against sadism.

Klein adds a crucial dimension to the understanding of "unreal
reality." The essentially "unknown" external reality, which has to become known in order to equate it with one's own sadism, is the inside of the mother's body. To the extent that anything outside oneself
is experienced as unknown, the inner contents of the mother's body
become the "symbolic equivalent" of an "internality" that can be
known only by forced entry. "Knowledge" then becomes a dedifferentiating sadistic attack: epistemophilia is invasive symbolic equivalence. Here we can again return to the problem of concreteness. Recall the patients cited in Chapter 1, for example, Frosch's patient who
"knew" that her analyst was a "jerk" just like her, the student analyst's
patient who "knew" that he was angry at her for being late, and Caper's patient who "knew" how exhausted he was. All these patients
can be understood to be claiming to have an invasive knowledge of
the inside of the analyst's mind. This "knowledge" is actually an aggressive identification of a part object fantasy with a transference af-

fect. From the patient's point of view, however, such "knowledge" is indubitable. From the analyst's point of view, the entire treatment then seems to take place in an "unreal reality." This is the problem noted in all the descriptions of concreteness.

For Klein, the anxiety that motivates such global defense is fear of one's own sadism. For me, the tension of differentiation generates fantasies of omnipotent dedifferentiation. In Chapter 1, I cited Freedman (unpub.; Freedman and Berzofsky 1995) on this topic. He calls the destructive narcissism directed against the possibility of psychic space "desymbolization." Like Klein, Freedman sees the equation of inner and outer as an act of destruction which operates "in a sphere 'beyond the pleasure principle'" (p. 372). Unlike Klein, however, he takes into account the problem of psychic space—the minimum internalization of differentiation necessary for the symbol not to be equated with what it symbolizes.

Why does Klein see this process as the origin of symbolism, while for Freedman it is an active process of desymbolization? Loewald is of help here. He understood Eros and the death drive in terms of internalization and identification, the maintenance or collapse of differentiation. Reinterpreting Klein in these terms, one can say that she has grasped the sadism intrinsic to dedifferentiating identification, something Loewald himself did not do. She takes symbolic equivalence to be a derivative of the death drive and also posits it as an essential forerunner of the "true relation to reality [that] is gradually developed out of this unreal reality." But Klein does not imagine a sadistic need to destroy psychic space, to dedifferentiate symbol and symbolized, as defense against registered differentiation. Klein's sadistic symbolic equivalence would not be possible if there were not some registration of a non-equivalence between the infant's mind and the mother's body. This non-equivalence can be conceived as the "membrane" between mother and baby within the organization of primary narcissism. It is the minimal psychic space necessary for symbolization. If it is eliminated in fantasy by sadistic destruction, then symbolic equivalence takes its place. Klein is actually describing desymbolization.

Loewald understood internalization of environment as the possibility of the observing ego. As a description of concreteness, desymbolization also implies destruction of the internal psychic space necessary for self-observation. Wherever dedifferentiation dominates the relation to the external world, so, too, it dominates the internal world. The space necessary for an observing ego is also collapsed. Klein's idea that sadistic epistemophilia is the origin of symbolism promotes the unwarranted clinical assumption that such formations can still be interpreted symbolically. Interpretations of fantasy content, or even of defense, that do not address the collapse of the space for the observing ego bypass defense against the possibility of symbolism. Therefore, they cannot modify symbolic equivalence.

This reinterpretation of Klein does not correspond to her intent. She understands symbolic equivalence as a literal and original process deriving from a literal and original death drive. From her point of view, the death drive originally dominates the psyche, and thus the infant lives in a world that is "wholly phantastic." Klein theorizes a pure autoerotism of destructiveness. If one simply follows Klein's emphasis on original sadism and her non-consideration of Eros, the derivation of symbolism from symbolic equivalence is inexplicable. There would be no dynamic account of symbolic equivalence as a sadistic, dedifferentiating response to unconsciously registered differentiation.

Without such reinterpretation Klein's very important emphasis on the projection of self-destructiveness is too easily dismissed. It can appear as unreal as the "unreal reality" she describes, since no baby lives in such a wholly fantastic world. This would be unfortunate, because Klein's thinking does add an essential dimension to understanding concreteness or enactive remembering. If one reinterprets symbolic equivalence as a defensive response to differentiation, then Klein has explained the aggression intrinsic to repudiation of "originally unconscious thought" (Freud) or "traces of interactions" (Loewald). Once such thoughts or registrations become painful, to repudiate them is to attempt to create a "wholly phantastic," "unreal reality." The creation of a dangerous, persecutory, external objectivity is then sustained by an illusion of justified counteraggression. But because a persecutory objectivity and the justified aggression against it are both narcissistic formations, aggression against the persecutory object is always aggression against oneself. This would explain the evident self-destructiveness of concreteness or enactive remembering.

Is this sadism a projection of a literal death drive, as Freud at certain points says and as Klein believes? If we follow Loewald's integration of the problem of the death drive with the tendency toward dedifferentiating primary process identifications, Klein's ideas can again be reinterpreted. She has demonstrated the vicious cycles of projection and re-introjection of sadism intrinsic to such identifications. Because such identifications re-create a picture of oneself and the world minus the repudiated difference, they are narcissistic and destructive in the sense in which we have understood secondary narcissism. They create an "unreal reality" in order to repudiate the tensions of primary narcissism. The primary narcissism of care for oneself equaling care for the "object" of processive interaction is replaced with a destruction of interaction which equals self destruction.

Clinically, this is exactly the problem of the concrete patient, who necessarily repudiates the self-preservative, libidinal function of interaction with the analyst and replaces it with sado-masochistic power struggles over "knowledge" of reality. Klein's concept of sadistic epistemophilia is very enlightening in this respect. The concrete patient's claim to "know" what the analyst thinks or feels, the omnipotent access to what is "inside" the analyst's mind, is a sadistic defense against internalization. Interactions with the analyst geared toward change are repudiated. The projected sadism of epistemophilia replaces (Loewald's) *conscire*.

It must constantly be emphasized, however, that Klein's theory seems to be caught up in the contradictions of an inherently hostile relation between "ego and reality," as delineated by Loewald. She takes the way in which symbolic equivalence creates a world of persecutory objects as a complete description of the infant's original psychic reality. When one takes this description as the means to formulate interpretations, one creates the possibility of using theory itself as an omnipotent system. Should the analyst in any way share the tendency to believe that perception guarantees reality, then the analyst also engages in symbolic equivalence. The patient who creates symbolic equivalents will experience interpretation as the analyst's own version of symbolic equivalence in any event. Thus, one can arrive at an impasse where enactive remembering meets enactive interpretation.

Klein at no point discusses this problem, which of course was anticipated by Abraham in "A Particular Form of Neurotic Resistance."

Just as one senses the frustration of therapeutic aims in Abraham's description of globally resistant patients, so one senses a kind of blinkered omnipotence in Klein's failure to rethink interpretation where symbolic equivalence dominates. It is entirely conceivable that the analyst's "pattern matching" interpretations, guided by Klein's innovative and precise descriptions of sadistic fantasies and early defenses, will eventually have some effect. The question is whether they operate as magical interpretive hallucinations that promote identification between patient and analyst instead of internalization of the analytic interaction.

The theory of depressive anxiety, which Klein first articulated in 1935, itself illustrates this dilemma. Klein is taking up an essential issue. If splitting and sadism reinforce each other, how is such splitting overcome? This is another way of putting Abraham's question about how the dominance of sadism is transformed. Simultaneously, for Klein this is also the question about how one emerges from the "wholly phantastic" "unreal reality" to a "real reality." Her crucial idea is that it is intrinsically anxiety provoking to undo splitting: the way out of the vicious cycles of projection and reintrojection of sadism may feel worse than entrapment within them. The essence of the depressive position is that "the ego comes to a realization of its love for a *good* object, a *whole* object and in addition a *real* object, together with an overwhelming feeling of guilt towards it" (p. 125; my emphases). The guilt is the result of a realization of "the disaster created through . . . sadism," which always threatens the internalized good object with destruction and disintegration. One's own aggression can lead to the loss of the good object and subsequent return to the "unreal reality" of pure destructiveness—the paranoid-schizoid position.

As one looks at the logic of the "good," "whole," and "real" object, all the problems of the conflation of reality and fantasy reemerge. Klein confidently believes that the early incorporation of the persecutory part objects—"a phantastically distorted picture of the real objects upon which they are based" (p. 116)—is the "psychic reality" of the infant. Since the operation of symbolic equivalence makes the external world conform to the vicious cycle of projection and introjection, at first the only way out of this nightmare is "scotomization, the *denial of psychic reality*; this may result . . . in the denial of external reality" (p. 117). A short detour around Klein's use of the peculiar word "scotomization" is useful here.

"Scotomization" means the creation of a blind spot. Freud discussed the term in "Fetishism" (1927b) in a manner directly relevant to Klein's argument. (Did she have this passage in mind?) In his first description of the little boy's defense against his perception that the woman does not possess a penis, Freud writes: "If I am not mistaken, Laforgue [who coined the word] would say in this case that the boy 'scotomizes' his perception of the woman's lack of a penis" (p. 153). Freud's brief dissection of scotomization is significant. He wants to explain why one would be tempted to describe the apparent non-registration of the mother's "lack of a penis" as scotomization but also why the term is particularly unsuitable. It suggests that the unwanted perception is "entirely wiped out, so that the result is the same as when a visual impression falls on the blind spot in the retina. In the situation we are considering, on the contrary, we see that the perception has persisted" (pp. 155–56). This is exactly why Freud wants to call it "disavowal," *Verleugnung*—simultaneous "registration and repudiation."

In the passage just cited, Klein is discussing psychosis. She understands the denial of external reality as a projected version of the denial of internal reality. One could argue that there would be no reason to question her comparison of denial to scotomization. Fetishism is not psychosis. However, in 1940, five years after Klein's paper, Freud was moved to state that even in psychosis what looks like denial is actually a version of disavowal. Klein's description of denial does not take into account the simultaneous registration and repudiation of whatever is being defended against—precisely what led Freud to reject the term "scotomization" in "Fetishism." In other words, the registration of "reality"—however one takes the term—as the precondition of every defensive process is not a question for Klein. Her conception of unconscious processes, like a certain version of Freud's and like Abraham's, assumes a simple opposition between internal fantasy and external reality. Something must eventually interfere with the dominance of fantasy in order to inaugurate a relation to reality as it is conventionally conceived. "Reality" is a psychic factor only after this relation is inaugurated.

Clinically, there is every reason to attend to Klein's description of global fantasies and defenses that produce an invasive "knowledge" of external reality. Yet as she begins to describe the modification of these global structures, she is able to say no more than that as "the ego becomes more fully organized, the internalized imagos will approximate more closely to reality and the ego will identify itself more fully with 'good' objects" (p. 118). For Abraham, externality and ambivalence suddenly impose themselves with the first "bite." For Klein, a "real reality," as opposed to an originally "unreal reality," suddenly imposes itself with an even more puzzling incorporation of a good object. Differentiation somehow intrudes from the outside.

Once the leap to the incorporation of the good object takes place, the depressive position essentially begins. As Klein says, "dread of persecution, which was at first felt on the ego's account, now relates to the good object as well and from now on preservation of the good object is regarded as synonymous with the survival of the ego" (ibid.). Klein attributes the survival of the object to that moment in the oral phase when the "goodness" of the object suddenly dawns on the developing ego. As soon as preservation of the good object becomes synonymous with the survival of the ego, she writes, there is

> a change of the highest importance, namely, from a partial object
> relation to the relation to a complete object. Through this step
> the ego arrives at a new position, which forms the foundation of
> that situation called the loss of the loved object. Not until the
> object is lived *as a whole* [author's emphasis] can its loss be felt as
> a whole. . . . With this change in the relation to the object, new
> anxiety contents make their appearance and a change takes place
> in the mechanisms of defense. . . . This leads to a weakening of
> oral fixations. . . . [As] consideration for the object increases, and
> a better acknowledgement of psychic reality sets in, the anxiety
> lest the object should be destroyed in the process of introjecting
> it leads—as Abraham has described—to various disturbances of
> the function of introjection . . . there is . . . a deep anxiety as to
> the dangers which await the object inside the ego. . . . [T]he ego
> becomes fully identified with its good, internalized objects, and
> at the same time becomes aware of its own incapacity to protect

and preserve them against the internalized, persecuting objects and the id. . . . [A]t this stage, the ego makes a greater use of introjection of the good object as a mechanism of defence. This is associated with another important mechanism: that of making reparation to the object. . . . The ego feels impelled (and I can now add, impelled by its identification with the good object) to make restitution for all the sadistic attacks that it has launched on that object. . . . [N]ow that good and bad objects are more clearly differentiated, the subject's hate is directed against the latter, while his love and his attempts at reparation are more focused on the former; but the excess of his sadism and anxiety acts as a check to this advance . . . *every access of hate or anxiety may temporarily abolish the differentiation and thus result in a "loss of the loved object"* [my emphasis]. . . . [T]he loss of the loved object takes place during that phase of development in which the ego makes the transition from partial to total incorporation of the object. (pp. 118–22)

This argument is intended to demonstrate why the good breast equals the whole breast equals reality. The ego emerges from the "wholly phantastic" relation to an "unreal reality" via its identification with the good, whole breast. Via this identification, concern for the survival of the good, whole breast becomes concern for the ego's own survival. When Klein says that "the ego endeavours to keep the good apart from the bad, and the real from the phantastic" (p. 123), she does not notice that what she calls the "real" is actually fantastic. The whole object is the idealized antidote of the part object and just as illusory. In fact, this is why fantasies about part objects are inevitably fantasies about whole objects, as in Abraham's description. Incorporation of the good object creates the possibility of *a* wholeness, which allegedly introduces differentiation into the unmitigated sadism of the early oral phase.

Thus, Klein's theory also has a two-fantasy structure and depends upon the notion of an originally undifferentiated state (of unbridled destructiveness). Once differentiation results from the introjection of the "good" object, it is unrelated to ongoing registration of processive aspects of reality. The depressive position then contains within it an idea like the "reality of castration." Loss of the incorporated whole object becomes the loss of reality and differentiation. Just as Freud equates sexual difference with the two fantasies "castrated" and "not castrated," so Klein equates the possibility of difference with the two fantasies "part" and "whole."

Klein could potentially counter this argument by citing her own close attention to the way in which idealization of the good breast is the defensive counterpart of persecutory anxieties. Because of the projection of sadism, she says, the loved object is in a "state of dissolution." A "beautiful and 'perfect'" image of it defensively counteracts the idea of disintegration (p. 182). But she does not notice that her own theory repeats this maneuver when it makes differentiation and reality dependent upon incorporation of a whole object. When a fantasy of absence is conflated with reality—the "reality of castration"— so, too, the presence of the potentially lost object becomes conflated with a fantasy of intactness. Just as the physical presence of a "thing" provides magical reassurance for the fetishist, the physical presence of an organ—a penis, a breast—may be put to the same illusory use. Fetishism teaches us that the physical presence of a thing can have the same defensive-fantasy potential as its physical absence.

Klein's account, even more pointedly than Abraham's, shows why something like fetishism is possible from the oral phase on. The conflation of the absence of the breast with the loss of a part of one's own body ("primal castration" as both Freud and Abraham called it) is precisely what made Abraham compare the part object to the fetish in general. But the homology of the part object and the fetish require one to reconceptualize the relations between reality and defense. Klein does not take this step.

Klein's 1946 introduction of the defense of projective identification in "Notes on Some Schizoid Mechanisms" (1946) illuminates this analysis (1986). Considering its eventual fate, Klein's first formulation of the concept is low keyed. She curiously does not refer to her earlier work on symbolic equivalence, although the concept of projective identification is clearly an extension of it.[8] She repeats the conflation of the good, whole breast with reality: "the frustrating breast—attacked in oral-sadistic phantasies—is felt to be in fragments;

the gratifying breast, taken in under the dominance of the sucking libido, is felt to be complete. This first internal good object acts as a focal point in the ego. It counteracts the processes of splitting and dispersal, makes for cohesiveness and integration, and is instrumental in building up the ego" (pp. 180–81). Klein then makes her essential point that "the ego is incapable of splitting the object—internal and external—without a corresponding splitting taking place within the ego" (p. 181).

Here Klein is both close to and far from the Freud who began to envision the "splitting of the ego in the process of defense." She is close to Freud, one could say, for all the wrong reasons. The "Kleinian baby," who defensively splits bad and good, is like the fetishist who oscillates between castration and non-castration, as if both were realities. Nonetheless, this emphasis on early splitting defenses does move beyond the repression model. It leads to the question of how to conceive the reintegration of what has been split off. But for this very reason, Klein is far from the Freud who spoke of the registration and repudiation of reality implicit in every defense. Certainly Klein knows that the processes she describes are "bound up with the infant's phantasy life . . . the anxieties which stimulate the mechanism of splitting are also of a phantastic nature. It is in phantasy that the infant splits the object and the self, but the effect of this phantasy is a very real one, because it leads to feelings and relations (and later on, thought processes) being in fact cut off from one another" (p. 181). The implication here is clearly that reality equals the non-split, or whole, object and ego. If depressive anxiety concerns the possible loss of this good object and therefore the loss of a relation to reality, then again it is difficult to distinguish between reality and the defensively created fantasy of an idealized object. This idealized object is ideally present, first externally and then internally.[9]

This again is not to say that Klein does not consider idealization to be a defense. The question is to understand exactly how she thinks idealization functions. She first reiterates that idealization "is bound up with splitting of the object, for the good aspects of the breast are exaggerated as a safeguard against the fear of the persecuting breast . . . idealization is thus the corollary of persecutory fear" (p. 182). Since persecutory fears are the result of symbolic equivalence, so, too, would be idealization. Klein then goes on to an extremely interesting discussion of hallucinatory wish fulfillment, in both its gratifying and defensive aspects. She says that "infantile hallucinatory gratification" always demonstrates idealization as a protection against persecutory fears, with concomitant splitting:

> The main processes which come into play in idealization are also operative in hallucinatory gratification, namely, splitting of the object and denial both of frustration and of persecution. The frustrating and persecuting object is kept widely apart from the idealized object. However, the bad object is not only kept apart from the good one but its very existence is denied, as is the whole situation of frustration and the bad feelings (pain) to which frustration gives rise. This is bound up with the denial of psychic reality. The denial of psychic reality becomes possible only through strong feelings of omnipotence—an essential characteristic of early mentality. . . . In hallucinatory gratification, therefore, two interrelated processes take place: the omnipotent conjuring up of the ideal object and situation, and the equally omnipotent annihilation of the bad persecutory object and the painful situation. These processes are based on splitting both the object and the ego. (p. 182)

In this passage, Klein has reinterpreted Freud's basic ideas about wish fulfillment. While she does not use the concept of negative hallucination, it clearly underpins her analysis of the splitting and idealization intrinsic to every wish. For Freud, negative hallucination explained how bodily tensions appear to be assuaged by the positive hallucination of the wish. Klein here thinks in an analogous way. In her account bodily tensions represent frustrations, and frustrations do not come from within oneself but are imposed by the bad object. Therefore, the negative hallucination implicit in every wish fulfillment would also imply the elimination of the source of frustration, that is, the same bad object. Since the bad object is also within oneself, to eliminate it is to deny psychic reality, an expression of omnipotence.

For Klein, idealization is intrinsic to the way in which every wish implies that hallucinated images can serve as gratifications. If one conceives an "original" state of the psychic apparatus entirely under the sway of symbolic equivalence, one understands exactly what Klein means. Hallucinatory wish fulfillment must be expanded to include the omnipotence of denial of the bad object and the creation of the idealized object. The idea that the wish itself, on its "subatomic" level, could not exist if there were not registrations of the primary reality of processive interactions (the experience of satisfaction) has no place in Klein's account. The omnipotence intrinsic to secondary narcissism becomes for Klein the original condition of the psyche. The problem of theory replicating fantasy is then acute.

We can finally meet projective identification with these points in mind. Klein writes that we must think about the aggressive relation to the "inside" of the mother's body not only in oral but also in anal and urethral or excretory terms:

the attacks on the mother's breast develop into attacks of a similar nature on her body, which comes to be felt as it were as an extension of the breast. . . . The phantasied onslaughts on the mother follow two main lines: one is the predominantly oral impulse to suck dry, bite up, scoop out and rob the mother's body of its good contents. . . . The other line of attack derives from the anal and urethral impulses and implies expelling dangerous substances (excrements) out of the self and into the mother. Together with these harmful excrements, expelled in hatred, *split off parts of the ego are also projected on to the mother or, as I would rather call it, into the mother.* These excrements and bad parts of the self are meant not only to injure but also to control and to take possession of the object. In so far as the mother comes to contain the bad parts of the self, she is not felt to be a separate individual but is felt to be *the* bad self. Much of the hatred against parts of the self is now directed towards the mother. This leads to a particular form of identification which establishes the prototype of an aggressive object relation. I suggest for these processes the term "projective identification".
. . . It is, however, not only the bad parts of the self which are expelled and projected, but also good parts of the self. . . . The

identification based on this type of projection again vitally
influences object relations. The projection of good feelings and
good parts of the self onto the mother is essential for the infant's
ability to develop good object relations and to integrate his ego.
(pp. 183–84; my emphases)

We find here an expansion of the logic of symbolic equivalence and
sadistic epistemophilia. Splitting now also implies a fantasy of forcing
"bad" parts of the self into the externality that is the inside of the
mother's body. Separation therefore is eliminated: the inside of the
mother is oneself, another version of destructive narcissism. However,
the same holds true for the "good" parts of oneself. They, too, can be
projected "into" the mother, so that by becoming her, one becomes
a more integrated version of oneself. Just as there seemed to be no
way out of symbolic equivalence in Klein's earlier theory, there seems
to be no conception of object relations that does not depend upon
dedifferentiation, upon undoing separation.[10] If Klein had said something like "the projection of the good parts of oneself is as much a
fantasy as the projection of bad parts of oneself, and therefore still has
a defensive function," one would have less to criticize. But because
Klein makes this process the condition for integration, there seems to
be no relation to reality except via defense. Klein's theory then repeats naïve objectivism. Projective identification is taken to be the literal process whereby part objects, defensively idealized as whole objects, become objectivity (reality) itself. Such a reality is as fetishistic
as the reality of persecutory bad objects.

Klein's clinical technique is problematic for just this reason. She
seems to promote "pattern matching" based upon her fetishistic theory. Further, the central concern of Kleinian analysis, the transition
from the paranoid-schizoid to the depressive position, depends upon
the incorporation of a "good, whole, real" object within the analysis.
Because the analyst has to move from being a part to a whole object
for the patient, the analyst promotes a fetishization of himself or herself. Identification with an object, not internalization of an interaction, becomes the mode of therapeutic action. The necessity of analyzing defense against differentiation in the transference, particularly
where projective identification is operative, does not become a ques-

tion—thus the ineluctable progression from a naïve view of interpretation to a naïvely experiential view of analytic change.

Despite this criticism of Klein in terms of Loewald, it is also true
that Loewald conspicuously lacked anything like a theory of the depressive position. In fact, with all her shortcomings, Klein must be
given full credit for introducing the idea that throughout life we may
defensively oscillate between reality and fantasy, because the anxiety of
undoing the splitting may feel catastrophic. The question is whether
anxieties about the integration of reality and fantasy are anxieties over
the loss of the "intact object" that makes one whole. When primary
process dominates consciousness, as in enactive remembering or symbolic equivalence, there will be prominent illusions about catastrophic
losses. (I outlined five such forms of loss in the discussion of Loewald's
conception of the repetition compulsion.) However, such fantasies of
loss always oscillate with fantasies of wholeness. Both serve to repudiate the registration of differentiating traces, of self-preservation as care
for the object. As a function of Eros, differentiation "binds." The near-
traumatic anxieties associated with differentiation are not about loss
but about contact.[11] To conceive depressive position reintegration
only in terms of anxieties over loss disavows the inevitable resistance
to interpretation produced by projective identification.

As dedifferentiating defenses, projective identification and symbolic equivalence do lead to the domination of consciousness by fantasy. This is why Klein analyzed the fundamental tie of projective
identification to hallucinatory wish fulfillment. Something like projective identification or symbolic equivalence would always occur
when fetishistic part or whole object fantasies are conflated with reality. In this sense the projective identification of the idealized whole
object is just as controlling, and inherently aggressive, as the projection of the part object. Without such a conception, it is all too easy
to construe the breast and the penis as concretely intact. Both Freud
and Klein fall prey to this kind of thinking in their respective ways
(the "reality of castration," the "good, whole, real" object). When they
do, they become entangled in the conflation of concrete absence or
presence with projected fantasies and calling the result "objective" or
"real." This is why depressive anxiety as Klein conceives it is essentially a version of castration anxiety. Defense against integration is ac-

tually sustained by castration-depressive anxiety, which regulates internalization anxiety.

In Chapter 2 I examined Ferenczi's idea that defenses create characteristic reality organizations. What Klein could not see was that projective identification, in its link to hallucinatory wish fulfillment, creates the reality organization of an outer space into which "real" inner objects can be expelled. This is another reason why her theory is an extreme form of naïve objectivism. But it also illuminates why the theory of repression accommodates a similar objectivism. Repression treats memories, drives, wishes, and affects as concrete objects that can be forcibly lodged elsewhere within oneself. Repression would be a more internalized version of fantasy about mind made possible by projective identification: the fantasy of mind as having various internal compartments, so that objectified contents can be expelled out of one place and into another. When Freud began to rethink repression as a version of ego splitting and disavowal, he essentially provided the groundwork for this analysis.

Whenever the unconscious is construed in terms of an originally undifferentiated state, internalization anxiety also operates on the level of theory construction. Differentiation and reality are imposed from outside as "objective" losses. Mind then reflects a pathology of loss. Clinical technique risks doing the same. The result is the fetishization of either interpretation or identification with the analyst, and often both, as is the case with Klein.

WINNICOTT

In 1954 Winnicott gave what he called "a personal account of Melanie Klein's concept of the depressive position" (1975, p. 262). Winnicott's earlier writings are indebted to Klein, but he increasingly distanced himself from her. His paper on the depressive position is as much a statement of fundamental disagreement as it is a tribute. The specific bone of contention is the role of reality and environment in depressive position integration, an obvious link to Loewald. Winnicott's rethinking of the depressive position, in fact, will extend Loewald's conception of primary narcissism and Eros as forces of integration with environment.

.Winnicott situates the depressive position between early infancy, in which the mother adapts to the baby's needs, and the triangular oedipal period, in which "instinctual life in interpersonal relationships" is being worked out (ibid.). From the outset he posits a dividing line within development. Before the depressive position one sees more severe psychopathology and after it neurosis. The problem with this idea is not in its understanding of the more severe pathologies but in its assumption that questions of integration and depressive anxiety are not also central to neurosis:

> The child (or adult) who has reached that capacity for interpersonal relationships which characterizes the toddler stage in health, and for whom ordinary analysis of the infinite variations of triangular human relationship is feasible, has passed *through and beyond* the depressive position. On the other hand, the child (or adult) who is chiefly concerned with the innate problems of personality integration and with the initiation of a relationship with environment is not yet at the depressive position in personal development. (ibid.)

The oedipal child by definition has passed "through and beyond the depressive position." Winnicott then would not consider sexual difference in the oedipal phase an environmental issue, an issue that can become entwined with depressive—or internalization—anxiety.

Between early infancy and the oedipal phase is the position in which the mother "holds" the child over a "phase of living," giving the infant "the chance to work through the consequences of instinctual experiences" (p. 263). Like Abraham, who wanted to figure out how concern for the object became possible, and Klein, who wanted to understand the emergence from unmitigated sadism, Winnicott wants to understand how "instinctual experience" comes to have consequences. For Klein, the introjection of the whole object gives rise to fear of its loss, an operation that takes place only in fantasy. Winnicott introduces the issue of the mother's actual care for the baby as a decisive environmental factor: "The mother holds the situation, and does so over and over again, and at a critical period in the baby's life. The consequence is that something can be done about something.

The mother's technique enables the infant's co-existing love and hate to become sorted out and interrelated and gradually brought under control from within in a way that is healthy" (p. 263). The rather light-handed phrase "something can be done about something" is actually decisive. Winnicott's idea is that love and hate need to be integrated so that one does not always feel controlled by external forces. This is essentially the problem of the paranoid-schizoid position, although Winnicott never uses the term. Once there is some control from within, it is possible to feel that one can do something with and about one's instinctual experiences. Clinically, if a patient is struggling with depressive position integration, the assumption that he or she comes to analysis in order "to do something about something" may not be warranted.

This is precisely what the concrete patient brings so forcibly to the analyst's attention. He or she seems to come to analysis in order not to "do something about something." In treatment this often takes the form of non-concern with time, manifested as endless analysis. Winnicott understands time as an essential dimension of depressive position integration. Because the mother holds the infant "over a phase of living . . . a *time factor* has entered" (ibid.). Time itself makes it possible "to do something about something." If there are problems either in working through the depressive position or in the mother's "technique," time will be of as little consequence as instinctual experience. The failure to work through the depressive position will then reemerge in analysis. In general, when the analyst senses that time does not count, he or she can begin to think about the anxieties that prevent integration.

Winnicott's idea that environment is temporal is close to Loewald's thinking about the temporality of internalization. Loewald contrasted the time of identification, in which a loss is magically made good in a frozen present, to the time of internalization, in which there is always the possibility of a future integration with environment. Klein's bias in favor of the introjection of a "good object" is an undiscerning reinforcement of the frozen time of identification. Within such a temporal framework one can only repeat the mechanism of making good a "loss" in the present. Winnicott tackles this issue, as light-handedly and elliptically as ever: "Analysts are faced with this difficult problem, shall we ourselves be recognizable in our patients? We always are. But we deplore it. We hate to become internalized good breasts in others, and to hear ourselves being advertised by those whose own inner chaos is being precariously held by the introjection of an idealized analyst" (p. 276).

What then is the essence of Winnicott's revision of the depressive position? He proposes to rebaptize it the "Stage of Concern." At some point in development the infant begins to grow concerned about the consequences of its drives, concerned about the survival of the object, and concerned about its own survival. Before reaching this point, there is a kind of "ruthlessness" to the infant's instinctual experience: "there is no concern yet as to results of instinctual love. This love is originally a form of impulse . . . it affords the infant the satisfaction of self-expression and release from tension; more it places the object outside the self. It should be noted that the infant does not feel ruthless. . . . The stage is one that is pre-ruth" (p. 265).

Winnicott does something quite important in these few sentences. Without formally saying so, he makes it clear that domination by the pleasure principle—release from tension—places the object outside oneself. The *appearance* that the object is external is a result of *apparent* domination by the pleasure principle. According to the pleasure principle, one makes part of oneself what is agreeable and expels what is disagreeable. Thus, hate and projection seemingly create the external object. However, even when the baby is "ruthless," it is ruthless within the context of primary narcissism. Winnicott says that initially "it is only the observer who can distinguish between the individual and the environment (primary narcissism)." One has to speak of "an environment-individual set-up, rather than of an individual" (p. 266). Within this organization, "the mother needs to be able to combine two functions, and to persist with these two functions in *time*" (ibid.; my emphasis). One is the environmental caretaking function, the active adaptation to the baby's needs. The other is the offering of herself as "the object of assault during phases of instinctual tension" (ibid.).

The depressive position for Winnicott is the "coming together in the mind of the infant of these two functions of the mother" (ibid.). Although Winnicott immediately pays tribute to Klein for her pioneering work in studying this process, he is clearly saying something quite different. For Klein, the depressive position is about the coming together of the part and the whole object. For Winnicott, it is about the coming together of environment and instinctual fantasy. The coming together of the environment mother and the instinct mother allows the "beginning of the recognition of the existence of ideas, fantasy, imaginative elaboration of function, the acceptance of ideas and of fantasy related to fact *but not to be confused with fact*" (p. 267; my emphasis). Elliptically again, Winnicott has said something quite important. He has demonstrated that the entire problem of concreteness, or symbolic equivalence, or enactive remembering, is a question of the non-integration of environment and instinct. However, Winnicott's view that environment is simply the mother's adaptation to the baby's needs leads to an empiricist conception of how depressive anxiety is mitigated: "Integration in the child's mind of the *split* between the child-care environment and the exciting environment (the two aspects of the mother) cannot be made except by good-enough mothering and the mother's survival over a period of time" (p. 267; my emphasis). This empirical description does not do justice to the processes that occur within primary narcissism. Drives, or instincts, for Winnicott, are not also intrinsically environmental forces, as they are for Loewald. The mother has two functions (to care, to be an object of the drives), but the baby is not intrinsically divided between drive as differentiating integration with environment and drive as dedifferentiating tension reduction. It is obvious that "good enough" adaptation to the baby's needs over time is essential for healthy development. However, one cannot let this truism obscure a more difficult idea: the mother's adaptation to need and survival will not necessarily prevent the repudiation of differentiating tension. In fact, the mother's care and survival are not only empirical questions, they are also coextensive with the integration of tension-raising, nonrepresented registrations.[12]

In 1924 Abraham had already grasped the fetishistic function of the part object. If the part object always replaces processive integration with environment, then anxiety about integration is an issue wherever part object formations appear, including the castration conflicts of the phallic phase. It is not only, as Winnicott says, that the "mother of the dependent relationship (anaclitic) is also the object of instinctual (biologically driven) love" (p. 268). It is rather that there is an inherent tendency to repudiate the registration of environment, precisely because of its differentiating function. Winnicott, both temperamentally and theoretically, cannot conceive that there could be a traumatic aspect to the registration of care.

When dynamic, processive reality is not factored into accounts of integration of reality and fantasy, theories tend to become symptomatically inconsistent. Winnicott is no exception. In elaborating his view of depressive anxiety, he says that it has two components: anxiety about the impact of instinctual expression on the mother and anxiety about the infant's "own inside" (p. 268). Winnicott says that he can presume anxiety about the infant's inside because of the "attainment of unit status; the infant has already become a person with a limiting membrane" (p. 269). So far, Winnicott has intended to describe how the working through of depressive anxiety made such a "limiting membrane" possible. The integration of environment and instinct was to explain "the acceptance of ideas and of fantasy related to fact but not to be confused with fact." Why is the "limiting membrane" now presumed? Meanwhile, he says, as "the mother is holding the situation in time," "physical digestion and also a corresponding working-through take place in the psyche" (ibid.). The empirical, external reality of the mother's holding the situation in time now has as its counterpart the empirical, internal time of digestion.

Because Winnicott does not conceive of environment in terms of primary reality, he makes it a concrete issue of the mother's actual care and the passage of time in a process like digestion. He does not think about the temporalization or spatialization of either internal or external reality. As a manifestation of primary reality, the "limiting membrane" is processive, is never achieved once and for all. Environment is everything that makes boundary formation possible. (This is why sexual difference is such an important environmental issue.) It simultaneously is not oneself and yet one is irreducibly related to it. The "membrane" between oneself and the environment is the internalization of temporal or spatial division. But this means that there are no units, intact wholes, on either side of the boundary. This more difficult conception of a processive environment is not taken into account by Winnicott with the result that, first, he presumes the existence of a "membrane" whose genesis he intended to describe, and second, he concretizes reality.

When Winnicott examines the role of environment in psychoanalytic therapy the inconsistency is even more striking. In a famous passage from "Metapsychological and Clinical Aspects of Regression," also from 1954, Winnicott (1975) repeats that in neurosis there has been adequate environmental provision for the infant, so that integration with the environment can be taken for granted. Since Freud himself was manifestly a neurotic, he did not concern himself with "the early mothering situation." "Mothering" then automatically *"turned up in his provision of a setting for his work*, almost without his being aware of what he was doing" (p. 284). Winnicott says that in order to clarify the question of environment, he has to divide Freud's work into two parts: the technique of interpreting the patient's material, the ordinary task in neurosis, and the setting in which the interpretive work takes place.

Winnicott gives a detailed list of all the things the analyst does to create the setting (such as regularity of sessions, reliability of the analyst, concentration on the patient, provision of a comfortable room and couch, absence of retaliation, "survival" of the analyst). In short, says Winnicott, "the analyst *behaves.* . . . If Freud had not behaved well he could not have developed the psychoanalytic technique or the theory to which the use of his technique led him" (p. 286). Winnicott says that Freud always assumed that there were three people in the analytic relation, which again calls for interpretive technique, while if "there are only two people involved then there has been a regression of the patient in the analytic setting, and the setting represents the mother with her technique, and the patient is an infant" (p. 286).

If a patient concretely appears to be an "infant," does the analyst adapt to need, or does the analyst have to intervene processively in a situation that is not interpretable in the conventional sense? In other words, is there simply a failure of adaptation, which can be remediated by the setting, or is there the kind of compromise formation in which, to use Winnicott's own categories, the difference between fact and fantasy, the sense of time, and the integration of the individual are subject to primary disavowal? If Winnicott had taken environment less empirically, he might have seen that the analytic environment itself, the setting or frame, is not only an adaptation to need but also a differentiating factor. In this sense, it is quite artificial to separate the analyst's interpretive activity from the setting, because interpretation presumes the analyst's different level of organization. Interpretation can be separated from the setting only if both are conceived conventionally: interpretation is objective observation; the setting objectively adapts to need.

Winnicott calls for "the scientific study of environmental adaptation" (p. 291) in the name of understanding the regressive needs the analyst has to meet when treating more disturbed patients. Because he segregates interpretation from the setting, however, he cannot conceive that interpretation is an environmental issue. This is where he become entirely inconsistent:

> In teaching psychoanalysis we must continue to speak against
> reassurance. As we look a little more carefully, however, we see
> that this is too simple a language. . . . What is reassurance? What
> could be more reassuring than to be in a reliable setting with
> a mature person in charge, capable of making penetrating and
> accurate interpretation, and to find one's personal process
> respected? It is foolish to deny that reassurance is present in
> the classical analytic situation. (p. 292)

Winnicott's point here, like Loewald's, is that there is always interaction in analysis—including the "classical situation." But what the concrete patient shows us is that everything that Winnicott finds reassuring can be quite distressing. The concrete patient specifically resists "penetrating and accurate interpretation" and consistently tries to remodel the frame in terms of his or her fantasies. This is why interpretation cannot be separated from the setting and why the setting does not only reproduce the early mothering situation. Internalization anxiety can prevent differentiating integration with the analytic environment, especially the frame element of interpretation.

The dynamics of concrete resistance to interpretation can take the scientific study of environment out of the simplistic mode to which

Winnicott confines it. Winnicott assumes that "holding" over time will promote integration in the patients for whom the depressive position is the issue. However, the concrete patient does not improve any more with prolonged "holding" than with traditional interpretation. The temporality of the analytic environment is a critical issue here, as Winnicott intuited with his analogy to the time of digestion. Freud spoke briefly (in *Beyond the Pleasure Principle*) of potentially traumatic unconscious time. In its differentiating function, the entire analytic environment is a derivative of this tension-raising time. Simply to "hold" over time, without processive interpretation of the defenses against internalization, is to stay on the level of conscious time. Its protective, defensive function, the way it serves as a "stimulus barrier" (Freud), then does not become an analytic issue. It is all too tempting, then, to slip into temporal modifications of the frame, as if in and of themselves they will provide the "holding" the patient needs. Winnicott in fact advocates this practice with more regressed patients. With the concrete patient especially, one would lose sight of the fact that such temporal modifications support the defensive need to control the differentiating function of time.

Can the modification of the time of the session serve as a therapeutic measure? Concrete patients often have to impose all kinds of frame violations (medication, adjunct treatments, less frequent sessions, persistent changes in normal routine) as a result of their splitting off of differentiation. The analyst may often have no other choice than to tolerate the violation for a while. But would the analyst tolerate changing the timed regularity of the session? Certainly, the patients themselves will attempt to modify the temporal framework, for instance, by frequent, extreme lateness or sudden, unnecessary cancellations. But it is crucial that the analyst neutrally maintain the time of the session. "Neutrally" means neither a power struggle that makes the patient submit to the analyst's control nor a modification in which the analyst submits to the patient's control. Rather, the analyst needs to understand that analysis of the frame's disruptive unconscious impact depends upon the maintenance of a regularly timed session. In analysis, the clock time of counted minutes is also the unconscious time that differentiates the analytic environment from conscious time. When primary process dominates consciousness, conscious time is conflated with the dedifferentiating time of wish fulfillment. As in the dream, there is only the present. By neutrally maintaining the time of each session, the analyst does not gratify the patient's wish to place the entire analysis under autoerotic control, for "within" the "now" of conscious time conflated with the "now" of wish fulfillment, there is also the trace of unconscious time, the time of Eros. This is the unconscious time of primary reality, the paradoxical time of binding-differentiation. Winnicott's empirical focus on the mother's holding and the infant's digestion does not adequately encompass environmental time.[13]

An example from the analysis of the man who used the tissue box to see me at will from the couch: The patient went through a long period of coming later and later to almost every session. He contemplated reducing the frequency—what was the point of maintaining it, if he was getting barely half of his allotted time? On a Friday, the patient was again quite late. He spoke about his own tendency to isolation and withdrawal over weekends. I said that what he was most afraid of was contact, that he came later and later for almost every session because of his extreme anxiety over contact with me and the analytic process. Isolation and withdrawal were actually a relief. The patient responded humorously, telling me that a friend of his had remarked that he seemed to have "people avoidance syndrome." He then went on to speak quite seriously about his father. Exceptionally, he said that he knew he had created difficulties with his father by his own childish provocations. These had tended to make his father treat him dismissively. He knew that he had done the same thing with me. He had actually hoped that I would dismiss him as a patient.

This was quite striking. This man had almost never before been able to observe himself in the transference. He went on to say that he did not understand why he was suddenly thinking about sexual fantasies, fantasies of being watched, of having his hands tied. He said that he had once read a magazine about fetishes and had thought that he really envied people who could experience wild excitement just in relation to an inanimate object. We were very close to the end of a truncated session, and I had said nothing about the patient's associations. He suddenly stopped speaking and said, "You're sleeping. I *know* you're sleeping." Given my own intense interest in the relations between fetishism, time, and concreteness, if anything, I had been on the edge of my seat, fully intending to take notes after the session. I had a fantasy of repeating back to him everything he had just said in order to show him *concretely* that his perception was wrong. That we were at the end of a Friday session only added to the tension of the situation. I thought that the best course would be to maintain a differentiating neutrality in the moment. Anything I said at this point would join the patient on his level. It was already my conviction that a processive stance is most important in relation to perceptual identity operating in the moment ("I *know* you're sleeping"). Content interpretations are an invitation to a power struggle. So I said nothing and, after a few minutes of silence on both our parts, ended the session on time. The patient left very angry.

On the Monday, he came in on time. He said that he had had a surprisingly good weekend. He had thought about dropping out of the analysis and was still mad at me for "falling asleep." But he said, "If I can't sustain the contact with you and come on time, how will I know whether I should drop out or not?" At this point I did interpret that he had had to make sure that contact between the two of us was broken before the end of the session, particularly when he had been speaking to me so freely. The patient went back to speaking about his father and his sexual fantasies. He compared his fantasies and his tendency to withdraw to a "vortex," into which he wanted to drag himself and others. The analysis continued, with no change in frequency; the patient began to come on time regularly. While there were many areas of concreteness still to be worked through, interpretation of fantasy content became more therapeutically viable.

The patient had certainly offered many opportunities for the analyst to think about temporal modifications in order to "hold" him better. It was particularly tempting to extend the time at the end of the truncated Friday session in order to promote integration of the "instinct" analyst of part object fantasies (exhibitionism, sado-masochism, fetishism) with the environment analyst who was providing care through alert, awake listening. But there is no avoiding the tension of registration of the analytic process. Metapsychologically, the patient's concrete conviction that I was asleep was the result of internalization anxiety. He could not sustain the differentiated integration with the analytic environment that began with his increased capacity to observe himself and then led to a free associative process. The unconscious, defensive need to split off the self-preservative aspect of speaking to the analyst produced dedifferentiating destructiveness. While seemingly directed against the analyst, the destructiveness was also directed against himself. He "closed" the space he had "opened." One cannot avoid such angry moments if concreteness is to be modified effectively. Neutral silence, maintained because any words would have produced the dedifferentiating relief the patient thought he needed, facilitated an integrative registration. After the weekend, the patient could both maintain his anger at my purported sleep and take a step toward internalization of the frame by coming on time. Environment and instinct were integrated and differentiated without "adaptation to need" or indefinite "holding."

Winnicott introduced the concept of transitional phenomena in order to account for the capacity to sustain space, the space necessary for the move from symbolic equivalence to symbolism. In a summary statement, he says that the transitional object "gives room for the process of becoming able to accept difference and similarity . . . there is use for a term for the root of symbolism in time, a term that describes the infant's journey from the purely subjective to objectivity" (pp. 233–34). The transitional object, for Winnicott, is the fetish viewed from the side of "normality." However, he seems unaware of Freud's late thinking about fetishism in relation to reality, even though he is explicitly making a claim for an aspect of reality that is usually ignored.

Winnicott defines transitional phenomena *processively*. He speaks about them not in terms of experience, but experienc*inging*:

> there is the third part of the life of a human being, a part that we cannot ignore, an intermediate area of *experiencing*, to which inner reality and external life both contribute. It is an area which is not challenged, because no claim is made on its behalf except that it shall exist as a resting-place for the individual engaged in the perpetual human task of keeping inner and outer reality separate yet inter-related (1975, p. 230).

The last phrase, "separate yet inter-related," can be read as a description of a differentiating process, in which "separation" *is* "relation."
Separation-as-relation takes one back to the concept of the "limiting
membrane," the permeable boundary of integration with environment. In that case transitional phenomena would not simply be a
third area but the first area out of which internal and external, subjective and objective emerge.[14] Winnicott says something close to
this when he calls the transitional object the first "not-me" possession, a possession that arises in the "intermediate area between the
subjective and that which is objectively perceived" (p. 231). His assumption, however, is that subjective and objective already exist and
not that this intermediate area somehow includes and precedes them.

Throughout the study of transitional phenomena Winnicott stresses
another topic that has preoccupied us, illusion. He links illusion to the
intermediate area of experiencing and puts a much more positive spin
on it than I have so far:

> I am here staking a claim for an intermediate state between a
> baby's inability and ability to recognize and accept reality. I am
> therefore studying the substance of *illusion*, that which is allowed
> to the infant, and which in adult life is inherent in art and reli-
> gion. We can share a respect for *illusory experience*. . . . Yet it is a
> hallmark of madness when an adult puts too powerful a claim on
> the credulity of others, forcing them to acknowledge a sharing of
> illusion that is not their own. (pp. 230–31)

When Winnicott says that his intermediate area lies between the
baby's inability and growing ability to recognize reality, he again operates from an empirical point of view. He does not take into account the non-recognized registrations of differentiating reality, only
the more commonsense "objective" reality that the baby at first does
not consciously recognize. Illusion, as I have understood it, is the possibility of fetishism—the conflating of fantasy and reality via perceptual identity. This is why Sandler (see Chapter 1), for example, understood that conscious illusions imply what he called "*unconscious
secondary process*." The conscious use of the mechanisms of wish
fulfillment to create illusions implies defense against unconscious reg-

istration of "reality." In this conception illusion is akin to symbolic equivalence or enactive remembering. Winnicott claims that illusory transitional phenomena keep inner and outer reality "separate yet inter-related," implying that illusion is not defensive. Is it contradictory then to describe transitional phenomena in terms of illusion?

An analogous question emerges in Winnicott's familiar description of transitional objects. The object chosen "is vitally important to the infant for use at the time of going to sleep, and is a defence against anxiety, especially anxiety of depressive type" (p. 232). Winnicott is very careful to say that although the transitional object comes from "without" from our point of view, from the point of view of the baby it comes neither from without nor within and "is not an hallucination" (p. 233) or a conflation of reality and fantasy. However, if depressive anxiety is taken in Winnicott's sense as anxiety over the integration of environment and instinct, what does it mean to posit the transitional object as a defense against depressive anxiety? When depressive anxiety is too great, the integration of environment and instinct cannot be sustained. Illusion then functions to split fantasy from the time and space of separation-as-relation. Rigorously speaking, transitional phenomena sustain the tension of integration with primary reality. The question is really whether Winnicott can conceive them to function intrinsically either in terms of the working through or the defense against "depressive" anxiety. In that case one could say that when the transitional object functions defensively it becomes a fetishistic illusion. When it functions non-defensively, Winnicott's innovative understanding makes the most sense. He famously asserts that the fate of the transitional object is not to be "forgotten" or "mourned." In other words, the transitional object is potentially not an idealized object whose loss is inevitably feared. Rather, it "loses meaning, and this is because the transitional phenomena have become diffused, have become spread out over the whole intermediate territory between 'inner psychic reality' and 'the external world as perceived by two persons in common,' that is to say over the whole cultural field" (p. 233).

Winnicott is describing the maintenance of an intermediate space between what is usually considered internal and external reality. This means that although transitional phenomena do seem to be conventionally "unreal," they are not illusory in the sense of the conflation of reality and fantasy. There is no imperative ("ruthless") demand that transitional phenomena be taken as "real" in the moment. Winnicott's description of transitional phenomena in health and illness corresponds to the idea that they may function either to sustain or defend against depressive anxiety: "At this point my subject widens out into that of play, and of artistic creativity and appreciation, and of religious feeling, and of *dreaming*, and also of *fetishism*, lying and stealing, the origin and loss of affectionate feeling, drug addiction, the talisman of obsessional rituals, etc." (p. 233; my emphases). In this statement Winnicott makes transitional phenomena the possibility for various creative states in which something conventionally unreal does not immediately have to be taken as real ("depressive" anxiety sustained) and the various pathological states in which illusion is imperatively taken as reality (fetishism, lying, stealing, addiction, the magic obsessional thing, falling in and out of love—"depressive" anxiety defended against). Is it design or coincidence that makes Winnicott place dreaming between health and pathology here? In either case, his point is well taken. The dream mechanisms of perceptual identity and temporal immediacy are the mechanisms of imposed illusion. But, of course, the dream also implicitly contains the trace of the experience of satisfaction. If understood in terms of these dynamics, the dream itself functions both as illusion imperatively conflated with reality and as the trace of integration with environment. As Winnicott seems to suggest, the dream is the pivot between transitional phenomena and fetishism.

The specific relations of the transitional object to the part object and to symbolism carry a similar sense. Here Winnicott is more consistent than when he says that the transitional object may serve as a defense against depressive anxiety. About the part object and symbolism he writes: "It is true that the piece of blanket (or whatever it is) is symbolical of some part object, such as the breast. Nevertheless the point of it is not its symbolic value so much as its actuality. Its not being the breast (or the mother) is as important as the fact that it stands for the breast (or mother)" (p. 233). Thus, on the one hand, the transitional object can function as the tension-relieving presence of the part (whole) object. But, on the other, because the transitional object is other than the mother, it opens up the space in which inner and outer reality remain "separate yet inter-related." The "actuality" of the transitional object does not have the extra defensive burden of concreteness. When the transitional object functions in this way, it embodies the "limiting membrane" of differentiating integration with environment.

Nonetheless, the "transitional object may eventually develop into a fetish object and so persist as a characteristic of the adult sexual life" (pp. 236–37). Here one wishes that Winnicott had taken into account all of Freud's thinking about the defenses that make fetishism possible. He then could have proposed a dynamic explanation of how the transitional object may become a fetish. It is not that Winnicott avoids the problem altogether but that he typically falls back upon the limited empiricism of the mother's care as explanation. He says that the infant can use a transitional object when the internal object is not too persecutory. Whether or not the internal object will be persecutory depends upon whether "general environmental care" provides good enough "adaptation to the infant's needs." If there is environmental failure, then "the internal object fails to have meaning to the infant, and then, and then only, does the transitional object become meaningless too" (p. 237).

By "meaningless" Winnicott seems to intend that the "actuality" of the transitional object becomes "fetishistic." It *is* the breast. It then does not keep inner and outer separate and yet related. This process is due to the more complex understanding of the trauma of Eros (primary and secondary disavowal, the oscillation between internalization and identification). When Winnicott says that transitional phenomena are meaningful only if the inner object is not too persecutory due to environmental failure, he overlooks the idea that transitional phenomena cannot be separated from anxiety over integration at all levels of development. He makes it sound as if they are possible only *after* there is some depressive position integration of environment and instinct, as if they are not continuously a question whenever there is new integration of environment and instinct. When internalization anxiety heightens depressive anxiety, environment and instinct are split. Aggression is exacerbated in ways that are persecutory, and fetishistic illusions are produced.

For example, in the Oedipus complex, if sexual difference cannot be integrated with drives, the illusion of phallic monism replaces it. The well-known result is an intensification of the aggression of the super-ego in the form of castration anxiety. This is a form of internal persecution. The controlling aggression of the super-ego and the anxieties over conforming to super-ego demands are examples of fetishistic repudiation of integration with differentiating primary reality. The neurotic not only has symptoms but adapts to super-ego demands out of a concrete fear of castration. Such conformity with super-ego demands implies castration anxiety, as well as internalization anxiety. If integration of environment and instinct only has to do with integration of the mother's empirical care, then of course it would have nothing to do with neurosis, as Winnicott says. The concreteness of the neurotic super-ego demonstrates that anxiety over integration is as much an oedipal as it is an oral issue.[15] We are not used to thinking about sexual difference as a transitional phenomenon. But the internalization of sexual difference is as much a question of separation-as-relation as is internalization of the environment mother.[16] It can always be replaced with dedifferentiating illusion.

Winnicott concludes his discussion of how the transitional object may become meaningless by saying that it "is never under magical control like the internal object, nor is it outside control as the real mother is" (p. 237). In other words, transitional phenomena cannot be included in the oppositions fantasy-reality, magical control–loss of control. If so, one can understand that whenever the transitional object functions fetishistically, magical control and loss of control are conflated with the traditional opposition of fantasy and reality. This occurs at every level of development and in all psychopathology, including neurosis. Ferenczi's early point about the relation between each neurosis and a specific form of the development of the sense of reality can be expanded: transitional phenomena become fetishistic illusions whenever environment and instinct are split.

Winnicott's insistence on illusion as the essence of transitional phenomena suffers from not seeing clearly enough that illusion itself is a form of magical control. He is clear that normal, good-enough infant care is experienced by the baby as wish fulfillment and thus initially heightens omnipotence: "The mother, at the beginning, by an almost 100 per cent adaptation affords the infant the opportunity for the *illu-*

sion that her breast is part of the infant. It is, as it were, under magical control. . . . Omnipotence is nearly a fact of experience" (p. 238). Omnipotence makes it possible to "experience a relationship to external reality, . . . to form a conception of external reality" (ibid.). What Winnicott overlooks here is that omnipotence is made possible by wish fulfillment and perceptual identity. To reach reality in this way is to set in place the equation of objectivity and perception. Transitional phenomena are possible not because of the inevitable fantasies of omnipotence but because the registration of differentiation raises tension enough, but not so much, that internalization anxiety can be sustained.

Despite Winnicott's descriptions of the "third area of experience," of difference as relation, in the end he cannot free himself from a conventional conception of reality. This is why he thinks that we reach reality through illusion—both are perceptual phenomena. He repeatedly says that the mother has to help the infant by "disillusioning" it, that is, by introducing frustrations that diminish omnipotence. The infant then has the experience of a "real mother" who is beyond its omnipotent control. This is again an obvious truth, but it does not take into account that the process is more complicated. The mother does not have to concern herself with the registration and integration of processive reality, which make transitional phenomena possible. These non-objectifiable processes are not observable unless they become solidified in a fetishistic formation. For example, a child may demand that the mother carry with her the transitional object at all times. At that point the mother or parents may grow troubled, but it is doubtful that either the tolerance of omnipotent illusion or attempts at disillusionment will resolve the problem. At best, normal parenting not overly concerned with these issues may allow the child to work out such a conflict on his or her own, although of course without consciously knowing so. The analyst, on the other hand, must be concerned with such processes, especially when illusion is the issue in the transference. Otherwise, based on Winnicott's assumption that one reaches objectivity through illusion, the analyst can fall back upon parenting, first tolerating illusion and then promoting disillusionment. Such an approach to treatment would not promote the working through of depressive and internalization anxiety.

Winnicott's conception of creativity poses all the same dilemmas:

> the breast is created by the infant over and over again out of the
> infant's capacity to love or (one can say) out of need. A subjective
> phenomenon develops in the baby which we call the mother's
> breast. The mother places the actual breast just there where the
> infant is ready to create. . . . From birth, therefore, the human
> being is concerned with the problem of the relationship between
> what is objectively perceived and what is subjectively conceived
> of, and in the solution of this problem there is no health for the
> human being who has not been started off well enough by the
> mother. *The intermediate area to which I am referring is the area that is*
> *allowed to the infant between primary creativity and objective perception*
> *based on reality testing.* The transitional phenomena represent the
> early stages of the use of illusion, without which there is no
> meaning in the idea of a relationship with an object that is
> perceived by others as external to that being. . . . The mother's
> adaptation to the infant's needs, when good enough, gives the
> infant the *illusion* that there is an external reality that corresponds
> to the infant's own capacity to create. (pp. 238–39)

Loewald thought almost exactly the opposite. In his discussion of how
perception is shot through with memory, he said that when there is
a correspondence between a memory-perception and the external
world there is an "objectivation of reality" taken as the "unquestioned
standard of truth." The idea of transitional phenomena demands a
conception much closer to Loewald's, a conception that takes into account that internalization does not occur through the creation of objectivizing schema. If the baby can use an "actual" piece of blanket in
a way that is not concrete, in other words, that is not a defense against
internalization anxiety, then the baby also has the beginning of a capacity for creative questioning of illusion. Analytic interpretation evidently depends upon such a capacity. Where interpretation is globally or fleetingly repudiated, interventions (including silence) must be
geared to re-opening the possibility of questioning illusion. When
Winnicott compares transitional phenomena to the "play area of the
small child who is 'lost' in play" (p. 241), he leaves out the difference

between the child who can be interrupted and then return to play and the child for whom interruption is catastrophic because play is a form of magical control.[17] In concrete transferences the patient's illusory objective "knowledge" of the analyst cannot be "interrupted" by interpretation. Transference analysis cannot be effective unless it is temporalized, unless its apparently objective "nowness" is accompanied by a non-traumatized response to its "not-nowness."

Winnicott's concluding remarks bring us back to the generalization of fetishism. He devotes two paragraphs to a critique of those who describe infantile attachments to objects only as a form of fetishism:

> I would prefer to retain the word fetish to describe the object
> that is employed on account of a *delusion* of a maternal phallus. I
> would then go further and say that we must keep a place for the
> *illusion* of a maternal phallus, that is to say, an idea that is universal
> and not pathological. If we shift the accent now from the object
> to the word illusion we get near to the infant's transitional
> object; the importance lies in the concept of illusion, a universal
> in the field of experience. Following this, we can allow the
> transitional object to be potentially a maternal phallus but
> originally the breast, that is to say, the thing created by the infant
> and at the same time provided from the environment. In this way
> I think that a study of the infant's use of the transitional object
> and of transitional phenomena in general may throw light on the
> origin of the fetish object and of fetishism. There is something to
> be lost, however, in working backwards from the psychopathol-
> ogy of fetishism to the transitional phenomena which belong to
> the beginnings of experience and which are inherent in healthy
> emotional development. (pp. 241–42)

The presence of the breast is to some degree always conflated with the presence of an intact, magical, relieving object. Wherever there is such an illusion, there is always the counterpart illusion of the absence of the magical object. The maternal phallus is the phallic phase equivalent of these oral formations. The illusory equation of the breast with one's own creation—certainly a universal occurrence—would then not be a transitional phenomenon but the foundation of objectivity as the projected counterpart of subjectivity: reality conforms to wishes via perceptual identity. Winnicott does not realize that the differentiating registration of the experience of satisfaction within primary narcissism is the foundation for transitional phenomena. In this original setup, environment both is and is not "oneself," difference *is* relation. In this sense, from the oral phase on the breast can also function as something like a "maternal phallus." Transitional phenomena become fetishistic formations.

Winnicott's concept of illusion carries with it the same problem as Freud's "reality of castration"—the illusion that is the counterpart of the illusion of the maternal phallus. To "disillusion" a patient from the illusion of magical control of the analytic process can slip into an equivalent of accepting the "reality of castration." Through the study of transitional phenomena, Winnicott invaluably attempts to understand how inner and outer can be both separate and interrelated. Yet his inconsistencies illustrate that without a rigorous rethinking of reality, such attempts wind up contradictorily reasserting premises they wish to contest. The clinical result is retreat from interpretation (which is not understood as intrinsic to the analytic environment) to a naïve reassertion of experience with the analyst, that is, concrete "holding" and "adaptation to need." If this worked, there would be no argument against it. The problem is that it does not work for the patient with fetishistic difficulties any more than does traditional, objective interpretation.

A scientific rethinking of psychoanalytic treatment can only take place if psychoanalytic theory does not presume the traditional link between science and conventional objectivity and temporality. Loewald developed his theories of primary reality and Eros in line with this way of thinking. To make internalization of the analyst's different level of organization the crucial environmental factor in psychoanalytic therapy is to place transitional phenomena within interpretation itself. It is the processive implication of every analytic intervention that it attempts to open the closed system of the patient's symptoms and/or character structure and the reality organization that supports them. These reality organizations, first described by Ferenczi, are themselves versions of secondary narcissism, of the subtle or overt ways in which the conflation of fantasy and reality supports omnipotence and control. The sadism of part object relations (Abraham, Klein) describes a crucial aspect of such control. In their respective ways, Abraham, Klein, and Winnicott all understood that part object formations are related to depressive anxiety and to the issue of concern or care. To varying degrees, every analysis would have to come up against resistance to interpretation as a repudiation of care, a repudiation motivated by internalization anxiety. At such moments, a patient will always take a perception of the analyst—an illusion—as objectively true. As a scientific therapy, psychoanalysis needs to understand why both clinically and theoretically it promotes change through the modification of conventional objectivity.[18]

This is the sense in which Winnicott's call for a "scientific study of environment" in psychoanalytic treatment is always a necessary imperative. Winnicott himself could not see that conceiving transitional phenomena in terms of illusion forecloses any view of reality except in terms of traditional objectivity. Thus, he saw environment only in terms of concrete care and not in terms of care as differentiating process. Like Loewald, in a sense, Winnicott did not see that transitional phenomena contain their own tensions, which is why they so readily merge into fetishistic formations. Winnicott's revision of Klein's original conception of depressive anxiety, when integrated with a revised concept of environment, makes transitional phenomena another way to think about primary reality and the registration and repudiation of difference.

CHAPTER 5

Analysis of Surface, Analysis of Defense

Freud's interpretive technique developed out of an integrated view of mind, nature, and science. The original model of the unconscious, based on the primacy of repression, inevitably led to the stance of interpreting the objective content of the repressed past, whether past events or past wishes (usually both). Later in his career, Freud even understood that past defensive operations can themselves be repressed (for example, in *Inhibition, Symptom, and Anxiety* [1926]). Resistance analysis was expanded to include resistance to uncovering defenses. The renewed emphasis on resistance analysis, however, did not change Freud's basic understanding of how technique is integrated with basic therapeutic aims. Interpretation of the past always presumes the model of the unconscious based on repression.

The concrete patient's defensive response to traditional interpretation puts this entire model into question. Primary disavowal, motivated by internalization anxiety, dedifferentiates past and present, memory and perception. The fetishized, immediate perception of something apparently "objective" protects against the trauma of differentiation. Defense is not primarily directed against internal mental contents but against internalization of environmental interaction. In such constellations, there is still a question of past defensive operations —difference can be repudiated at any phase of psychic development. However, the past repudiations of difference translate into present, processive repudiation of difference—as in the global rejection of the possibility of interpretation. Content interpretations, whose unspoken aim is always to reverse repression, have no effect upon such compromise formations.

There are odd moments in Freud's theorizing that come up against the constraints of the repression model, and there are similar moments in his writings on technique. In fact, Freud's conception of technique quickly became paradoxical. The repression model is what made psychoanalysis a "depth psychology." It made perfect sense at the outset to attempt to reverse repression by inferring "buried" psychic contents. However, by 1914 Freud began to emphasize what he called "surface" in his technical approach. In the same year, he also began to speak of the "narcissistic attitudes" of neurotics, which, like narcissism in general, posed an enormous problem for the original theory and technique. The two most familiar rules of Freudian analysis became start from the surface and interpret defense before content. Why did a "depth psychology" evolve into a clinical approach that emphasizes surface? How does inevitable narcissism affect the theory of technique?

The processive approach to primary disavowal also abides by the rules of starting from the surface and interpreting defense before content. Narcissism, of course, is also an essential question: the concrete patient defends against integration with environment (primary narcissism) via omnipotent control, the global imposition of a narcissistic reality sense (secondary narcissism). Because analysts in fact have always encountered concrete patients (as evidenced by Abraham's early description), they have always encountered these dynamics. It is actually demonstrable that the transformations of classical technique have unwittingly, but consistently, been informed by the limits of interpretation from within the repression model. From Freud's own conception of surface and defense analysis to today's most sophisticated practitioners, the paradoxical evolution of technique is explicable in terms of the primary registration and repudiation of differentiating reality. This unnoticed trend also opens up the possibility of a new integration of theory and practice, an integration that fully takes into account a psychoanalytic rethinking of the question of reality.

ACTION AND SURFACE

In the opening paragraph of "Remembering, Repeating, and Working Through" (1914) Freud explains his new emphasis on defense analysis. Quickly reviewing the history of technique, he emphasizes that the abandonment of hypnotic recall of the buried past did not change the aim of treatment. The only change was technical. It became a question of "discovering from the patient's free associations what he failed to remember" (p. 147). However, this transition from hypnotic recall to "the work of interpretation" demanded the patient's "willingness" to associate. Once the focus shifted to the associative process, Freud had to rethink how recall of the past was to come about. Resistance due to repression produces breaks in association. The analyst has to help the patient "to overcome his criticism of his free associations, in accordance with the fundamental rule of psychoanalysis" (ibid.). Thus, Freud writes, the evolution of the

> consistent technique used today, in which the analyst gives up
> the attempt to bring a particular moment or problem into focus.
> He contents himself with studying whatever is present for the
> time being on the *surface* of the patient's mind, and he employs
> the art of interpretation mainly for the purpose of recognizing
> the resistances which appear there, and making them conscious
> to the patient. From this there results a new sort of division of
> labour: the doctor uncovers the resistances which are unknown
> to the patient; when these have been got the better of, the
> patient often relates the forgotten situations and connections
> without any difficulty. *The aim of these different techniques has, of*
> *course, remained the same. Descriptively speaking, it is to fill in gaps*
> *in memory; dynamically speaking, it is to overcome resistances due to*
> *repression.* (pp. 147–48; my emphases)

The shift to surface and resistance analysis leads Freud to anticipate a problem that will preoccupy him in his later works. Resistances are "unknown" to the patient; the analyst has to "uncover" them. This clinical finding will produce a major theoretical change. As Freud will say from 1920 on, parts of the ego are unconscious. Special analytic work is demanded to help the patient become aware of the ego's resistances. There will even be resistance to the uncovering of resistance. Is this resistance to resistance a result of repression? If not, how does one explain that defenses themselves come to be defended against?

Some of the earlier theories of defense in fact explain the "resistance to resistance" better. In 1913 Ferenczi had conceived of an ego split between its defensive maneuvers and reality. Farther back, in the *Project for a Scientific Psychology* (1895a), Freud himself had understood defense as the counterpart of wish fulfillment in the primary process of eliminating undue tension. Once defense is more broadly conceptualized in terms of primary process tension reduction and splitting, the analysis of surface resistances can be conceptualized more coherently. Analysis of surface resistances is directed at the tendency to eliminate tensions that begin to disturb the patient in the course of associating. Such tensions are so automatically split off that the patient is not consciously aware of it. It takes "special work" to bring this tension reduction and splitting into consciousness.

Freud, of course, did not integrate these aspects of existing clinical theory. However, his uneasy amalgam of repression theory with clinical focus on surface resistances did produce the first formal discussion of "acting out." Freud observes that some patients begin treatment by producing something like hypnotic recall but "later cease to do so"—in other words, when their resistances enter the treatment. Other patients, however, do not even begin by producing memories. This kind of patient "does not *remember* anything of what he has forgotten and repressed, but *acts* it out. He reproduces it not as a memory but as an action; he *repeats* it, without, of course knowing that he is repeating it" (p. 150). Repetition in action is then the largest form of resistance. Just as the patient is not aware that he or she resists, the patient is even less aware that he or she repeats. Surface actions can keep repressions in place by actively defending against understanding. Action becomes a general principle: "As long as the patient is in the treatment he cannot escape from this compulsion to repeat; and in the end we understand that this is his way of remembering" (ibid.).

Is the resistance of repetitious acting out a manifestation of conflicts due to repression? Freud himself envisages a wider possibility, while maintaining the primacy of repression:

remembering in the old manner—reproduction in the psychical
field—is the aim to which [the analyst] adheres, even though he
knows that such an aim *cannot be achieved in the new technique*. He
is prepared for a perpetual struggle with his patient to keep in
the psychical sphere all the impulses which the patient would
like to direct into the motor sphere; and he celebrates it as a
triumph for the treatment if he can bring it about that something that the patient wishes to discharge in action is disposed
of through the work of remembering. (p. 153; my emphasis)

"Remembering" as "reproduction in the psychical field" actually
means something like "internalization": the expression of affects,
thoughts, wishes, and fantasies such that they are interpretable. Freud
now sees it as inevitable that the compulsion to repeat will produce
acting out as resistance to interpretation, but he does not offer a conception of the dynamics of immediate discharge through action.

In Chapter 2 I examined the passage from "Two Principles" (1911a)
that envisaged "originally unconscious thought." The same passage is
relevant here, because it deals with the question of action. To cite it
again:

Restraint upon motor discharge (upon action) . . . was provided
by means of the process of *thinking* [author's emphasis], which
was developed from the presentation of ideas. Thinking was
endowed with characteristics which made it possible for the
mental apparatus to tolerate an increased tension of stimulus
while the process of discharge was postponed. . . . For this
purpose the conversion of freely displaceable cathexes into
"bound" cathexes was necessary, and this was brought about
by means of raising the level of the whole cathectic process. *It
is probable that thinking was originally unconscious, in so far as it went
beyond mere ideational presentations and was directed to the relations
between impressions of objects* [my emphasis]. (p. 221)

In other words, Freud had already begun to think about action in
terms of immediate discharge and about postponing action in terms
of increased tension levels. He had also begun to think about such

raised tension levels in terms of originally unconscious thought—registrations of the "impressions [traces] of objects" (*Objekteindrucke*). As Freud began to think about action as the most general form of resistance in 1914, he could have referred to an inevitable resistance to raised tension levels. This idea is perfectly consistent with the general thrust of his theory. More subtly, such raised tension levels can also be linked to originally unconscious thought. From this more complex point of view, action can be seen as discharge that defends against unconscious registration of the "trace of the analyst." This would imply repudiation of the analyst's interpretive function. By definition, interpretation intrinsically interferes with automatic tension reduction.

The question of action also brings up the question of "reality." Freud at first says that the compulsion to repeat clarifies the basic tenet that the patient's neurosis is "a present day force" that must be brought into the treatment. "[W]hile the patient *experiences it as something real and contemporary* we have to do our therapeutic work on it, which consists in a large measure in tracing it back to the past. . . . Repeating, as it is induced in analytic treatment according to the newer technique . . . implies conjuring up a piece of real life; and for that reason it cannot always be harmless and unobjectionable" (p. 152; my emphasis). If repetition in action is indeed neither harmless nor unobjectionable, and if it cannot be conceived exclusively in terms of repression, will tracing it back to the past modify it? Freud's hope is that the transference neurosis, as "an intermediate region between illness and real life," is only provisionally "real," meaning that it will be modified by interpretation. The concept of "working through" is introduced in conjunction with the compulsion to repeat: resistance is always operative and must be interpreted time and again. The aim of interpretation, however, is to "discover the repressed instinctual impulses which are feeding the resistance" (p. 153). Is the resistance of action fed by repressed instinctual impulses alone? Does their "discovery" promote the move from action to interpretation?

Freud has come up against the intrinsic limitation of the repression model. He knows that action is related to conflict between patient and analyst over the possibility of interpretation, but he does not conceive of dynamic reasons why a patient might resist interpretive help. Here we have the entire problem of defense against integration with environment—specifically the analytic environment. If we take environment as the surface context of analysis, we can begin to conceive of defense organized against registration of the surface. In Freud's characteristically "military" way, he only envisages a "perpetual struggle" between analyst and patient over action versus remembering. Surface resistances are analyzed with the expectation that repressed contents will reemerge and for no other reason. One cannot expect Freud to have thought about surface in terms of primary narcissism, Eros, and unconscious registration of difference. However, he easily could have integrated his thoughts about action as tension reduction from "Two Principles" with narcissism as he already conceived it. Action in the service of tension reduction manifests the narcissistic resistance to "analytic influence" Freud had found even in neurotic patients. Since action itself is also a manifestation of the compulsion to repeat, repetitive action is always a defensive assertion of omnipotence, of secondary narcissism.

Freud returns to the problem of action in *Beyond the Pleasure Principle*. In chapter 3 he quickly reviews the history of psychoanalytic technique, for the same reason as he had six years earlier in "Remembering, Repeating, and Working Through"—to address the questions of action and repetition:

> Twenty-five years of intense work have had as their result that the immediate aims of psychoanalytic technique are quite other today than they were at the outset. At first the analyzing physician could do no more than discover the unconscious material that was concealed from the patient, put it together, and, at the right moment, communicate it to him. Psychoanalysis was then first and foremost an art of interpreting. Since *this did not solve the therapeutic problem*, a further aim quickly came in view: to oblige the patient to confirm the analyst's construction from his own memory. In that endeavor the chief emphasis lay upon the patient's resistances: the art consisted now in uncovering these as quickly as possible. . . . But it became ever clearer that the aim which had been set up—the aim that what was unconscious should become conscious—*is not completely attainable by that method*. The patient cannot remember the whole of what is

repressed in him, and what he cannot remember may be precisely the essential part of it. . . . He is obliged to *repeat* the
repressed material as a contemporary experience instead of, as
the physician would prefer to see, *remembering* it as something
belonging to the past. (p. 18; my emphases).

Freud's major example of this kind of repetition is the transference
neurosis. However, he immediately notes a clinical problem. The analyst must attempt to "keep this transference neurosis within the nar-
rowest limits: to force as much as possible into the channel of memory and to allow as little as possible to emerge as repetition" (p. 19).
    What kind of "force" can the analyst exert in order to "channel"
the transference neurosis into interpretable memory? Is it always effective? Freud cursorily envisages the paradox built into his conception:

The physician cannot as a rule spare his patient this phase of the
treatment. He must get him to re-experience some portion of
his forgotten life, but must see to it, on the other hand, that the
patient retains some degree of aloofness, which will enable him,
in spite of everything, to recognize that what appears to be
reality is in fact only a reflection of a forgotten past. If this can
be successfully achieved, the patient's sense of conviction is
won, together with the therapeutic success that is dependent
on it. (ibid.)

Should the analyst be unable to "force" the transference neurosis into
"the channel of memory," then one has the entire problem of the
"real" transference. The "aloofness" that makes it possible "to recognize that what appears to be reality is in fact only a reflection of a
forgotten past" is the psychic space that differentiates past and present, memory and perception. If this space is eliminated, dedifferentiation dominates the transference. Freud's images of "forcing" and
"channeling," and the vagueness of "seeing to it" that the patient retains the necessary "aloofness," speak to his non-dynamic grasp of the
problem of the observing ego.
    Freud has certainly described the "real" transference. Is he still pre-
vented from thinking about it dynamically because of his focus on

repression? In his familiar mode, he says that unconscious contents, "the repressed," offer no resistance to the analytic process because they are always trying to force their way into consciousness, seeking discharge. Resistance, he says, arises from "the same higher strata and systems of the mind which originally carried out repression" (ibid.). But—and here is the problem anticipated in "Remembering, Repeating, and Working Through"—"the motives of the resistances, and indeed the resistances themselves, are unconscious at first during the treatment. . . . We shall avoid a lack of clarity if we make our contrast not between the conscious and the unconscious but between the coherent *ego* and the *repressed*" (ibid.).

This distinction is clarifying to the extent that Freud now understands that the ego protects its "coherence" by carrying out repressions. Resistance to making the unconscious conscious is an effort to maintain that coherence. In the next sentence Freud says that it "is certain that much of the ego is itself unconscious, and notably what we may describe as its nucleus" (ibid.). If "the patient's resistance arises from his ego," and if much of the ego is unconscious, then of course we have the beginnings of an explanation of why resistance itself has to be made conscious. It is an aspect of the "unconscious ego." However, confusion sets in when Freud reiterates that "the compulsion to repeat must be ascribed to the unconscious *repressed*" (p. 20; my emphasis). Within the ideal domain of a transference neurosis that is exclusively "channeled" into memory and interpreted, this statement is comprehensible. However, action is the most general principle. At some point, every patient will not retain the necessary "aloofness" and will specifically defend against the observing ego. Can the compulsion to repeat then most generally be ascribed to the repressed?

Loewald spoke about the observing ego as an internalization of the analyst's different level of organization. If the analyst is to understand why a patient might use action to defend against the "aloofness" necessary for transference interpretation, then the analyst has to understand that the different level of organization may be defended against in and of itself. The ego split between registration and repudiation of differentiation will then use repetitive action as a resistance to "memory" in the broader sense of internalization. Since internalization only takes place in an interaction, such global, surface resistance will be directed against interpretation as interaction. Would not the compulsion to repeat itself be better understood in terms of de-differentiation? Loewald ascribed it to the wish to remain embedded in an all-embracing totality. In enactive remembering, he said, the dedifferentiation and timelessness of primary process dominate consciousness, and the integrating-differentiating function of *conscire* is absent. The "action" of enactive remembering can then be used as a global defense against interpretation as *conscire*. Or, to synthesize Winnicott and Loewald, due to internalization anxiety the transitional, environmental function of interpretation is split off and replaced by instinctual actions whose "fact" and "fantasy" components are fetishistically dedifferentiated.

In this conception, the patient is still protecting the coherence of the ego, but the coherence of the secondarily narcissistic, omnipotent ego. Nothing is to "break into" this closed organization. Therefore, interpretation cannot be registered. The analytic environment has to become an all-embracing totality in which the analyst is the reflection of the patient. And as in Narcissus's repudiation of "interaction," this coherence is protected in a self-destructive way. The patient remains in analysis while strenuously resisting change through interpretation, particularly interpretation of concreteness in the transference.

Freud does in fact begin to think about repetitive action in relation to narcissism. If the compulsion to repeat derives from the repressed, then presumably what is repeated would ultimately be pleasurable, even if anxiety provoking. However, clinical experience does not support this assumption. Freud says, "we come now to a new and remarkable fact, namely that the compulsion to repeat also recalls from the past experiences which include no possibility of pleasure, and which can never, even long ago, have brought satisfaction even to instinctual impulses which have since been repressed" (p. 20). Freud's examples of the repetition of painful experiences center on the idea of narcissistic wounds: repetition of the sense of failure to understand where babies come from and to make a baby oneself, repetition of the failure to bring oedipal love to fruition. Such "unwanted situations and painful emotions" will be repeated in the transference "with the greatest ingenuity" (p. 21). The content of such repetitions still seems to come under the rubric of repetition of repressed oedi-

pal wishes. But the form of such painful repetition is the "real" transference. As Freud puts it, "no lesson has been learnt from the old experience of these activities having led . . . only to unpleasure" (ibid.).
Thus, the way in which such experiences are repeated is concrete.
Such patients

> seek to bring about the interruption of the treatment while it
> is still incomplete; they contrive once more to feel themselves
> scorned, to oblige the physician to speak severely to them and
> treat them coldly; they discover appropriate objects for their
> jealousy; instead of the passionately desired baby of their child-
> hood, they produce a plan or a promise of some grand present—
> which turns out as a rule to be no less unreal (ibid.).

In all of Freud's examples the transference is "real." This reality effect is organized in terms of secondary narcissism—"real" wounds,
"real" compensations. Such narcissistic resistance preempts interpretation. Even though Freud does not think about this issue dynamically,
he does explain the repetition compulsion in relation to the death
drive, the force of tension reduction, and dedifferentiation. Thus, it is
noteworthy that the clinical reason for this explanation is the repetition of "real," painful experience in treatment. Such seemingly instinctual concreteness has something to do with self-destruction and
dedifferentiation.

The drive to dedifferentiating action is in fact the defensive counterpart to the drive to differentiating integration with environment.
Once the repetition compulsion is ascribed to the death drive, the
questions of action, surface, and resistance gain a new status: repetitive
action is no longer due only to the discharge-seeking force of the
repressed. Action is certainly a form of discharge. The repetition of
"real," painful experience in analysis becomes an expression of the
dedifferentiating, tension-reducing gradient of unconscious processes.
Such surface actions work against understanding and interpretation.
But Freud did not grasp that this reality of the analytic process is derived from the tension-raising, differentiating gradient of unconscious
processes—Eros.

Analysts are often stumped by concrete patients who come to analysis but who do not seem to remember what it is for. Abraham was pessimistic about patients who manifested this "special form of resistance." Freud's images of "forcing" and "channeling" give the impression that he felt the need to compel patients who repeated "real" narcissistic wounds to maintain the necessary "aloofness." The failure to remember that the analyst's function is to maintain the frame and to interpret is the defense against memory as internalization. The possibility of interpretation is remembered through its repetitive repudiation. This is another way of understanding Freud's original conception of action. As he says, action is a way of remembering that does not know it remembers.

If the analyst does not understand these dynamics, the most typical countertransference problem is a lapse into enactive interpretation. The analyst uses a preferred schema of development to formulate genetic interpretations that apparently match the patient's material. Such "pattern matching" is usually the analyst's own attempt to exert omnipotent control. This amounts to an objectification of the patient, which does not take into account the surface repudiation of interpretation. If the analyst remains unaware of these dynamics, the treatment of the concrete patient can resemble a folie à deux. The analyst continues to make "pattern-matching" genetic interpretations, while the patient resists interpretation altogether. Each may be lost in the defensive creation of a picture of the other that conforms to narcissistic fantasies. Both may be situationally delusional. Freud already knew that the structure of delusion depends upon "pattern matching." In "The Loss of Reality in Neurosis and Psychosis" (1924a) he said that in psychosis there is a constant search for a match of experience to delusion. Such a match buttresses the apparent "truth" of convictions that serve to deny a piece of reality. In the potential analytic folie à deux analyst and patient remain unaware that each is involved in a repetitive effort to disavow the reality of the other.

Freud actually began to conceptualize this clinical dilemma in his late paper "Constructions in Analysis" (1937b). He did not intend to do so. Most of the paper is concerned with a problem intrinsic to the repression model. The aim of treatment is still conceived archaeologically as the unearthing of repressed contents. Because interpretation does not lead to recall any more consistently than hypnosis originally did, repressed contents may have to be "constructed." Freud offers a set of clinical criteria for the validation of constructions, a topic that does not directly concern us here. What does concern us is his excursion into the topic of delusion, interpretation, and disavowal.

Freud raises the topic of delusion in order to examine defenses against reality. He is first interested in the idea that some patients will respond to the analyst's constructions with especially vivid memories of related details. "These recollections might have been described as hallucinations if a belief in their actual presence had been added to their clearness" (p. 266). Freud's idea here is that when the analyst correctly constructs a piece of the forgotten past, he or she promotes the return of the repressed. However, the repressed does not return directly but via distorted, sensorily vivid, associated details, as in dreams. The almost hallucinatory, compellingly "real" recall of details shows that the construction *has* modified a piece of repression. Freud adds that his linkage of delusion to recall is not new, but he "emphasizes a point of view which is not usually brought into the foreground": there is a "fragment of *historical* truth" (p. 267) in every delusion. The recognition of the kernel of truth in every delusion would provide the ground for "therapeutic work," as the basic theory of dreams had always implied.

None of this is remarkable. What is remarkable is what Freud calls a "seductive analogy":

> The delusions of patients appear to me to be the equivalents of
> the constructions which we build up in the course of an analytic
> treatment—attempts at explanation and cure, though it is true
> that these, under the conditions of a psychosis, can do no more
> than replace the fragment of reality that is being disavowed in the
> present by another fragment that had already been disavowed in
> the remote past. It will be the task of each individual investiga-
> tion to reveal the intimate connections between the material of
> the present disavowal and that of the original repression. Just as
> our construction is only effective because it recovers a fragment
> of lost experience, so the delusion owes its convincing power to
> the element of historical truth which it inserts in the place of the
> rejected reality. (p. 268)

Freud intends to say that just as there is a grain of truth in every delusion, there must be a grain of truth in a construction that leads to hallucinatorily vivid recall. This truth is historical, not material. In other words, it is the truth of something already constructed, the truth of the psychic processing of the material of the "rejected reality." This idea is consistent with Freud's late conception of delusion as a substitute for a lost reality. Psychosis and delusion illustrate the intrinsic link between disavowal of the past reality and disavowal of the present reality. Since disavowal implies that the reality is registered and repudiated, the delusion that replaces the reality has to have that reality embedded within it. This is a theory of memory via repudiation.

We know that Freud will soon come to see fetishism as the model for both neurotic and psychotic disavowal. Once he does so, both repression and denial are the after-effects of primary disavowal. One can speculate that the term "disavowal" is so prominent in this passage precisely because Freud at this time was beginning to think of it as the most general defensive process. In any event, Freud overtly compares construction to delusion in terms of unconscious disavowal of reality. If one factors in that an exclusively "objective" view of reality disavows processive reality, then the construction of the repressed past can be delusional in exactly Freud's sense. It would be the analyst's construction of a historical truth that unknowingly registers and repudiates the patient's past-present disavowal of the "material truth" of processive reality.

An analyst may sense, more intuitively than not, that the aim of interpretation is to help the patient gain the necessary "aloofness" that will modify concrete repetition. However, he or she may not understand global, surface resistances and thus will fall back upon constructing the past. As an unconscious response to primary disavowal, the analyst's interpretations will then have the disavowed processive reality embedded within them in the form of a genetic story. Such a story itself, as Freud says, is an attempt at "explanation and cure." The analyst's "delusional" genetic reconstructions are a kind of waking therapeutic dream. In the present the analyst registers but repudiates the reality that a different kind of intervention is called for.

This analysis is indebted to a similar one proposed by Humphrey Morris (1993). In Chapter 1 I mentioned Morris as one of the few to have realized that Freud, in his late work, was beginning to replace the repression model with a disavowal model. For Morris, the entire topic of disavowal and "delusional construction" "brings us to the limits of practice and theory, limits that confront us in the compulsion to repeat, and in the related inaccessibility to representational memory of the fateful archaic past" (p. 33). He states that in the late work

> Freud brings a challenge to his lifting-of-repression model of historical recovery and interpretive understanding by pointing to constraints that come . . . from within that model. Through his inquiry into the defences of denial and disavowal, and his formulations about what he calls "splits" in the ego, Freud offers a revised, more portentous analysis of the part played by enactments in the psychoanalytic process. Enactment as an obstacle to the analyst's historical understanding is no longer simply located in the analysand, as it was in "Remembering, Repeating, and Working Through." Now, as Freud suggests that enactment is a constitutive element of a dialogic structure at the basis of psychoanalytic understanding, the analyst–theoretician is also implicated. In this more complex and ironic vision, elusive enactments would be both a constraint upon and a condition of possibility for all psychoanalytic representations of history: both the representational rememberings of the analysand, and the representational theorisings of the analyst. (pp. 34–35)

Morris says that if Freud can compare the analyst's constructions to the patient's delusions, then he also opens up the possibility that "enactment might work as a form of action *within* the language of an analytic dialogue" (ibid.). This leads to a theory of surface much more sophisticated than the usual ones. These tend to assume, along with Freud, that one starts from the surface because the surface is what is most immediately apparent to both patient and analyst. Morris contends that in psychoanalysis "narrative enactments" are acts "that are in some sense unconscious, but that are not hidden 'under' repression" (p. 37). In other words, such enactments demonstrate the workings of unconscious processes on the surface, in the use of words itself. Dynamically, Morris understands enactive language as "primary process intrusion into secondary process attempts at accurate representation of some 'reality'" (ibid.). He cites Loewald's view that originally there is no distinction between word and thing. Non-referential, enactive language is built into referential language. Morris's overall aim is to show how disavowal, as a non-repressive defense, explains the surface use of enactive language.

Morris says that when Freud speaks of the link between delusions and constructions in terms of disavowal in "Constructions in Analysis" (1937b), he has perhaps unwittingly found

> underneath repression . . . an earlier form of turning away from
> reality. . . . Disavowal, a turning away that is at the same time a
> primitive registration, constitutes psychical prehistory not in
> the archeologically reconstructable historical object, but in the
> fragment . . . the "fragment of historical truth'" (pp. 267, 268
> [of "Constructions"]); the "fragment of reality" (p. 268); the
> "fragment of lost experience" (p. 268). As the fragment takes
> precedence over the object . . . Freud verges on a theory of
> what lies beyond interpretation. (p. 45)

When Morris speaks of disavowal as "underneath" repression he means that it might be temporally prior. All of his analysis, however, alerts us to the fact that such disavowals operate between analyst and patient. Therefore, they are not "underneath" in the sense of a more deeply buried past but in the sense of the repetition of defenses that "turn away from reality" in the immediacy of the present, on the surface. But because this surface turning away from reality is the result of disavowal, it is paradoxically not immediately observable.

How does one account for a "surface" that is not what is most immediately observable? The "fragment of historical truth" itself is a compromise formation which has embedded within it the material truth of processive reality. Freud's distinction between historical and material truth is quite useful, provided that "materiality" is no longer considered in the conventionally objectivist sense. Such a conception is deliberately Loewaldian. It emphasizes the repudiation of primary reality by both patient and analyst. Although Morris does not consider the question of primary reality, he does understand enactment within the analytic dialogue in the same way that Loewald understands enactive remembering: the intrusion of primary process equivalence of word and thing into consciousness. Loewald did not formulate the defensive function of enactive remembering in relation to primary reality, and neither does Morris. Before repression, defenses inherently operate not only against contents, of which "fragments" remain, but also against the trauma of Eros, differentiating primary reality.

When reinterpreted, Freud's generalization of fetishism makes this problem conspicuous. Like Loewald, Morris does not integrate the theory of fetishism with his understanding of enactment and disavowal. The result of this omission is apparent when Morris follows Freud in linking disavowal to phallic phase conflicts. He clearly delineates the parallel between the little boy's fantasy that everyone might have a penis and the construction of analytic theories. He calls such "theorizing" "thought as aversive action." Aversive thought, as in the boy's phallic phase "theory," is the result of "early and necessary denials and disavowals" (p. 49). Morris's point, however, is that disavowals create the need for the construction of a narrative about how things came to be so. Therefore, he says, just as disavowal contains within it the reality it defends against, by instituting the need for narrative, it also creates the "reality" of narrative action: "early denials and disavowals directed against 'external reality' would at the same time, as primal acts of exclusion, establish another external reality, that of the narrating self to itself" (ibid.).

Here Morris appends a footnote citing Laplanche and Pontalis's (1973) crucial question about disavowal: "does not disavowal—whose consequences in reality are so obvious—bear upon a factor which *founds* human reality rather than upon a hypothetical 'fact of perception'?" (p. 120). In other words, Laplanche and Pontalis are aware that when Freud speaks of disavowal in relation to the boy's repudiation of his perception of the absence of the penis, Freud is somewhat inconsistent. For Morris, the answer to Laplanche and Pontalis's question is in narrative theory: because disavowal creates the demand for narrative, it also institutes the reality of the "externality" of "the narrating self to itself." However, to presume an institution of the "external reality . . . of the narrating self to itself" is to skip over the question of the observing ego. Both clinically and theoretically one would have to say the opposite of what Morris says: primary disavowal tends to collapse the division between the narrating self and itself. Narration can then be taken as historical truth that accurately depicts reality. Its apparent accuracy is precisely what allows it to function as a disavowal of the material truth of primary reality.

Morris says something like this when he examines Freud's theorizing about constructions as narrative:

> The process of establishing historical reference in psychoanalysis now comes to seem more elusive, as the theoretical narration about analytic constructions is itself not able to avoid the kind of referential loss that constructions attempt to get around [that is, constructions are necessarily compared to delusions]. As a narrator, the theoretician eludes his own referential search. At the *observable surface* of the narration, he is separated from himself by a version of the defence to which he would devote his next paper after "Constructions," "The Splitting of the Ego in the Process of Defence" (1940b). . . . The inter- and intra-personal narrative splits that are determining conditions for the dialogic narrative process of a psychoanalysis repeat this past referential loss in the present. Preserved in language, the lost prehistoric reality of the narrating self cannot be equated with the dynamic unconscious, and cannot be recovered by repairing memory through lifting repression. Its *traces* remain referentially split off in historical narratives, for example in the hallucination-like details that constructions can evoke. (ibid.; my emphases)

Morris locates the enactive use of language on the surface of Freud's theory. Just as Freud never stops to examine the phrase "fact of castration," he glosses over his startling comparison of delusion to construction. This very act, according to Morris, is the "trace" of the distance between the "narrating self" and "itself." But what for the observer is a loss of referentiality is for the "theoretician" or the enacting patient not a loss of referentiality at all. When Freud uses a phrase like "reality of castration" he clearly believes that he is describing reality as it is. This is true in every example of concreteness. The use of perceptual identity creates a reality effect.

Morris does not consider how and why the space of the observing ego, which holds open the "space" or "time" of reference, come to be collapsed. For lack of considering the dynamics of defense against differentiation, he does not really tell us how enactive defenses on the surface of a theory or a patient's discourse come about or how they can be modified. Certainly he tells us how this cannot be done, that is, "by repairing memory through lifting repression." He contends that Freud's interest in disavowal revives "his early theorising about defensive dissociation, and about the basis in *traumatic experience of what is radically unconscious*" (p. 50; my emphasis). This is precisely the point at which a conception of the "trauma of Eros" is necessary. As soon as differentiating integration raises tension too much, it is repudiated. Invisible, surface use of dedifferentiating language is the result. In such a situation, the distance between narrator and narration is no more "instituted" than any processive reality can ever be instituted.

Without such a conception, one inevitably falls back upon perception and an originally undifferentiated state as the foundations of reality:

> Far back in Freud's archeology of the mind, the child's denials or disavowals are discovered to be inevitable accompaniments of primitive attempts to institute the primal differences upon which reality testing depends—between internal and external reality, between perception and memory, between the sexes. These differences, in Freud's theory of development, do not appear as pre-existing biological givens; they are the personal theoretical constructions of each individual. The child's use of denial and disavowal to construct experience into perceived differences is narcissistic in the most basic sense: it not only protects the self, it establishes it. Proceeding over time and through numerous transformations, this narcissistic process becomes inextricable from the self-referential dimension of language. (p. 50)

Morris wants us to think of disavowal as instituting primal differences through narration. In other words, there is a hypothetical state "before" such differences are instituted, an originally undifferentiated state. Once the "externality of the narrating self to itself" is instituted, differences are perceivable, in the sense that one putatively perceives the differences between internal and external, perception (present) and memory (past), male and female. The difference between the sexes is the most difficult question here. Who could deny that we perceive the differences between male and female? Yet my account of fetishism worked toward showing that defense against difference creates a perceivable opposition as a substitute for processive differentiation. Eros and primary narcissism imply that such differentiating registrations are neither subjective nor objective, neither internal nor external, the model always being the registration of the experience of satisfaction. As the ur-trace of primary narcissism, the registration of the experience of satisfaction is the memory of something other that is also oneself. Processive differentiation always implies that the trace of the other operates as the foundation of memory. This foundation of memory is both radically unconscious and non-perceptual: it registers an environmental surface. If sexual difference is not to become fetishistic, it cannot simply be conceived in terms of perceivable attributes. As "originally unconscious thought," the trace of the other has to create a tension-raising delay, the possible trauma of unconscious time *within* male and female, subject and object.

To call differences "personal theoretical constructions" is to "narrativize" them as the products of the need to tell a story. Once one does so, one assumes the externality of the narrating self to itself, just as one might assume the possibility of the observing ego clinically. But boundary formation is always poised between differentiating integration with environment and the splitting from environment, which creates perceivable opposition. This process is indeed, to use Morris's terms, radically unconscious and yet on the surface. What better illustration of the way such mechanisms operate to produce surface concreteness and referential aberration than Freud's "fact of castration" or his comparison of construction to delusion? Such defensive theorizing on the surface is radically unobservable for him. In enactment or concreteness one does not "perceive" anything other than an "accurate depiction of reality" at exactly those points at which differentiating process is defended against.

The clinical implications can be grasped if one begins to think of what it might be like to try to explain this to Freud. One would have

to demonstrate to him the unobservable surface concreteness he repeats whenever he encounters the necessity of rethinking reality. For
example, one would have to show him that because he automatically
repudiates sexual difference as process, he objectivizes it. This objec-
tivization would not be possible if it were not also possible to conflate
reality and fantasy through the creation of waking illusions. The unobservable operation of primary defense "on the surface" also modifies the classical rationale for starting from the surface. Conventionally,
this rule assumes that the surface is immediately observable for patient
and analyst, creating a shared point of departure for interpretation.
This shared point of departure presumes that analyst and patient agree
that if they both perceive the same thing, it must be real. As in fetishism, concreteness, or dreams, seeing is believing. This is why the
repression model accommodates a conventional view of reality.

Morris clearly states that the temptation to disavow surface enactments is very strong when traditional interpretation works well:

> Like Freud's enacted disavowals in "Constructions," denials and
> disavowals can remain invisible in a clinical psychoanalysis while
> the work of interpretation seems to proceed smoothly. . . . Even
> the analysand whose well developed representations of inner
> life express the "symbolizing capacity" often associated with
> "analyzability," and even the well analyzed analyst, paradoxically
> depend upon the narrative enactment of denials and disavowals
> to establish a referential basis for their respective psychoanalytic
> narratives. (pp. 50–51)

This is the point implicit in Freud's generalization of disavowal. Once
repression itself is secondary in relation to disavowal, then repression
is made possible, and sustained by, the disavowal of difference. Precisely because the analyst can construct a more coherent narrative, the
temptation to disregard the more disruptive and non-narrativizable
disavowals of differentiation is very strong. It is not only that disavowal can "remain invisible . . . while the work of interpretation
seems to proceed smoothly." It is that disavowal, to recall Anna Freud's
expression, is a "silent and invisible" processive defense against a "silent and invisible" processive reality. Thus, disavowal is all the more

"invisible" where narrative reconstruction seems to "fit." This defensive operation takes place on a surface that, as Morris says, is radically unconscious. This is why the analyst may be unable to observe his or her own use of enactive interpretation. But just as the analyst can observe the enactments that are invisible to the patient, the reverse is equally true. The enacting patient's accurate observations of the analyst's own enactments through interpretation can be quite disturbing. The question is whether or not the analyst will be able to register them. How difficult this is can again be illustrated by Freud's inability to observe his own theoretical enactment when he speaks of the "reality of castration."

WORDS, ACTIONS, TIME

Morris makes clear that any simple distinction between actions and words in psychoanalysis is problematic. Fenichel, in his book on technique (1941), had already said that even when a patient appears to be associating according to the fundamental rule, there may also be "a duplicate of what is being spoken about in wordless action on a different level" (p. 43). This is good clinical advice, but it does not take into account that when the analyst speaks or constructs a theory, there may also be "a duplicate of what is being spoken about" through the action of words. Further, the analyst always acts in order to maintain the analytic frame. In discussing Winnicott on environment I said that it was artificial to separate provision of the setting from the interpretive function. The setting, or the frame, is the differentiated surface that makes interpretation possible. When Winnicott humorously said that "the analyst behaves," he did not take into account that such behavior is action in the service of Eros. So, too, is interpretation, in the widest sense of reopening a defensively closed system. Thus, the essential question is not so much one of words or actions but of the dynamics of words and actions, their differentiating or dedifferentiating functions—for both patient and analyst.

Many of these points were anticipated in a seminal paper by Luisa Alvarez de Toledo, first delivered in 1953 and published in English only in 1996. She examined the action potential of the analyst's and the patient's words, the problem of concreteness on both sides of the couch. Her general contention was that "analysis of 'speaking,' in the form of *both 'associating' and 'interpreting'* could bring unconscious fantasies into the present. . . . In connecting countertransference sensations and emotions with the act signified by associating and interpreting, I understood the *concrete* significance of 'speaking and words,' as distinct from and in addition to their content" (p. 293; my emphases). She also raises the question of global resistance to the analytic process and understands that the patient may use interpretation to recreate magical control:

> The patient treats and manipulates his analyst in the same way as he treats and manipulates his internal objects, and he in turn feels treated and manipulated by the analyst in that way. On a magic level, *interpretation as the behavior of the analyst* completes the *Gestalt* of the unconscious primal fantasy that he is then carrying out. To the patient the analyst is an unknown, who can be understood and learnt about only on the basis of the known, by a process of comparison, which takes place by an interplay of projective and introjective identifications. The analyst thus acquires the qualities of the introjected objects and the capacity to be manipulated by the patient, who will control him in the same way as he controls his internal objects. *Good or bad*, he will be manipulable. . . . By knowing and understanding someone or something, at a deep level we believe that we are controlling him or it. *What arouses the most anxiety is the unknown, because it cannot be controlled.* . . . In this situation, *instead of forming a link with the object, words become the object projected and introjected by the analysand as he superimposes his internal reality on an external reality.* (pp. 293–95)

In analysis itself, the external reality on which the patient's internal reality is superimposed is the analyst's neutrality and different level of organization. They are what makes the analyst "uncontrollable" and "unknown." Alvarez de Toledo captures the essential affective problem: this reality may feel so anxiety provoking that the patient must bring it under magical control. The aggressive components of this superimposition of "internal reality on an external reality" are well captured by Klein's concept of sadistic epistemophilia. The clinical result is conflation of interpretation with fantasies of "goodness" or "badness": the patient feels concretely gratified and relieved or frustrated and threatened by what the analyst says. And, of course, the analyst's words will lose their therapeutic leverage if they are used to enact the countertransference fantasy of controlling the patient.

Alvarez de Toledo is clear that when interpretations fit the patient's fantasy of what is "good or bad," the analytic process is stalled. Thus, she would not see modification of splitting as an integration of the "good" and the "bad," as does Klein in her reified way. To modify splitting is rather to analyze the anxieties that compel the patient to control the "uncontrollable unknown" implicit in interpretation. Alvarez de Toledo does not conceptualize the nature of this unknown reality. However, she does capture quite well the unconscious hostility toward the analyst's different level of organization:

> Words as a magic act are used in analysis for attack and defense. . . . The defensive aspect takes the form of control of thought concerning associations, with the aim of watching over thought and hence also the analyst's interpretations, which are experienced at a deep level as hostile. In this way too, the subject avoids the emergence of anything unforeseen, whether from himself or from the analyst in interpretation. . . . Hence, the anxiety and hostility aroused by an unexpected interpretation, which, after all, not only acts by virtue of its content, but also demonstrates the failure of the magic of the patient, who then accommodates all his lost omnipotence in the analyst and in his interpretation, seen as both act and object. . . . This allows [the patient] to transform the interpretation, in accordance with his fantasy needs, into something good or bad. (p. 303)

The transformation of the interpretation into "something good or bad" is the transformation of its transitional function into a fetishistic one. The idea that an unexpected interpretation represents the failure of the patient's magical omnipotence is very much to the point. The "unexpected" is eliminated by negative hallucination and replaced with the positive hallucination of the "goodness" or "badness" of the interpretation.

These dynamics explain how to intervene such that the analyst neither retraumatizes the patient nor maintains a naïve faith in the power of traditional interpretation. The analyst can use words as actions in the service of differentiation. Words as differentiating actions address the unobservable surface and interfere with the use of perceptual identity on a moment-to-moment basis. The same principle would also have to apply to analysis of countertransference and to the analyst's hostile-magical use of words with a patient who poses a threat to the analyst's reality sense.

Clinical theories tend to address spatio-temporal difference when they consider the use of fantasy to defend against interpretation. Alvarez de Toledo is no exception, and her remarks are again quite pertinent. She is in the process of extending her conception of magical control to the questions of depersonalization and depression:

> . . . depersonalization and depression are due to the object loss involved in understanding that the analyst and other objects are *different* [my emphasis] from the objects accommodated in them by the subject . . . the individual projects something known, which is himself. . . . Since these objects are an image of the subject himself—indeed they *are* [author's emphasis] the subject himself—when he loses them he loses his own person, and that is why he becomes depressed and depersonalized. At a deep level, he and the object were one. If the object becomes different and strange, the subject too becomes different and strange to himself. . . . When he understands that the object is different from himself, he withdraws his libido completely. . . . When the individual becomes depersonalized, withdrawing his libido into himself . . . , he loses the notion of external time. . . . In turning himself into his own object, he becomes his own object world, a space and time that he controls totally. The analysand then manipulates the passage of time with his body, thought or words. He mobilizes or *immobilizes it in accordance with his wishes, and superimposes his own internal time on external time.* . . . [my emphasis] He is also afraid of losing himself through the loss of his control over space and time, and of being absorbed by the space-time world of the object, in which he needs to accommodate his lost omnipotence. (pp. 305–7)

"If the object becomes different and strange, the subject too becomes different and strange to himself." Recall the clinical examples in Chapter 1, in which it was clear that the patients adapted their analyses to their own frames of reference. The "strangeness of difference" was categorically rejected, precisely because it was outside the "certain knowledge" gained by the conflation of fantasy and reality. Freud originally conceived the "narcissism of minor differences" in terms of the "strangeness of difference." The analyst as object can become "strange"—or "new," in Loewald's sense—only when the patient can internalize that he or she also is different from what had seemed to be certain. To the extent that the entire analytic process represents the threat of this difference, the patient will indeed, as Alvarez de Toledo says, attempt to control time and space totally. The control of time through the repetition of the dedifferentiated "now" of immediate perception works as the "stimulus barrier" against the differentiating strangeness of unconscious time. The patient will only see the analyst as a non-strange version of himself or herself, as someone who also attempts to impose his or her own "control over space and time." Thus the endlessly enacted power struggle over who will become "absorbed" by whose "space-time" and the constant push toward frame violations. If the analyst does not grasp the profoundly defensive nature of the patient's need to objectify analytic space and time, it is almost inevitable that the analyst will attempt to "repossess" what the patient attempts to control. The analyst may rationalize that the patient is being brought back to reality, or the analyst may not intervene in such a process at all and may rationalize that "holding" or "experience" will do the trick over time.[1]

The question of theoretical enactment, as Morris has called it, or of internalization anxiety in theory construction, is intrinsic to this clinical approach. Alvarez de Toledo also discusses it:

> the difficulty of symbolization in the field of analysis . . . and in
> metapsychology . . . arises from the need to see everything as a
> single good or bad thing, and to deny the different and hence
> also the unforeseen that cannot be dominated . . . the difficulty
> of attributing reality to the abstract has to do with what the
> abstract symbolizes on the instinctual level, and lack of a concrete

form (evidence or experimental material) prevents us from
understanding—that is, from accepting—just as we reject and
avoid everything we cannot control, by which we are therefore
afraid of being controlled. (p. 310)

What Alvarez de Toledo here calls "the abstract" is what I have been
calling non-perceptual reality. It appears as abstract only in opposition
to the concrete. The material reality of difference as "the unforeseen
that cannot be dominated" is exactly what the concrete patient repudiates and is afraid of being controlled by. The analyst, then, must not
fear the material difference of the patient who compels one to give
up the false security of "concrete evidence." When Alvarez de Toledo speaks of "what the abstract symbolizes on the instinctual level,"
she does not really say what she means. However, she has pointed out
exactly what the problem is: the relation between the instinctual and
the abstract. This would be drive as Eros, which both integrates "vital difference" and raises tension levels.

Although she does not make explicit her conception of the abstract as the instinctual, Alvarez de Toledo describes it as the crux of
therapeutic change:

The *new* notion . . . [the patient] acquires is that he has a capacity
for development, which, even if not as sudden or magic as he
would like, takes place inexorably, deny it as he will. This notion
also arouses anxiety, because the analysand realizes that his
knowledge, whether of reality, of objects or of himself, is relative
and that there is something inside himself which does not know
and over which he does not therefore have total control. The
idea of the impossibility of change, the feeling that "it is always
the same" . . . is merely a defense against the anxiety aroused by
the unknown in oneself, in the world, in objects and *in time*,
and which, being unknown, cannot be controlled . . . even if
this frustrates and depresses [the patient] and arouses his anxiety,
since he loses the hope of finding something *definitive, stable
and immutable that will protect him*, he is compensated by the
newly won increase in his capacity for symbolization. (p. 313;
my emphases)

The "definitive, stable and immutable" protection against the un-known, uncontrollable, instinctual force of time is, of course, the fetish. Transferentially, the fetish defends against anything new or strange. In Alvarez de Toledo's terms, we can call the analyst who does not fit into the patient's fantasy system of "good" and "bad," the analyst who can-not be used as a fetish, the strange object.

As therapeutic change occurs, time itself, as an infinite repetition of identical "nows" that guarantee that it "is always the same," be-comes strange. Internalization always implies the shift from the con-trollable time of identification to the uncontrollable time of the fu-ture. It is not possible to potentiate the shift to the "strange time" of analytic change by modifying the temporal aspects of the frame itself. In longer or shorter sessions, the "clock time" of the session is con-trolled. Time itself is then manipulated as something "good" or "bad" by the analyst or by the patient. The patient will inevitably feel con-trolled by the analyst's fantasized control of the time, and will attempt to exert a counter-control. However, by beginning and ending the session at fixed times, the analyst is not treating time as a manipulable possession. The analyst must be aware of the strangeness inherent in "clock time" and in the maintenance of fixed, regular sessions. This is the strangeness of unconscious time, the time against which a stimu-lus barrier is erected. As Freud said, conscious time itself is this stim-ulus barrier. Variable length sessions intensify the perceptual focus on conscious time. The opening of the fantasy system of the controllable "good" and "bad" to what it excludes, to uncontrollable instinctual time, is another way of conceptualizing the overall analytic aim of re-integrating environment and instinct. "Unconscious time" constitutes the invisible surface of analysis. Thus, in enactive remembering or concreteness the patient's defenses are conspicuously mobilized against registration of it and against integration with the analytic environ-ment. This is why those patients who most openly defend against the possibility of interpretation itself have the most trouble with analytic time, making it endless as they simultaneously manipulate the regu-larity of session time by lateness and absence. Processive interventions aim at these unconscious, surface defenses mainly by attempting to make them observable. This can occur only if the analyst does not at-tempt to control the patient by having him or her fit into the analyst's

reality sense, that is, if the analyst does not engage in enactive interpretation. The latter is a frame violation on the analyst's part, inevitably leading to power struggles over whose sense of reality will prevail. Once the analyst can shift the focus to the complex unconscious
defenses used to create the counter-surface, the therapeutic task is to
make conscious both gradients of internalization anxiety—the near-
traumatic anxiety over integration and all the fears of loss. Alvarez
de Toledo warns us that our metapsychology suffers if we are afraid of
the abstract. Our clinical work suffers equally if we do not conceptualize the "silent and invisible" dynamic processes on the analytic
surface.

The classical setup of neutrality, of frequent sessions of regular duration, of insight rather than experience as the major vehicle of therapeutic change, and of a focus on transference analysis, is inherently
the one that maximizes the encounter with a differentiating framework. But it, too, is limited if the kinds of questions raised by Morris
and Alvarez de Toledo are not part of its theory of technique. Even
when there is more and more agreement that the most effective clinical work focuses on surface manifestations of resistance within the
transference, the nature of the reality of the analytic frame can remain
unexamined. A version of concreteness will then be left in place in
the rote maintenance of the classical frame.

TWO TEST CASES:
PAUL GRAY AND BETTY JOSEPH

The general trend of integrating resistance and surface analysis initiated by Freud was powerfully continued by Fenichel. The latter famously said that when interpretations do not have therapeutic effect,
analysts tend to make the mistake of thinking that the interpretations
have not been "deep" enough. The real problem is that they have not
been "superficial" enough (p. 44). Today's most sophisticated practitioners, who maintain the classical framework, converge on the issues
of surface and defense analysis. Contemporary Freudian and Kleinian
practice emphasizes analysis of resistance to the analytic process. This
trend is exemplified in the work of Paul Gray and Betty Joseph. Gray
is a Freudian ego psychologist, Joseph a Kleinian. Each has elaborated

a technique that expands and enriches the ideas of defense-and-surface analysis. Both offer important correctives to those within their own traditions who focus too much on content analysis. Neither, however, has even remotely begun to think about all the issues implied in Freud's generalization of fetishism, disavowal, and ego splitting. Therefore, both are also limited by unquestioned assumptions about reality. There is a great deal to be learned from the similarity between Gray and Joseph, despite their divergent theories. But there is as much to be learned from their convergent objectivism, which repeats some of the most questionable conceptions of Freud and Klein.

Gray (1994) is interesting both for his innovations and his traditionalism. The innovations stem from his technique of "close process monitoring" of defense. Gray has done more than anyone to show why close process monitoring is such a difficult clinical task. His focus on surface and process makes some of his clinical formulations quite similar to the ones advocated here. His traditionalism stems from his limitation of the technique of surface-and-defense analysis to the classical neuroses. Neurosis for him is the specific disorder of defense against sexual and aggressive drives—no more, no less. He has no interest in its narcissistic aspects. Narcissism for Gray is only a matter of self-esteem regulation and has no relation to the question of reality. In fact, Gray would view concrete patients with narcissistic defenses as outside the purview of the close process technique.

His most general point is that analytic listening itself has not been adequately reconceived in line with the unconscious workings of defense (p. 5). The familiar conception of analytic listening, he contends, is based on an antiquated sense of the function of the analyst—the use of the analyst's unconscious to pick up derivatives of unconscious fantasies. Gray calls this the "missing content" approach. It became outmoded as soon as Freud formally spoke of resistance and surface analysis in 1914. The problem, Gray thinks, is that the analyst cannot pick up the unconscious workings of defense the same way as he or she picks up "missing content." Freud advocated non-purposeful, evenly hovering attention as the counterpart of the patient's free associations. For Gray, this kind of listening has to be complemented by a much more purposeful, finely honed attention in order to perceive the "subtle and invisible" workings of defense in the moment.

Gray says that the "crux of the difficulty in making the unconscious ego conscious is that the elements the analyst wants to bring into awareness are not 'driven' toward the analysand's awareness, as are the id derivatives" (p. 65). Evenly hovering attention goes halfway to meet the discharge-seeking force of whatever is actively defended against. However, it does not facilitate awareness of unconscious defensive operations (p. 66). Gray cites Freud's intuition, from *New Introductory Lectures* (1933b), that the theory of the unconscious workings of defense would affect his (imaginary) audience "differently [than] the introduction into the psychical underworld which preceded it. . . . I now believe that is somehow a question of the nature of the material itself" (p. 58). Gray's explanation of the nature of the difficulty is that "self-observation of the process of the mind's intrapsychic activity at its encounter with and defensive solution to conflict—conflict not ordinarily in the scope of attention—makes an even stranger demand on the autonomous ego apparatus" (p. 70). The strange demand is for the "meticulous registering of the sometimes fast moving surface changes" (p. 101) in the operation of defense. The ego has no intrinsic motivation to register its defensive surface.

Gray thinks that Freud himself could have initiated a consistent rethinking of standard technique but did not because he lost interest in defense-and-resistance analysis after writing *Inhibition, Symptom, and Anxiety* in 1926. While Gray is right to a certain extent, he completely overlooks the revision of the theory of defense with the introduction of disavowal and ego splitting. Certainly Freud did not even begin to consider how the generalization of disavowal and splitting would affect defense analysis. However, Gray seems unaware that Freud did begin to reconceptualize neurosis itself in the light of his new theory. Therefore, Gray does not apply the concept of the "splitting of the ego in the process of defense" to the ego's inherent resistance to observing its own defensive activities—even in neurosis. By alleging that Freud simply lost interest in the topic of defense after 1926, Gray avoids the more difficult question that Freud did maintain his outmoded insistence on filling in gaps in memory as the major therapeutic goal of analysis, while initiating profound innovations in the theory of defense and the theory of mind.

Gray also thinks that Freud never really relinquished dependence on the positive transference for therapeutic effect. He contends that only a thoroughgoing process approach allows for the fullest analysis of the transference. Whenever the analyst bypasses surface analysis of how derivatives are automatically eliminated from consciousness, Gray says, he or she lapses into a suggestive technique, consciously or not. The analyst then depends upon either tacit permission or authoritative coercion to readmit the repressed into consciousness. The anxieties that motivate defense are simply alleviated by the transference, leading to a cure by identification. To maximize the therapeutic potential of analysis, Gray says, optimal focus is on the defenses at work in the registration of psychic reality as it includes registration of the analytic process.

What are the results of defense against registration of the analytic process? For Gray, this is a matter of analyst and patient colluding to avoid the operation of defense in the moment, an essential clinical point. But Gray does not take into account that wherever there is defense, including repression, there is always a processive splitting of the ego and a less differentiated reality organization. Defense against registration of the analytic process, for him, has nothing to do with defense against the analyst's different level of organization and interpretive function. Conversely, he thinks that wherever there is defense against the different level of organization, one does not use the close process analysis of defense in the transference. He says: "many wider-scope patients are beset with deeper, often intractable resistance against developing a capacity for relative autonomy and acceptance of reality. The egos of such patients require protective measures that *preclude some of the aims of essential psychoanalytic methodology*" (p. 140). In other words, if the patient does not share the analyst's objective reality sense, one does not analyze defense against registration of the analytic process. This thinking fails to understand the dynamics of non-acceptance of reality, particularly non-acceptance of the reality of the analytic process.

Reality for Gray is only what is objectively observable. He is quite cogent about the analyst's tendency to bypass surface-and-defense analysis. But he assumes that this surface is immediately observable if pointed out by the analyst—thus his insistence that his method works only if the patient's ego functions well enough to observe what is brought to its attention. If the analyst consistently overcomes his or her own resistances to surface-and-defense analysis, the patient can "learn" (p. 52) through "practice" (p. 67) that he or she can do the same. There is a certain empirical justification for this attitude. Defenses against the possibility of an observing ego do not globally dominate the analysis of the neurotic. However, Gray never considers that there might be moments when the neurotic, too, has the same defensive attitude to observation as the more impaired patient, precisely because the surface can be radically unobservable.

For Gray, then, defense against registration of the analytic process does not demand a rethinking of reality. Nonetheless, he is acutely aware of the problem of a defensive "reality effect" in recall of the past. He says that memory and fantasy are "closely linked" (p. 55). The consequence is that the ordinary experience of recall is experienced "as a *reference* to something that happened in the past, something that is perceived as a former, recent or distant past reality, *external* to the intrapsychic here-and-now . . . there is . . . a great temptation to yield to the natural tendency of giving memory a priority in its function as referring to *past external reality*, over its role as an *internal event of immediate intrapsychic importance*" (pp. 55–56). Gray's idea is that the hyper-referential functioning of memory points to a vivid past in order to divert attention from the present defensive organization. He incisively goes on to raise the problem of "pattern matching," saying that the analyst's genetic theories may be used to support listening to memory *only* as direct reference to the past (p. 57).

Without knowing it, Gray has put his finger on the problem of enactive remembering and enactive interpretation in the treatment of neurosis.[2] When analyst and patient share the "illusion of referentiality," and especially when reference to the past fits the analyst's preferred genetic theory, the inevitable resistances to analysis of the "defensive surface" may be intensified. Gray has to be given full credit for offering a corrective to potential "referential aberrations" on both sides of the couch. However, because he is uninterested in the narcissistic dimensions of neurosis, he does not at all consider the dedifferentiating, destructive implications of treating the past concretely. In his most eloquent statement of the issue he writes:

> To the extent that analysts are able to use an optimum surface, they will provide analysands with the best chance to use their self-observing equipment. . . . Analysands are not familiar with the nature of the activities in which the mind-at-surface quietly engages while they are speaking. Indeed, they are barely even aware of the existence of these activities. For instance, the natural orientation of their thinking is restricted to regarding the things they say as *references* solely to what they have been talking about. Patients must learn that they can yield this natural stance as they gain familiarity with another function of their mind, a function that consists of their *living out* a piece of mental behavior while they are speaking, and must also learn how and why they are doing so . . . experiencing and practicing these skills is obviously essential. Part of the manifestation characterized by "there is a resistance to uncovering of resistances" (Freud 1937a, p. 239) often results from the analyst's failure to provide the analysand with the best opportunity to perceive the resistance. (p. 76; my emphases)

When Gray speaks of having to "yield the natural stance" of the illusion of reference, he is as close as he comes to rethinking the problem of reality. The next step would be to question the equally "natural" assumption that what is on the surface is intrinsically what is most readily observable. For Gray, however, once the analyst acquires the necessary skill to communicate the intrinsically less observable defensive processes, the rest is an affair of "experience," "practice," and "learning." In other words, there is nothing more to analyze, no other dynamics at work in the resistance to uncovering resistance. Thus, when he says that the therapeutic aim of consistent surface and defense analysis is to reduce the "potential for anxiety" (p. 91), he means only the signal anxiety that motivates defense against drive derivatives. Gray does not conceive of forms of anxiety more intense than signal anxiety, anxieties that contribute to surface defense against something inherently unobservable. He would have no reason to analyze the neurotic's splitting of self-preservation from libido and its inevitable heightening of self destruction.

These issues converge in Gray's very pertinent remarks about the relations between super-ego analysis and neutrality. Gray believes that the analyst's typical wish "to be regarded as noncritical" is conflated all too easily with the patient's wish to avoid the "unconscious threat of censorship" (p. 134). The neurotic's need to create the image of a permissive analyst is a defense against "inhibiting, censoring images of authority." Gray's conclusion is that it "takes a long time for most patients to risk emotionally (and often intellectually) accepting the analyst as *analyst* and as actually working with a *morally neutral* attitude. It is often safer for the patient to choose between the fantasy of a critically restraining image or an affectionately forgiving one" (ibid.). Gray has described a fetishistic formation here. Two fantasies—critically censoring, affectionately forgiving—are taken as concretely real in order to replace the processive reality of the analyst's neutrality. What Gray casually calls the emotional "risk" of "accepting the analyst as *analyst*" speaks to the problem of internalization anxiety in neurosis and to the very typical ways in which neurotic super-ego conflicts lead to fetishistic transferences. Moreover, the self-directed aggression that classical analysts have no trouble conceptualizing when dealing with the super-ego can also produce subtle forms of aggression against the analyst's interpretive function. If, as Gray says, the neurotic responds as if the analyst "*really*" matches the "critically restraining image or [the] affectionately forgiving one," then one has a concrete defense against interpretation itself.

What Gray calls "moral neutrality" here is exactly what Alvarez de Toledo meant by the "uncontrollable unknown." This is why, as Gray says, there is significant emotional risk in "accepting the analyst as analyst." "Neutrality" has to become a threat when the analyst attempts to open the closed system of fantasy oppositions of "good" and "bad," "permissive" and "critical." Without analysis of these dynamics, learning and practice would bypass an even more superficial defensive operation: the neurotic's use of the analyst as a super-ego fetish. In the analysis of neurotic super-ego transferences, the emotional risk and the intellectual difficulty are actually one and the same. The patient resists the loss of control of the apparently certain knowledge that any fetishistic organization provides. Unsuspected forms of anxiety and concreteness enter the treatment. These can make the neurotic transiently look like the more impaired kind of patient for whom Gray thinks consistent surface-and-defense analysis is contraindicated. The examples of the patient who became momentarily concrete in the Freud museum and of the patient who developed a cardiac "symptom" (Chapter 2) speak to this point.

The strengths and weaknesses of Gray's approach are apparent in a study of actions and words in analysis by Busch (1995). On the contemporary American scene, Busch has importantly extended Gray's thinking, always stressing the limitations of the "absent content" approach. Busch clearly thinks that Gray's innovations can and should be extended to the treatment of patients whose "acceptance of reality" is conventionally impaired. As in Gray's position on memory, Busch is aware that problems with "acceptance of reality" are often manifested as hyper-referentiality. He makes the point clinically:

> By the end of analysis one would hope that an analysand, caught in the throes of a transference, would move from being convinced that an impression of the analyst's greeting as less than exuberant was an indication of the *analyst's* mood toward the analysand, to at least considering this as a possible sign of an important observation relative to the *analysand's* mind. The significance of this step is that the analysand moves from thinking of his thoughts only as realities, to thinking that can take itself as the object of its own inquiry. (p. 65)

Busch's explanation of why a patient would remain fixed in the illusion of reference is cognitive-developmental. Like several of the authors cited in Chapter 1, Busch refers to Piaget's description of the sensory-motor phase of thinking and to Flavell's extension of it in terms of immediate perception as action (the white circle behind the blue filter is only blue) (pp. 66–68). Busch thinks that words themselves can become actions if this earlier form of thinking is maintained. Certainly he is aware that there is immediately a question of the observing ego, enabling him to take Gray one step further. He says that when the analyst wants to interpret defensive conviction about the immediacy of perception, the analyst also has to interpret "layers of resistances that have led the behavior to stay at an action level, where the analysand's capacity to reflect upon himself is very limited" (p. 71). But Busch does not understand this limitation on self-reflection as in any way related to the dynamics of dedifferentiation, self-destruction, or fetishism. Therefore, although he, too, stresses the limits of genetic interpretation "when there is no observing ego," he falls back upon interventions that focus on "observational inclinations" (p. 73). Such interventions allow patients to express their wishes not to observe, that is, their defensive retreat to sensory-motor phases of thinking. This is a good beginning strategy for examining hyper-referentiality itself. It allows the patient to express a surface resistance that might otherwise be bypassed. However, its dynamic limitation becomes clear in a very interesting clinical example.

Busch writes about a patient who feels discouraged about the lack of progress in his treatment. While he speaks morosely, Mr. A rhythmically touches a plant at the end of the couch with his foot, an action Busch says he has not noticed before. As Mr. A becomes more entrenched in the reality of his perception of his lack of progress, Busch notices an edge in his voice and asks him about it:

> He said that while he felt he was talking about reality, I was
> suggesting that his thoughts meant something else. He then
> began a harangue against me for over interpreting, when things
> were sometimes just what they were. Upon finishing, he breathed
> deeply, laughed, and said, "I feel a lot better now." . . . He then
> remembered that we were two weeks from a week long break in
> the treatment. In his heart, he said, he wanted to fight with me
> about the meaning of this incident. At this point he noted the
> rhythmic touching of the plant with his foot. He wondered, with
> some sadness in his voice, if this was the expression of a wish to
> get close, and he wondered, too, why it was so difficult for him
> to know about these wishes. (p. 74)

By not rotely focusing on Mr. A's action with his foot as a resistance to verbalization and by asking him to observe the edge in his voice, Busch helps the patient to speak about the defensive function of his action. The patient's use of sensory-motor actions to conflate thoughts with perceptions emerges. The result is effective intervention on the surface: the patient wants to resist possible interpretation of the break in the treatment.

But Busch has no dynamic conception of the trauma of Eros. He cannot see that the patient's resistance to any interpretation of the break is a dedifferentiating attack on the analytic environment itself. The patient wants to "fight" with the analyst in order to use speaking as a form of discharge when the tension of possible interpretation is too great. The patient engages in a "harangue" against "over interpreting, when things were sometimes just what they were," and experiences relief—he feels "a lot better now." The harangue then is an autoerotic, sexualization of thought. It splits off the self-preservative and differentiating function of interpretation.

What does the patient fear? Is it simply a question of conflicts over wanting to be close to a male figure, acted out with his foot on the plant, as he and Busch eventually agree? From my point of view, it is predictable that the patient's concreteness would be linked to a fetishistic structure. Busch tells us that until his forties, the patient's mother, and then his wife, bought his clothes and shoes: "His ability to feel manly was severely interfered with, as exemplified by masturbatory fantasies of being a woman with a penis while wearing women's undergarments" (p. 75). The patient also had compulsive rituals: repetitive actions performed on the left side of his body were conventionally, and concretely, equated with femininity, the right with masculinity. He was touching the plant with his right foot, thus indicating a "fantasy of masculine closeness." As a response to "loss" of contact with an "intact" male figure, the touching of the plant is no less fetishistic than his fantasy of being a phallic woman. As an enactment, it is also an attack on the analyst's different level of organization. To be in the analytic environment always implies that one's thoughts might mean something else, as the patient says in order to repudiate it. The patient shows the two gradients of internalization anxiety—the panic over internalization of the analyst's interpretive function, as a transference repetition of the trauma of sexual differentiation, and all the fantasies of loss that replace integration with environmental process. The analyst interprets fear of loss of a presumably "intact" phallic replacement and regression to earlier forms of cognition. To eliminate consideration of the self-destructive, dedifferentiating attack on interpretation is to stop short of analyzing the patient's environmental conflict with the analyst.

The result has to be a concretization of the analyst's interventions themselves, a concretization Busch cheerfully assumes. Because he wants to apply Gray's technique of close process monitoring to the surface operation of sensory-motor, concrete thinking, Busch reasonably says that the analyst generally attempts to work with "what is most tangible, knowable, and concrete to the patient. To do this, it is most helpful to stay within the here-and-now of the transference" (p. 77). Thus his effective intervention about the edge in his patient's voice. However, if one does not understand concreteness in terms of the intrinsic conflict between the "two realities," the objective and the processive, the analyst inevitably feels justified in making the concrete more concrete, as the only way of helping the patient to observe what is presumed to be a cognitive defense:

> My purpose, then, is to concretize what is essential for a psychoanalysis to take place, while focusing attention . . . on resistances
> to these processes. . . . Most important, it is tangible, concrete
> behavior that is easiest to bring before the analysand for consideration, without danger of stretching his cognitive abilities
> beyond the level at which he is capable of operating. As the
> concrete nature of resistance is established with the patient, it
> becomes possible to look at some of the more subtle (but still
> concrete) forms of action that the resistances take. . . . These can
> be elaborated, over time, only in the context of the tangible goal
> of psychoanalysis to say whatever comes to mind as a method
> of understanding internal psychological states. Gray's method
> of close process monitoring, within the context of what he
> describes as the two methods of observation in analysis—i.e.
> observing that thoughts are occurring (free association) and
> observing these thoughts as expressions of intrapsychic states
> (self observation)—is an ideal method for the analysis of actions.
> To put it more succinctly, the method *concretizes* the analytic
> task, and the patient's response to it, at a time when the patient's
> thinking is most concrete. (p. 78)

Although he does extend Gray's technique beyond neurosis, Busch believes that he can teach the patient through experience about why he resists interpretation. Essentially he tries to show the patient why his own reality organization is just as concrete as the patient's. There is no analysis of all the complex, surface defenses that link the patient's fetishism to his resistance to interpretation. The analyst's dependence upon a "concrete pedagogy" in order to treat concreteness is an unconscious response to primary disavowal. It embeds the disavowed processive reality within a genetic "story" of cognitive development. The defensive nature of this cognitive-developmental story is made clear in the reliance on the security of concrete evidence (Alvarez de Toledo) to create "conviction" on both sides of the couch. There is no defense against an intrinsically unobservable, unconscious surface. The splitting off of primary reality in the transference remains unanalyzed.

The first of Betty Joseph's collected papers, *Psychic Equilibrium and Psychic Change* (1989), written in 1959, is devoted to the repetition compulsion. As a Kleinian, Joseph is committed to the concept of the death instinct, and as an original clinician, she attempts to show how the linkage of repetition and death gives the analyst purchase on certain very difficult patients. Joseph's thought-provoking integration of the repetition compulsion, the death instinct, and resistance to interpretation leads her to a brief discussion of "the trauma of Eros." She is the only author cited here to have envisaged primordial defense against contact with the analytic process, producing defense against interpretation itself.

Joseph discusses a patient who "somehow" always seemed to wind up in the position of having people depend upon her. The patient inevitably feels the same way about her analyst, as a defense against her own need for therapeutic help. Joseph notices that over time none of her interpretations "link up" for the patient, no matter how significant they had seemed at any given moment. As the patient becomes aware of, and then denies, her need for help from the analyst, she also shows "a growing awareness and a denial of the importance of gaps in time" (p. 22). Simultaneous awareness and denial are, of course, the hallmarks of disavowal. When they are related to the question of time, as is the case here, it is usually a question of defense against processive reality. Joseph reports her interventions:

[the patient] instanced how she had just been giving the interpretations about her worries herself, but seemed to have left a
great gap between that and the last sessions, so that no insight or
understanding derived from the analysis appeared to have been
carried over from one session to the next. . . . I showed her that
she had turned against and bitten great holes into what I had to
give and had become identified with the bitten-up analyst,
fundamentally the bitten-up breast. And she had at the same
time taken over the analysis herself, making her own links, her
own interpretations, she had identified with myself and become
me, the mother, doing the feeding herself. (p. 22)

Joseph does not connect her patient's resistance to interpretation to
Abraham's classic description of the "special form of resistance." Therefore, she does not consider, as Abraham did, that the patient's identification with the analyst's interpretive function is a form of autoerotic
control. Nor does Joseph consider anything like defense against internalization, the use of conscious time as a protective "stimulus barrier,"
and the splitting of environment from instinct. Nonetheless, her fine
clinical sense leads her to intervene around these issues. She points out
the patient's need to create "gaps," so that no "understanding derived
from the analysis appeared to have been carried over from one session
to the next." Joseph also interprets in typical Kleinian content terms:
oral aggression, the breast in bits, splitting of good and bad. Processive
interventions are translated into the content of the analyst's preferred
genetic theory.

Joseph goes on to say that the patient

could not keep the connection between the sessions and had to
make these gaps, since keeping the links meant links between her
own insight and my previous interpretations, between herself and
me, and this was tantamount to allowing myself and my work to
be loved and valued, and it was too painful . . . one could see in
all [the] material the patient's struggle against being dependent
on me and my work, or on her husband . . . she told me that she
had decided to join her husband for the weekend and had been
thinking how very enjoyable the few days might be; then this

idea became connected with the work we had been doing in the sessions and suddenly . . . all "the pleasure drained away like sand running through my fingers." We could see that when she was thinking happily of the weekend, this became a good experience like a good feed, then she saw that the experience, feed, was connected with my work, as if milk was seen to come from a breast which was mine and attached to my body—so she drained it away, could not use it and turned it into sand, like feces or urine. (pp. 22–23)

It seems that Joseph's finely tuned processive interventions do not satisfy her because she cannot account for them adequately. There is a rich Kleinian theory of oral and anal paranoid-schizoid fantasies and defenses but very little about defense against interpretation per se. Joseph seems certain that good experience with the husband and interpretive help from the analyst equal a "good feed" from a "good breast." However, she has described the patient's defenses against integration with the analytic environment: the patient treats internalization of the analyst's interpretive function as trauma ("it was too painful") and uses time as a possession (the manipulation of the "gaps" between sessions) to reinforce the splitting of self-preservation (help, dependence) and libido. The patient says that if she enjoys the analytic work, she immediately has to drain it away, like sand running through her fingers. This moment is akin to the one in Busch's clinical example in which the patient had to discharge tension through a harangue against interpretation. Can we infer that Joseph's patient analogously retreats to tension release ("draining") in the face of tension-raising registration of the analyst-object? Such a defensive-economic, processive account of the patient's dynamics does not concretely conflate "good interpretation" with "the good breast." It also takes into account the registration and repudiation ("awareness" and "denial") of interpretive and temporal processes. Whatever therapeutic leverage Joseph may have gained from her processive interventions may also have been lost by her content interpretations. One does not know whether the patient felt that Joseph was attempting to impose her own version of (fantasy conflated with) reality.

The mapping of a fine intuitive grasp of the patient's processive dynamics onto a Kleinian grid takes Joseph to her most original point. Joseph understands that when the patient claims all insight as her own, in the transference she (Joseph) has

> ceased to exist as a separate analyst. This total identification with
> the idealized object . . . means that so long as the object is part
> of, and fused with the self, it can be kept alive and not lost. I
> think that this situation is comparable with what Freud described
> when he spoke of love at the oral stage being indistinguishable
> from the annihilation of the object . . . the object is annihilated
> as a separate object, but nevertheless maintained. This type of
> love is of a highly narcissistic nature. . . . It is clear that this object
> has to be kept internally paralysed; if it comes alive and is felt as
> separate and creative and with a life of its own, it arouses great
> hostility and destructiveness—as happened with A., when she
> momentarily experienced my help . . . and "drained it away like
> sand." (p. 25)

Joseph has again described just what Abraham described: the part object is a possession that can be controlled and manipulated. One can totally identify with it because it serves as a defense against separateness, that is, against intrapsychic and interpersonal differentiation. Such total identification with a part object allows one to defend against the differentiating function of interpretation: all insight is one's own; there is no need for another. As we saw with Abraham, even in oral terms the part object is a fetishistic formation. It repudiates the self-preservative–libidinal registration of care. There is peremptory insistence on primary wish fulfillment and primary defense (immediate repudiation of any tension-raising registration). Interpretations can be drained away like sand—or even like feces or urine, provided that one understands the "excretion" of a raised tension state.

As Joseph says, patients who repeat such patterns in their lives are motivated by a need to avoid an anxiety that is "very apparent in their constant unconscious attempts to avoid any really close relationships with significant figures in their *environment* . . . these repetition-compulsion patients *suffer more from closeness than from loneliness*" (pp. 28–29; my emphases). Joseph has intuitively understood that environment implies relation through differentiation. Thus, any integration with environment ("closeness") becomes enormously anxiety provoking. Joseph's example here is very much like the example of the concrete patient from Chapter 3, for whom withdrawal and isolation were relief. Where internalization anxiety dominates, the patient is more afraid of contact than loss.

Joseph's grasp of her patient's repudiation of analytic help logically leads her to Freud's formulations from *Beyond the Pleasure Principle*:

> Freud postulated that the repetition compulsion was a manifestation of the death instinct at work, describing the death instinct as tending towards the reinstatement of a previous state of existence, in the final issue to an inorganic state. . . . I feel that these [repetition compulsion] patients do feel most free from anxiety when they can become near to inorganic—that is, free of emotions. . . . In any case, conflict is constantly introduced, as Freud showed, by the life instinct. It manifests itself in a need to love and be dependent, and in the need for relationships with desirable and significant people, of whom the analyst is the prime and most disturbing current representative. *Each time these carriers of the life instinct disturb the patient's peace, a situation akin to trauma arises, and they react in a way which seems aimed at restoring their quasi-inorganic state.* . . . (p. 32; my emphasis)

Joseph grasps that the analytic environment, particularly the analyst's interpretive function, embodies the tension of Eros. The ineluctably repetitive encounter with this environment is defended against as if it were a trauma. While Freud's notion of a literal return to an inorganic state is itself somewhat concrete, Joseph understands that the patient regresses to less differentiated part object relations, because in fantasy part objects are "inorganic" possessions. In other words, fetishistic ("inorganic") compromises are intensified.

Here there is the possibility of a rigorous integration of Klein and Loewald. Loewald knew that defense itself always creates a less differentiated internal and external reality but did not consider that integration itself could be anxiety provoking. Joseph in this passage has clearly grasped that there are patients for whom interpretation repeats the trauma of Eros. She herself, however, does not grasp what Loewald, and eventually Gray in his own way, will explain: identification with a "good" analytic object is itself as magical-narcissistic as are part object fantasies. The "good, whole, intact" breast is no less fetishistic than its part object complement. In Busch's clinical example, too, there was a failure to see that contact with an "intact" phallic replacement was a concrete resistance against interpretation.

The "good, whole, intact" breast is the Kleinian version of unquestioned objectivism. This objectivism will prevent Joseph from integrating her earlier work on the repetition compulsion and the trauma of Eros with her important later work on surface-and-defense analysis. Very much like Gray, Joseph shows how many patients "live out" defense and fantasy on the surface of the transference. Her theory of effective analytic work is based on the analyst's ability to grasp subtle, moment-to-moment shifts in defense. But in the end, Joseph will still rely upon identification with a good, "whole" analyst in order to modify paranoid-schizoid splitting. As we saw in Chapter 4, Klein did not grasp the problem in her theory of the depressive position and did not see that it perpetuated "cure" by identification. Neither does Joseph.

In 1976 Joseph delivered a paper on psychic pain in which the theme of differentiation is placed in the clinical context of close process monitoring. She speaks of patients who in their lives and in the transference need relationships in which "distance, difference, separations were wiped out as far as possible" (p. 92). The pain such people suffer as treatment begins to affect them is "more unknown, more raw . . . , more connected with the emerging into a live world. Retreat from it involves . . . destruction of progress or of the self, or an attempt to return to an undifferentiated state, as if inside the object" (pp. 93–94). Right here Joseph would have had every reason to refer back to her discussion of the trauma of Eros. The patients who cannot tolerate distance can no more internalize the tension-raising "impression of the object" than can the patients who cannot tolerate closeness. Both repudiate differentiation. Although she does not make the connection to her previous thinking, Joseph does see that the overwhelming, "unknown" nature of the pain of differentiation should make the analyst cautious about the way he or she interprets:

If one assumes knowledge as to its content prematurely, I suspect that one helps a patient to harden up again. There is an additional technical point; that is, I think one cannot help patients to break out of the old methods of operating and emerge to the experiencing of this type of psychic reality and the beginnings of suffering pain and get through it, except by following minute movements of emergence and retreat, experiencing and avoiding within the transference. (p. 96)

Joseph's great contribution is to think about how to intervene in non-content terms in order to modify the "primal" defenses of such patients. She sees that "following minute movements of emergence and retreat . . . in the transference" is an alternative to content interpretations. Here is a close process monitoring that, like Gray's, requires a fine-grained focus on the surface. It goes beyond neurosis and is aware of the analyst's temptation to lapse into the kind of intervention that would foreclose the patient's acute anxiety. Joseph asserts that this kind of psychic pain is "on the border between mental and physical, between shut-in-ness and emergence, between anxieties felt in terms of fragmentation and persecution and the beginnings of suffering, integration, and concern" (p. 97). To delineate "border" pain shows an intuitive grasp of internalization anxiety, a pain on the border between "fragmentation" and "integration and concern."

In Joseph's own conception, integration itself is a question of differentiation: the patients "wipe out" "distance, difference, separation." Is "fragmentation" the "other side" of integration? If so, the implication is that integration equals "wholeness." It is more difficult theoretically and clinically to conceive integration-as-differentiation (Loewald's *conscire*) than as wholeness. The anxieties of which Joseph speaks cannot simply be fear of "fragmentation" but rather "raw" panic in the face of intrapsychic-interpersonal division (differentiation, distance). Such division is the possibility not only for literal separation from the object but also for enough internal "separation" to sustain the observing ego. This function itself derives from Eros or *conscire*: it sustains differentiated contact with one's intrapsychic processes.

But Joseph does not examine defenses that operate against self-observation, a point also made by Schafer (1994) in his excellent ap-

preciation of the group of Kleinians most influenced by Joseph. Schafer was struck by the emphasis on surface-and-defense analysis shared
by contemporary ego psychological and Kleinian practice. But he
criticizes Joseph for having "no well developed theoretical provision
for what standard Freudians call the observing ego" (p. 427). Schafer
himself seems to assume a conventional theory of the observing ego.
His point, however, is that not even to consider the question is to risk
sliding back into the kind of concreteness Joseph so subtly argues
against. Schafer writes:

> . . . the Kleinians . . . speak comfortably about attacks on the
> ego, the self, even the mind, in a way that refers in part to actual
> functional disturbance and in part to unconscious fantasies of the
> ego, self, or mind being a substance that can be ejected, spoiled,
> or broken into pieces. The concretistic fantasy of mind is not
> foreign to any analyst who works on primitive levels of function,
> but fantasy is not systematic theory, and primitive dynamics
> cannot account adequately for secondary process communication
> and organization. (pp. 427–28)

The assumption in this passage is that secondary process belongs to
consciousness, to the synthesizing function as usually understood in
ego psychological terms. Schafer no more conceives of "unconscious
secondary process" or of "originally unconscious thought" than does
Joseph. He has echoed the familiar argument against the Kleinians:
they make their patients' fantasies about mind into a theory of mind
that inevitably conflates fantasy and reality.

The way out of this dilemma is to synthesize Joseph's early remarks about the trauma of Eros with her understanding of the primal anxieties of patients on the border of "shut-in-ness and emergence." Unconscious traumatization by difference is then defended
against by concrete fantasies of mind as a manipulable "inorganic"
substance. Joseph is right that content interpretations would "harden
up" such patients but for a reason she does not quite grasp: if the analyst interprets content when the patient defends against process,
then the analyst, as Schafer says, operates from a concrete position. To
equate integration with wholeness is as much a product of a "con-

cretistic fantasy of mind" as the assumption that mental processes can be actually fragmented.

Joseph shares with Gray the conviction that ego's initiation of defense in response to anxiety is the primary concern of analysis. In 1977 she wrote: "I think that technically we listen to what our patients are telling us in the sessions in terms not of 'what does this mean?' but 'what is the main anxiety here?' And we start from the belief that the immediacy of the transference situation will keep us in contact with the most important anxieties" (p. 106). It is daring for an analyst, particularly a Kleinian, to go beyond listening for "meaning." Once one is listening for the main anxiety in the transference, Kleinian theory has a certain advantage. Projective identification always implies an attempt to compel the recipient to act in accordance with the projections. For Joseph, if the analyst attends to the entire emotional climate created by the patient in the session, and not just to meaning, the analyst will be able to interpret the patient's attempts to compel him or her to act in accordance with split-off fantasies. In this global sense, as Joseph elegantly says, the patient uses the analyst "to stand rather than understand" anxiety (p. 108).

Joseph's innovation is to attempt to describe the picture of the analyst created via projective identification. She says that to describe such a picture avoids premature interpretation of what the analyst presumes is "objectively" inside the patient. Moreover, such pictures often contain a globally projected perception of the analyst's negative feelings about his or her own work. Joseph frequently refers to the "awful" feeling created in the session when the analyst makes useless interpretations. In order to avoid such "awful," useless interpretation, she advocates close attention to the analyst's wish not to attend to certain aspects of the patient's material:

> I am . . . attempting to indicate . . . primitive concrete types of
> defences which it seems very important to recognize in the
> transference. And they raise, as I suggested, important technical
> issues. Thus I indicated in the case [of a patient who has been
> verbally sadistic to his wife] how one might have seen his anxiety
> in terms, for example, of his guilt about his nastiness to his wife;
> in the face of the pressure in the transference, which begged for

such an interpretation, this would have been more comfortable [relieving] for the analyst to interpret, but would, to my mind, have been not only an acting out in the transference on the part of the analyst, but *ipso facto* on the wrong level. . . . I think that our understanding of the nature and the level of anxiety is interlinked, and depends, in large part, on our correct assessment of the use that the patient is making of us. My impression is that frequently the guide in the transference, as to where the most important anxiety is, lies in an awareness that, in some part of oneself, one can feel an area in the patient's communications that one wishes not to attend to—internally in terms of the effect on oneself, externally in terms of what and how one might interpret. (p. 111)

Joseph is using important affective terms to explain why the analyst might make the most relieving interpretation. When the patient employs global defenses to use the analyst to "stand, rather than understand" anxiety, the analyst will feel uncomfortably affected by what the patient is doing. As in any traumatic situation, the analyst will attempt to repudiate registration of the discomfort and will find himself or herself perplexed about what to say to the patient. The temptation is to match the patient's words to a preferred theory in order to feel more "comfortable." To avoid such countertransference enactment, Joseph advocates paying close attention to one's disturbance and using it to understand the patient's picture of the analyst. In playing back the patient's projected picture, the analyst articulates unstated transference configurations and does not attempt to control the patient. This kind of intervention begins the process of analyzing the global use of defense. It brings into focus the frame of reference —the defensive counter-surface—created by conflating fantasy and reality in the very act of speaking to the analyst.

Joseph's theory of therapeutic change integrates Gray's sense that surface-and-defense analysis reduces the potential for anxiety with Klein's overall theory of "phantasy":

I have been describing how we can see the phantasy nature of mental mechanisms . . . being enacted in the session; how the

> patient unconsciously attempts to use the analyst as part of his
> defensive system, attaching his phantasies to him; and how we
> can see conflicts and defences shifting in the session as these
> phantasies are analysed. Indeed, I doubt if we can achieve real
> change in our patients' defensive organizations, unless both they
> and we can experience the defences and phantasies as they are
> being lived in the analytic situation. (p. 123)

In the largest sense, to "live out" one's defensive system is to use the
analyst as a fetish. As in any fetishistic formation, wish-fulfilling perceptual identification is used to reduce the anxiety of integration
with environmental reality. Joseph has eloquently described this process in terms of projective identification. She offers important technical refinements, both in terms of the analyst's inner reactions and
methods of intervention. But just as she does not consider the question of the observing ego, she at no point asks herself what the "reality" of the analytic situation must be if the patient can globally replace
it with defensive fantasy. In her paper on the repetition compulsion
she described the analyst as the "prime and most disturbing current
representative" of the "life instinct." The analyst's neutrality and interpretive stance function as a disturbance "akin to a trauma" (p. 32).
Joseph does not conceptualize that within the hypercathected picture
of the analyst there is also a repudiated registration of the analytic
environment.

This problem is very clear in one of Joseph's major clinical examples. She recounts a series of sessions with a man who has made significant progress in his analysis but who is now worried about sex
with his new wife. He speaks in a way that conveys "hopelessness and
despair" (p. 175). Joseph uses this material first to illustrate the com-
plexity of the analyst's affective response. This is one of the sessions
that first feels "awful," because analyst and patient momentarily enact
a futile exchange of lifeless interpretations. Joseph then acutely interprets that the patient is encouraging her to "make false interpretations and to pick up his pseudo-interpretations as if I believed them"
(ibid.). The patient is creating a picture of her as having to reassure
herself that "interpretations, now empty of meaning and hollow, were
meaningful" (p. 176). Joseph says that this intervention helped the

patient to speak about his fear of the analyst's wanting to "cheat" by avoiding the reality of his despair and by offering him false encouragement. The affective tone of the session changes as the patient voices these concerns. Articulation of the picture of the analyst produces a shift in the material. In Busch's example, he, too, commented on the "edge" in his patient's voice in order to help the patient articulate his wish not to understand.

In the next session, Joseph's patient brings in a dream of being on a boat in the mist; without fear, he steps onto another boat that is going down. His associations contain a reference to an "excellent" but "too strong"–tasting steak and kidney pudding his wife had made, knowing his fondness for the dish. Joseph's overall sense of the material is that her "strong" and "tasty" interpretations of the day before had produced depressive position integration to which the patient responds anxiously. He gets off the "boat" of the analysis and masochistically drowns on his own. The analyst is again rendered impotent— she can only watch him drown. This is a paranoid-schizoid moment in which self-destruction equals an attack on the object. In my terms, the patient is threatened by the integration of self-preservation and libido momentarily achieved in the processive work of the day before. As the patient repudiates internalization in response to the tension of integration, dedifferentiating aggression is heightened. As Joseph says, he tries to "attack me and our work, by trying to drag me down in despair, when there was actually progress" (p. 177).

That patient and analyst are to go down together illustrates something fundamental about projective identification. Joseph writes: "At the very primitive end of projective identification is the attempt to get back into an object—to become, as it were, undifferentiated and mindless and thus avoid all pain" (p. 178). Once again, Joseph describes a retreat from effective processive work due to the pain of differentiation. The trauma of Eros precipitates internalization anxiety. The destructiveness of getting inside a dedifferentiated totality feels like a preferable alternative. Dynamically, however, Joseph thinks that the problem is that the patient has been given too much of a good thing—excellent, tasty interpretations that are too strong. Why does not Joseph take this as another picture of herself that the patient wants to live out?

She says that her patient moved back and forth between the paranoid-schizoid and depressive positions when there was

> movement, in the transference, towards more genuine whole object relations. At times he can really appreciate the strong containing qualities of his object; true, he will then try to draw me in and drag me down again, but there is now potential conflict about this. . . . As his loving is freed, *he is able to introject and identify with a whole valued and potent object, and the effect on his character and potency is striking.* This is a very different quality of identification from that based on forcing a despairing part of the self into an object, who then in his phantasy becomes like a despairing part of himself. (p. 179; my emphasis)

For Joseph, there is here no defensive "forcing" of the analyst to think that her "genuine, good, whole" aspects are the counterparts of her "false, bad, part object" aspects. In other words, Joseph does not apply a processive approach to material that matches her (Kleinian) conviction about cure by identification with the intact breast. She has no conception of fetishistic alternation between fantasies of the good and the bad, which themselves replace the processive reality of the pain of differentiation.

Busch's concrete patient predictably had fetishistic practices, and so does Joseph's. The patient first "came to analysis because he had a fetish, a tremendous pull toward getting inside a rubber object which would totally cover, absorb, and excite him" (p. 178). For Joseph, of course, this particular kind of fetishism illustrates what she calls the "primitive end of projective identification": the inorganic part object in which one can embed oneself in a way that globally reduces tension. But again, why would not an increase in the patient's potency due to introjection of a "whole and valued potent object" also be a use of the analyst as a fetish? The answer is that Joseph has no conception of reality that would include her astute description of the pain of differentiation. As in Klein, reality is objectively whole. Therefore, the "real analyst" is also whole. Psychic equilibrium is maintained by the part object fantasy-defense system that creates a less differentiated organization, but psychic change is a question of "experience" with a "whole, different, and properly separate person" (p. 179). Joseph does not notice that there might be a contradiction between the ideas of wholeness and difference.

This is an instance of the ineluctable progression from unquestioned categories of wholeness and realness to a cure by identification with a good object. Joseph is an important example of this progression, because her clinical descriptions, and some of her theory, provide a possible way out of this unquestioning repetition. Her excellent grasp of the subtleties of surface-and-defense analysis could have led to a theory in which the picture of the analyst as either a "bad" part object or a "good" whole object is a defensive counter-surface. But where "objective experience" with a whole object is thought to be the vehicle of therapeutic change, there is no need to analyze resistance to integration with a differentiating environment and no need to address identification as a defense against internalization.

Gray's work was extended by Busch, who described but did not understand why the close process approach requires a reconceptualization of surface. Joseph's work has been extended by Michael Feldman with similar results. In a recent article he began by citing Fairbairn, who wrote: "psychoanalytical treatment resolves itself into a struggle on the part of the patient to press-gang his relationship with the analyst into the closed system of the inner world through the agency of transference" (p. 385). A Kleinian does not usually cite Fairbairn, who famously rejected Klein's conception of early object relations. The significance of the citation is that whether one thinks of Freud on inertia versus raised tension levels, of Ferenczi on narcissistic or non-narcissistic reality organizations, of Loewald on closed and open systems, of Joseph on equilibrium and change, or even of Fairbairn as cited here by Feldman, it is clear that analysts of different persuasions most generally conceive treatment as the opening of a defensively "closed" organization. Feldman integrates Joseph's idea that projective identification is used to "live out" fantasy and defense with this conception. My thesis is that the surface itself is the opening intrinsic to the entire analytic environment. The repudiation of opening by fetishistic transferences, with their closed structure of opposed fantasies, becomes the most general form of compromise formation. Feldman will describe such formations wonderfully, but because he, too, will construe what he describes only in terms of projective identification, he will not be able to theorize it.

Feldman makes his point right away: "the projection of elements of a phantasied object relationship represents an attempt by the patient to *reduce the discrepancy* between an archaic object relationship and an alternative object relationship that might be confronting the patient and threatening him" (p. 228; my emphasis). Threatening discrepancy is the trauma of differentiation. Transference most globally functions as resistance precisely by repudiating any alternative, new, or strange object relationship. Feldman does not examine the metapsychological status of the threatening discrepancy or wonder why fantasies can be "lived out" as defense against it. Nevertheless, he describes the clinical problem in terms of concreteness. He says that projective identification is used to create "unconscious belief in the effectiveness of a concrete process" (p. 230). Conviction about the perceived reality of projected fantasies repudiates the tension of differentiated integration. This, too, Feldman describes: "it is not difficult to see the advantages of projection into a hallucinatory, delusional . . . object. Since it is an omnipotent process, there is no doubt about the object's receptivity, and the consequent transformation. . . . *The patient is not confronted with the contrast between phantasy and reality, which is disturbing, nor the differences between himself and his object*" (p. 231; my emphasis).

Feldman questions the Kleinian assumption that concrete projection of fantasy is motivated by envy. Both Abraham and Klein spoke about the envious aspects of narcissistic resistance to interpretation—the primary drive to destroy what is good or helpful. To make such envy primary is theoretically and clinically dangerous, since it does not question the idealization of the envied object. "Primary envy" has all the theological overtones of "original sin" and redemption through the acceptance of the idealized mother (Klein) or father (Abraham). Feldman puts his finger right on the difficulty:

> We sometimes assume that it is only the operation of the patient's envy that militates against [relief gained through analytic understanding]. However, it often seems that there is a different drive in operation, namely the pressure toward identity, which

seems paradoxical and difficult to reconcile with the longing for
a better, more constructive experience. It is as if the patient
requires the analyst's experience or behaviour to correspond in
some measure to his unconscious phantasy, and is unable to
tolerate or make use of any discrepancy. . . . The lack of this
identity between the internal and external reality may not only
stir up envy, or doubts about the object's receptivity, but create
an alarming space in which thought and new knowledge and
understanding might take place, but which many patients find
intolerable. (p. 232)

The "pressure towards identity" describes the use of wish-fulfilling
perceptual identity in waking life. It also describes the dedifferentiating
repetition compulsion, which compels action. In Freud's view, such
action was evidence of the conflict between Eros and death. Feldman
uses similar economic terms when he speaks of reduction of the tension of "discrepancy": because the difference between reality and fantasy implicit in interpretation may be intolerable, there is a "drive" to
make the experience of the analysis conform to a fantasy system. The
"alarming space in which thought and new knowledge . . . might take
place" interferes with omnipotent creation of correspondence between
fantasy and reality. Feldman does not refer to Joseph's idea of the "raw"
anxieties of differentiation, but his "alarming space" describes the same
phenomenon. The "alarming space" is also, in Alvarez de Toledo's
terms, the "uncontrollable unknown" of the analyst's neutrality. Resistance to internalization of the "uncontrollable unknown" is what produces the "collapse" of the observing ego.

Enlarging Joseph's conception of the resistance to psychic change,
Feldman takes the conflict between space and identity as the crux of
therapeutic efficacy:

The difficult and often painful task for the analyst is to recognize
the subtle and complex enactment he is inevitably drawn into
with his patient, and to work to find a domain for understanding
and thought *outside the narrow and repetitive confines unconsciously
demanded by the patient.* . . . While the achievement of real psychic
change is dependent on this process, it is threatening for the

patient and liable to mobilize further defensive procedures.
(p. 236; my emphasis)

Feldman offers an extended clinical example of a patient who hears about another therapist who has seduced a patient. The patient reports that she thought about Feldman and about her analysis when she received the information. Here we have Gray's situation of something external to the analysis' being registered along with the analytic process. The clinical question then is less one of the literal content (seduction) than of the way in which the patient brings the content into the session. Feldman approaches the material in just this processive way. Like Joseph, he is highly attuned to the emotional climate the patient creates as she speaks. This climate best indicates the "pressure towards identity" with the picture of the analyst created by projective identification. In this particular case, the way in which Feldman's patient spoke about the other therapist's abuse of his patient was "compulsively driven to involve me in interactions in which she either experienced a tantalizing, ominous withholding or exciting demanding sexual intrusion" (p. 238). Here again we predictably find a fetishistic transference: oscillation between opposed fantasies taken as reality. The two-fantasy structure globally defends against the possibility of interpretation as differentiation. The patient tells Feldman "that normally her main concern was to avoid saying things if she could foresee some sort of opening she might give me, so she has to make sure this doesn't occur" (ibid.). Feldman comments that whether he is tantalizingly withholding or excitingly intrusive, the patient is actually reassured. She maintains her conviction that "what is enacted in the external world corresponds in some measure with an object relationship that is unconsciously present [in the transference]. The alternative, when she is confronted with the discrepancy between the two, is painful and threatening" (p. 239). This is internalization anxiety.

Thus Feldman delineates the way in which projective identification and enactment can interfere with the opening of the space of interpretation. But then he stops. There is no reflection on why the patient's registration of space creates an alarm greater than anxieties over "withholding" or "intrusiveness." As in Busch's ego psychological expansion of surface-and-defense analysis, Feldman describes fetishistic transference against the space of interpretation but does not grasp the implications of what he describes so well. Busch and Feldman do not question the presuppositions of their respective commitments: the Anna Freud tradition of ego analysis, extended by Gray to a more sophisticated view of surface and defense; the Melanie Klein tradition of analysis of projective identification, extended by Joseph to a more sophisticated view of surface and defense. The idea that one would look to Freud's theory of fetishism, and to the defenses of disavowal and splitting, to explain fetishistic transferences occurs to neither.

However, the remarkable consonance of these clinical descriptions demonstrates the necessary integration of dynamic theories that agree on two basic principles: first, that the overall question of analytic therapy is the opening of a closed system, and second, that the most effective way to achieve this end is through surface-and-defense analysis. Freud's earliest conception of the inertia created by primary wish fulfillment and defense, his own move toward surface-and-defense analysis, his conception of action in terms of dedifferentiating repetition, and his final attempt to generalize disavowal and ego splitting all provide the groundwork for such an integration of theory and technique. Freud, of course, did not notice any conflict between most of these ideas and his general theory of mind. Only at the very end of his life, as he began to expand his conception of fetishism, did he even begin to question the centrality of repression. Nor did Freud have any general conception of the analytic environment as the most general question of surface. Such a conception has not been developed by the rigorous practitioners who maintain the classical framework, with increasing emphasis on surface-and-defense analysis. But just as Freud glimpsed the necessity of rethinking substitute formations in terms of disavowal and ego splitting, so contemporary classical practice focuses more and more on the resistance to interpretation itself. Both trends depend upon the rethinking of reality as differentiating process.

Afterword

In "Psychoanalysis in Search of Nature" (1988a) Loewald called the objectivist view of reality *natura naturata*. This model of nature informed all of Freud's initial discoveries. Loewald argued that no matter what Freud's presuppositions about reality and nature were, the "discovery" of the unconscious had to transform them. In order to move beyond a questionable objectivism, Loewald thought that psychoanalysis needed a view of nature as process, *natura naturans*. Conceived processively, the unconscious and nature share dynamic properties. Thus, Loewald emphasized unconscious integration with what he called "unconscious aspects of reality." However, he did not exactly say what he meant by this phrase. The generalization of fetishism demonstrates that Loewald's "nature as process" is "nature as differentiating process."

"Nature as differentiating process" in turn changes the basic model of the unconscious. The repression model of the unconscious and the interpretive technique that was its result presume the existence of *objectifiable* unconscious content. In this model, the unconscious is a place or a structure characterized exclusively by primary process, tension reduction, and timelessness. It is buried in the depths. As process, each of these characteristics becomes questionable. The "unconscious" is the possibility of nonconscious registration of differentiation—Freud's "unconscious time" and "unconscious thought." These are the manifestations of primary narcissism and Eros, of primal care and concern.

They are the possibility of unconscious memory (the trace of the experience of satisfaction). Loewald and Winnicott both understood the importance of primary narcissism and added to Freudian theory conceptions of integration with environment. However, neither saw that as a differentiating process registration of care necessarily raises tension levels and can verge on the traumatic.

Freud was right that mind has an intrinsic tendency to use primary wish fulfillment and primary defense to eliminate registration of trauma. He simply assumed, however, that repudiated trauma becomes unconscious content. He could not see that when he began to think about disavowal as the basis of defensive process, he would also have to move to a processive view of reality and of analytic treatment. The conundrum built into the original theory and technique—that interpretation backfires with a large group of apparently analyzable patients—can be resolved without modification of the classical framework. The possibility of interpetation calls for a metapsychology of the "alarming space" (Feldman) or of the "uncontrollable unknown" (Alvarez de Toledo) embodied by the differentiating reality of the analytic environment. The patients who most strenuously resist interpretation are the patients who teach us that there is a surface unconscious registration of this processive reality and a complex defensive response to it.

The general characteristic of this defensive response is the global projection of a dedifferentiated reality organization, constructed by primary wish fulfillment as primary defense. Within such substitute formations, repudiated difference is replaced by fantasy oppositions of perceivable presence and absence. Presence is generally idealized and relieving, while absence is "bad," persecutory, threatening. The threat of the loss of an idealized presence is the foundation of depressive or castration anxiety. When such a threat is taken as reality, objectified fantasy replaces processive reality. Concrete patients reveal a general characteristic of all patients, just as fetishism reveals the general structure of compromise formation. Integration with the analytic environment ("contact") inevitably repeats the "trauma of Eros." At such points, loss of the idealized object is taken as a reality (the "reality of castration," the "good, whole, real" object) in order to ward off what appears to be a chaotic loss of control if difference is no longer

repudiated. Depressive or castration anxiety oscillates with internalization anxiety. It is a basic unconscious process that primary narcissism oscillates with secondary narcissism, internalization with identification, Eros with the death drive.

Dreams remain central to this theory of defense, psychopathology,
and treatment. But they are key for the way in which they demonstrate the domination of consciousness by primary process, a domination that produces the reality effect of perception ("seeing is believing"). The elimination of the difference between memory and
perception in dreams is the basic structure of concreteness, which itself makes fetishistic compromise formations possible. The patients
who globally resist interpretation demonstrate that unconscious, surface registration of differentiating process always occurs and that the
dream mechanisms of temporal immediacy and perceptual identity
can globally defend against it. To the extent that any patient takes the
loss of an idealized presence as a signal of danger—for example, castration anxiety in neurosis—there is a fetishistic structure that will at
some point enter the transference as resistance to interpretation, in
other words, as primary defense against internalization of the analytic process.

The clinical consequence is that content interpretations that "make
the unconscious conscious" in the objectivist mode can perpetuate the
global repudiation of "unconscious secondary process." Loewald spoke
of interventions whose aim is not to make unconscious content conscious but to modify unconscious ego processes that maintain splitting.
Primary splitting must be considered in a revised sense. As Freud said,
it is the splitting of reality and fantasy. However, on the always active
primary level, it is the splitting of Loewald's primary reality and fantasy. Freud's idea of a stimulus barrier directed against unconscious
time is a good example of this process. Once primary reality is split
from fantasy, the mechanisms of wish fulfillment can enter consciousness in order to keep disruptive primary reality unconscious. Analytic
intervention in this domain aims at redifferentiation of perception and
memory, past and present, in order to reverse the effects of primary
disavowal.

Frequently, such interventions are directed to surface resistance to
integration with the analytic environment. What is on the surface of

the patient's mind in concrete or fetishistic situations is in fact an unconscious counter-surface used as a kind of stimulus barrier to protect against the threat of differentiation. Splitting of libido from self-
preservation is intrinsic to such primal defenses, with two results. The
patient's defensive counter-surface is an autoerotic formation, and aggression is enhanced. Processive interventions make this aggression
more conscious and finally bring near-traumatic internalization anxiety into the session, as libido and self-preservation are reintegrated.

Analysis of the overtly concrete patient is so difficult because the
analyst has to be ready to have his or her own assumptions about reality and interpretation questioned. The analyst cannot share the patient's view that "seeing is believing" and remain on a different level
of organization. Once the analyst has grasped that the surface is unconscious, he or she has to adopt a very subtle but simple approach.
This approach, in line with some of Gray's and Joseph's ideas, makes
conscious the process of defense that produces primary splitting in
the session. But the analyst has to expect a prolonged encounter with
intense aggression and anxiety when such interventions are effective.
However, if the analyst can go through a difficult change in his or her
own thinking, analysis remains the treatment of choice for concrete
patients, and, of course, the moments of concreteness in all patients
become understandable and treatable.

It took Freud his entire career to begin to question the primacy of
repression, the exclusive dominance of tension reduction in the unconscious, and the equation of reality testing with perception. He also
knew that there was something about fetishism that demanded rethinking the relations between the unconscious and reality and the
bases of defense. However, he did not integrate these major revisions
begun at the end of his life. Nor did he even begin to consider how
these revisions of the theory of mind in nature would have to modify
the basic theory of technique. Laplanche and Pontalis's idea that disavowal bears on the foundation of reality is the key to integrating what
is best in the Freudian traditions—both ego psychological and Kleinian—with a theory of the unconscious registration and repudiation of
a processive reality.

All the theorists who share a commitment to maintenance of the
"classical" frame of analysis, eventually have to come up against the

problem of resistance to interpretation. Many have valuably contributed to understanding it. However, they have not always understood that they were testing the limits of their own presuppositions. Loewald is to some extent the exception. As he made clear early in his writings, the presumption of a static objectivity has produced some of the most questionable theories and practices of classical psychoanalysis. If the dynamics of fetishism not only explain concreteness but are also the generalizable model of compromise formation, then the psychoanalytic view of mind and nature has to move beyond the presumed objectivity of the closed system. This move would have to include understanding why the subjectivist, experiential approach to analytic theory and practice is the counterpart of traditional objectivism and inherently leaves it in place. To abandon the interpretive stance and neutrality is to abandon the major therapeutic function of the analytic frame: integration with a differentiating environment. Neutrality itself is a manifestation of processive primary reality. This is why neutrality is never a once-and-for-all achievement but demands continuous effort on the analyst's part. As a function of an open system, neutrality internalizes the raised tension levels of unconscious thought, unconscious time, and binding: Eros as vital difference. Neutral maintenance of the analytic frame can only occur when the analyst is aware of the inevitable tendency to repudiate it, precisely because it does raise tension levels. Neutrality provokes internalization anxiety in the analyst as well as in the patient. Primary disavowal is an always active force on both sides of the couch and in the construction of analytic theories. But it is also an essential resource. Analysis of it, in the countertransference, in theory construction, and in clinical manifestations of concreteness, moves psychoanalysis toward integration with differentiating processes and toward a greater scientificity.

REFERENCE MATTER

Introduction

1. For an excellent survey of the challenges to "classical interpretation," including contemporary developments, see Pancheri (1998).

2. Winnicott, however, was among the first to advocate specific attention to environmental factors in all analyses; see in particular "Metapsychological and Clinical Aspects of Regression" (in 1975). His overall therapeutic practice certainly contained many modifications of the basic format. These modifications influenced his understanding of the function of the traditional framework, which he maintained specifically for psychoanalytic treatment.

Concreteness and Fetishism

1. Although he does not include Jacobson's article, Brown otherwise has an excellent survey of the literature on concreteness. Since I do not pretend to a thorough literature survey but am carefully choosing certain concepts in order to develop my later arguments, I refer the interested reader to Brown's comprehensive (as of 1985) bibliography.

2. Freud had actually already discussed this issue in terms of the early theory that anxiety is libido transformed by repression. In the *Three Essays on the Theory of Sexuality* (1905b), Freud wrote: "Children themselves behave from an early age as though their dependence on the people looking after them were in the nature of sexual love. Anxiety in children is originally nothing other than an expression of the fact that they are feeling the *loss* of the person they love. . . . They are afraid in the dark because in the dark they cannot *see* the person they love . . . " (p. 224; my emphases). Freud appends an anecdotal footnote to this passage that speaks directly to my point: "For the explanation of the origin of infantile anxiety I have to thank a three-year-old boy whom I once heard calling out of a dark room: 'Auntie, speak to me! I'm frightened because it's so dark.' His aunt answered him: 'What good would that do? You

can't see me.' 'That doesn't matter,' replied the child, 'if anyone speaks, it gets light.' Thus what he was afraid of was not the dark, but the absence of someone he loved; and he could feel sure of being soothed as soon as he had evidence of that person's presence" (p. 224, n.1). One can read this anecdote as the child's saying, when you do something that brings you into consciousness, i.e., when you speak, although I cannot literally see you, it is as if I were using my visual apparatus in the "light." In other words, the child "knows" that there is a state of consciousness that overrides reality testing, so that he can attempt to use the perceptual apparatus to regulate the tension of distance. Therefore, it is not exactly the absence of someone he loves that the child fears. He knows perfectly well that she is there or he would not call out to her. It is rather that the child resists internalization of the possibility of distance—difference in space —and conflates it with an absence that can be remediated by an illusion of visible presence.

3. Recall Renik's (1992) statement that the "use of the analyst as a fetish" implies "an "unusual degree of conviction about the reality of a reassuring idea" (p. 545).

4. "Denial" was the initial translation of Freud's *Verleugnung*, which Strachey more felicitously rendered as "disavowal" in the *Standard Edition*. Jacobson, for example, discusses concreteness and fetishism in "Denial and Repression." The conceptual point is that Jacobson's discussion explicitly understands concreteness in terms of disavowal and specifically contrasts disavowal with repression. Recall Frosch's use of disavowal to describe his patient's concrete stance that she understood the "reality" of the analytic situation, with its focus on transference, but simultaneously was convinced that she must not discuss her fantasies because of the effect on the analyst.

5. While there is a clear masculine bias in the expression "primitive dread of woman," it does help to explain why Freud would so consistently use a phrase like "fact of castration." As he says, expanding his thoughts about the inherent strangeness of minor differences, "It would be tempting to pursue this idea and to derive from this 'narcissism of minor differences' the hostility which in every human relation we see fighting successfully against feelings of fellowship. . . . Psychoanalysis believes that it has discovered a large part of what underlies the narcissistic rejection of women by men . . . in drawing attention to the castration complex . . . " (1918b, p. 199). Freud could not take this argument one step

farther and say that, because difference is a potential narcissistic threat, it always tends to be treated as a potential trauma and therefore will tend to be both registered and repudiated, primally disavowed. A repudiated difference is always replaced by an opposition between an idealized presence and its threatening absence. However, Freud here does open the possibility of understanding why femininity as difference is such a frequent figure of that which tends to be primally repudiated. Near the end of his life, he again speaks of the "repudiation of femininity" common to both sexes, as manifested by the "bedrock" penis envy of women and castration anxiety of men (1937a, pp. 250–52). One can reinterpret him to have stumbled upon the concrete conflation of reality and fantasy common to men and women which is always the result of the repudiation of difference. Perhaps Freud called it "bedrock" because he could not quite understand the way in which his theory of fetishism, based on the primary disavowal of sexual difference, provided a dynamic explanation of this supposedly "unanalyzable" "biological fact." Thus, the undoubted misogyny of the phrase "fact of castration" would also have to be understood as a form of theoretical "concreteness." I will pursue these ideas in relation to the theory of narcissism in Chapter 2.

6. Silverman (1996) provides a compelling illustration of these dynamics, although the intent of her description is quite different from mine. Writing in order to show the limitations of a polarized opposition between a "one person" ("classical Freudian") and a "two person" ("contemporary constructivist") psychology, Silverman presents the case of a woman who responded less to the content of her interpretations than to the way in which they were phrased. Anything outside the patient's preferred modes of communications "would affect her shaky equilibrium" (p. 256). Overall, the patient "felt comfortable in merged experiences, and had difficulty tolerating differences. . . . Differences, she insisted, were unacceptable. She worked exceedingly hard and quite convincingly to eliminate them" (pp. 256–57). Silverman notes that the patient "focused on ways to alter my responses consistent with what she believed were essential to achieving a state of equilibrium. . . . The patient's unconscious fantasy was that what was curative was the achievement of unity without difference" (p. 261).

7. To link secondary process with Eros creates a paradox to which I will return repeatedly: it implies an "unconscious" secondary process, an apparent contradiction in terms.

8. A clinical example in Bach (1985) illustrates these points. A patient subject to what Bach calls "the illusion of living in endless narcissistic time" was in the terminal phase of his analysis. Although consciously aware of the agreed upon termination date, he "both did and did not believe that it would really happen," which Bach tangentially links to Freud's ideas about the splitting of the ego in fetishism (p. 187). The patient became preoccupied with the difference between digital and analog time, associating them to the basic paradox that one lives both in each present moment and in a flow of time with a past and a future. He says: "'How to live in the moment, yet live in the flux of time; how to be separate from the world yet live in it. . . . What I'm looking for is a resolution of all the oppositions . . . not really a resolution but a recognition and acceptance of relativity . . . it's more than just accepting that there are men and there are women and I only have one chance at it— I can't be both. . . . It's inside of *me*, the man and the woman . . . it oscillates depending on what you're looking for and what you're willing to supply'" (p. 190). The patient seems to have grasped the idea of sexual differentiation as processive, as an oscillation, like the intrinsic oscillation between each present moment and the flow of time. He moves from wanting to resolve sexual and temporal opposition to internalizing the paradox that one is either sex only in relation to the other, just as one is only in each apparently identical moment because time creates change. Hypothetically, one can assume that the "recognition and acceptance of relativity" is a result of a successful analytic process that must have modified the primary disavowal—recognition and repudiation—of sexual and temporal differentiation. This primary disavowal of sexual difference had compelled the patient to live in "endless narcissistic time." See Chapter 2 for an extended discussion of all these issues in relation to the theory of narcissism. Bach importantly emphasizes that this progress only took place in the context of a disavowed termination, i.e., a disavowal of analytic time.

9. I will return to Gray in detail in Chapter 5.

10. This contrast between neurotic and concrete compromise formations is deliberately oversimplified for the moment. What Freud calls "the loss of reality in neurosis and psychosis" (1924a) would have to involve some use of negative hallucination. For the meaningful neurotic symptom to fulfill its role as the substitute for a lost reality, the problem of concreteness would have to be related to the finer structure of neuro-

sis. We will begin to see Freud's own adumbration of this problem in the next section of this chapter.

11. In An *Outline of Psychoanalysis* (1940a) Freud tangentially examined the equation of perception with objectivity. He once again considers the paradox that had haunted him from *Project* onward, i.e., that the "perceptual periphery of the cortical layer can be excited to a much greater extent from the inside" so that consciousness of ideas and thoughts becomes possible but, simultaneously, so do hallucinations. As always, he concludes that reality testing is necessary to distinguish between the two. Exceptionally, however, in this posthumous work Freud realized that since both possibilities imply perception, the "equation 'perception = reality (external world)' no longer holds" (p. 162).

12. Renik (1992) consciously echoes Freud's famous imposition of a termination in the Wolfman case. Freud's problem in this case is directly related to continuing to interpret fantasy as reality, quite specifically the "reality of castration." This occurs precisely as he begins to describe the structure of what he will later call disavowal. Freud writes about the Wolfman: "In the end there were to be found in him two contrary currents side by side, of which one abominated the idea of castration, while the other was prepared to accept it and console himself with femininity as a compensation. But beyond any doubt a third current, the oldest and deepest, which did not as yet even raise the question of the reality of castration, was still capable of coming into activity" (1918, p. 85). When Freud describes the "oldest and deepest" "third current" as "the reality of castration," he already creates the problem of the later analysis of fetishism, the problem that can only be resolved by understanding the "third current" as the "reality" of sexual difference. In order to maintain the disavowal of differentiation, the Wolfman can create a fetishistic oscillation between castration as abomination and castration as compensation. One wonders whether Freud's imposition of a termination is the result of a power struggle over the patient's difficulty with interpretation itself. Many of the authors who have reconsidered the Wolfman case have pointed out the specific anticipation of the theory of fetishism in Freud's description. In fact, the Wolfman seems to be one of the patients described in both "Fetishism" (1927a) and "The Splitting of the Ego in the Process of Defense" (1940b; see Abraham and Torok 1986; Rey-Flaud 1994). Moreover, Freud specifically mentions Wolfman in "Analysis Terminable and Interminable" (1937a) in a significant way. He says

that the apparent success of the original treatment, with its imposed termination, did not last; more than twenty years later, Freud speaks of the patient's "perennial neurosis" (p. 218). Is it possible to understand the apparent success and ultimate failure of the imposed termination in terms of conducting an entire analysis such that the analyst conceives his or her task as having to resolve the patient's defenses against the "reality of castration"? If so, there would have been no analysis of the patient's concreteness in the transference. One has to admire Freud's forthrightness in admitting the eventual failure of what had seemed to be one of his most striking successes. However, he remains oblivious to all the clinical and theoretical implications of thinking in terms of the "reality of castration." As discussed in Note 5, he seems not to have a conception of the dynamics of repudiated difference that would lead one to take a fantasy of castration as a reality.

13. I will return to Loewald's conception in depth in Chapter 3.

14. Here is an instance of the paradox mentioned in Note 7.

15. Chasseguet-Smirgel's (1984) theory of perversion, however, winds up equating difference with an opposition of essences. I have consistently tried to show that rigid oppositions are the defensive, fantasy replacements for nonobjective differentiating processes. By making difference something "objective" and "natural" that can be perceived, Chasseguet-Smirgel falls back into equating reality with perception. For more on this topic see Bass 1995.

16. I will return to Morris's thinking more extensively in relation to questions of technique in Chapter 5.

17. There is much more to be said about this form of "thinking." In Chapter 4 I will return to it in relation to the Kleinian problematic of "sadistic epistemophilia."

Narcissism, Thought, and Eros

1. These discussions also include references to the problem of the apparent "cruelty" of the early infantile sexual aims: "The history of human civilization shows beyond any doubt that there is an intimate connection between cruelty and the sexual instinct. . . . According to some authorities this aggressive element of the sexual instinct is in reality a relic of cannibalistic desires—that is, it is a contribution derived from the apparatus for obtaining mastery, which is concerned with the satisfaction of the other and, ontogenetically, the older of the great instinctual needs"

(p. 159). Later: "The cruel component of the sexual instinct develops in childhood even more independently of the sexual activities that are attached to erotogenic zones. . . . It may be assumed that the impulse of cruelty arises from the instinct for mastery and appears at a period of sexual life at which the genitals have not yet taken over their later role. It then dominates a phase of sexual life which we shall later describe as a pregenital organization" (pp. 192–93). In sum, there is an intrinsic connection between the drive for mastery and the infantile sexual aims. These considerations have to be integrated with the concept of the part object, to which I will return in Chapter 4.

2. In *Life and Death in Psychoanalysis* (1980) Laplanche also cites this passage in order to demonstrate that Freud never believed in the "vast fable of autoerotism as a state of the primary and total absence of an object . . . autoerotism is, on the contrary, a second stage, the stage of the loss of the object" (p. 19). Laplanche specifies that the "lost object" is a partial object, so that "*on the one hand there is from the beginning an object, but that on the other hand sexuality does not have, from the beginning a real object*" (ibid.). Although Laplanche starts out from the same analysis of *Three Essays* as mine, his intent is actually the opposite: he wishes to show why the concept of unconscious fantasy is necessarily an entity other than the "instinct of self preservation" from which it is derived. Throughout, I will attempt to demonstrate the theoretical and clinical necessity of integrating the instinct of self-preservation and sexuality, whether in terms of primary narcissism, of Eros and environment (Chapter 3), or of the defensively fetishistic nature of the part object (Chapter 4). Because Laplanche wishes to uphold the equation of the unconscious with the repressed, the modifications that ensue from the theory of fetishism remain closed to him at this point of his theorizing, especially the problem of the unconscious registration of "reality." Over the years, however, Laplanche has modified his understanding of sexuality; see Note 10.

3. Caper (1998) makes a similar observation: "there is some reality sense in even the most primitive of mental states . . . a stage of development entirely devoid of reality sense cannot exist at any point of life." Caper appends a note to this sentence that speaks to my point: "In Freudian terms, this means that the second of Freud's two principles of mental functioning, the reality principle, must exist alongside the pleasure principle even from the very beginning of post-natal life" (p. 540).

4. Four years later, in "Instincts and Their Vicissitudes" (1915a), Freud

speaks of an "original 'reality-ego'" that becomes a "purified 'pleasure-ego'" by means of projection (p. 136). While this later discussion is difficult in its own right, it can be cited here as another example of the idea that the narcissism or autoerotism of infantile sexuality develops out of a decontextualization of an intrinsic link to reality: the original "reality ego" is "purified" by projection and becomes the "pleasure ego." I will return to the idea of the original "reality ego."

5. In October 1912 Ferenczi had written to Freud: "I want to tell you briefly about the ideas . . . about the individual stages of development of the 'organ of reality' (lack of need = omnipotence, magic of gestures, magic of words, sense of reality)—with an indication of their significance for symbolism, hysteria, and obsessional neurosis . . . " (p. 420). When Ferenczi's paper was published in February 1913, Freud wrote him that it was "the best and most significant one that you have contributed" (p. 469).

6. As Strachey reminds us in his editor's introduction, Freud himself thought that the narcissism paper was marked by the difficult circumstances of his breaks with Adler and Jung. It is entirely conceivable that many of its puzzling and difficult aspects are related to these circumstances. It is not my intention to provide a detailed reading of the entire text. Unfortunately, Freud wrote his most extended treatment of narcissism in charged circumstances and did not greatly develop his ideas on the subject afterward.

7. The entire third chapter of *Totem and Taboo* (1913) is devoted to a discussion of the omnipotence of thought. Freud there demonstrates that the "magical thinking" of the child and the primitive is an autoerotic projection of wishes upon external reality and explicitly links magical thinking to narcissism.

8. This formulation does not imply that in specific cases the reality being defended against via delusion or hallucination is never the memory of a perception too disturbing to be accommodated by consciousness. Rather, such a defensive process in and of itself would not be possible if there were not different kinds of knowledge of reality, such that the conscious, representational knowledge of reality can substitute for nonrepresentational knowledge of reality.

9. The idea of integrating primary narcissism with Eros is originally Loewald's: "it is by no means the ego alone to which [Freud] assigns the function of synthesis, of binding together. Eros, one of the two basic in-

stincts, is itself an integrating force. This is in accordance with [Freud's] concept of primary narcissism" (1980, pp. 234–35). I will return to this question in Chapter 3.

10. It is striking that in his recent writings Laplanche, too, has clearly seen that there is a sexuality of the death instinct and a sexuality of self-preservation: "psychic conflict . . . is a drive conflict: between the 'sexual death drives' . . . and 'sexual life drives' . . . " (1997, p. 75).

11. In *Female Perversions* (1991) Kaplan develops the thesis that perversions are the attempts to conform to gender stereotypes, most typically the stereotypes female = castrated, male = not castrated. Given the intrinsic links between perversion, infantile sexuality, autoerotism, and secondary narcissism, one can begin to think of compulsive conformity to super-ego demands as conformity to gender stereotypes. This idea would open new approaches to super-ego analysis.

A Dialogue with Hans Loewald

1. A more thorough analysis of Loewald would have to spell out his ambivalent relation to Hartmann's ego psychology. By challenging the view that the ego adapts to reality, Loewald implicitly criticizes Hartmann's magnum opus, *Ego Psychology and the Problem of Adaptation*. Nonetheless, Loewald also explicitly states his debt to Hartmann. In too summary a fashion, one can say that Loewald uses his integration of primary narcissism and Eros to correct the "philosophical preconceptions" that unknowingly guided Hartmann's thinking. Given the subsequent influence of Hartmann on the development of American ego psychology, Loewald's 1949 paper seems to have been a cry in the desert. For more on this topic, see Notes 2 and 11.

2. Hartmann's theory of adaptation starts from a premise akin to Loewald's: "The requirements for the survival of the species can take a form . . . which may be independent from the pleasure principle, and from a reality principle that is secondarily derived from it. . . . A similar assumption may be made for the needs of self-preservation: for instance the libidinal activity of the oral zone 'leans,' to begin with, upon the alimentary need. Thus we arrive at a conception in which relations to reality are determined by a *reality principle in the broader* and a *reality principle in the narrower sense*. . . . The reality principle in the broader sense would historically precede and hierarchically outrank the pleasure principle" (p. 44). But what is the "reality principle in the broader sense"? Hartmann

does not say or leaves one to assume that it is simply external reality as conventionally conceived. He would not think of the "broader sense" of reality in terms of a primary reality that continues to develop. Later he writes that the infant is born adapted to its environment: "the individual has a relationship to the external world from the very beginning. The newborn is in close touch with his environment not only by his need for its continuous care but also by his reactions to its stimuli . . . " (p. 51). However, "we should not assume, from the fact that the child and the environment interact from the outset, that the child is from the beginning psychologically directed toward the object as object . . . " (p. 52). From the usual, objective point of view Hartmann is certainly correct here: it does not make sense to speak in terms of nonexistent representations of the object ("the object as object"). However, he cannot begin to consider Loewald's problem, that the usual, objective point of view is simply not relevant in this context, because the objective view of reality develops out of "another" reality. The fact that the infant is not directed to the object as object, yet certainly registers the experience of satisfaction, is precisely what led Freud to envisage nonrepresented registrations of the object. Again, this is an expansion of Loewald's idea of the "primary object," or the "nonobjectified object."

3. Loewald does not cite Winnicott in this paper, but the often noted congruence between him and Winnicott is evident in the ideas of the environmental provision necessary for development and the threat of too great a difference of levels between infant and environment (impingement, as Winnicott calls it). I will pursue these ideas specifically in the discussion of Winnicott in Chapter 4.

4. Along with many others, I prefer "drive" for Freud's *trieb*. Loewald, however, consistently uses the consecrated translation of "instinct" for *trieb*. Therefore, both terms will have to be used here.

5. In *Totem and Taboo*, however, Freud also used obsessional neurosis as the exemplar of the omnipotence of thought that characterizes all neurotic symptomatology, so that the neurotic lives in what he calls a "world apart." Loewald's emphasis on the obsessive *character* makes the point that this belief in the possibility of omnipotent control of a hostile reality becomes "ego syntonic," i.e., normalized to such an extent that this fantasy construction becomes synonymous with reality itself.

6. This criticism holds for any psychoanalytic theory that accommodates itself to an unquestioned view of subject and object and to an

equation of perception and reality testing, whether that theory construes drives, object relations, narcissism, language, intersubjectivity—or anything else—as its theoretical or clinical focus. See note 10 below for a continuation of this topic.

7. One could certainly ask whether there could be such "objectified mental contents." I will return to this question in the discussion of the relations between Klein's concept of projective identification and repression in Chapter 4.

8. An example: In the early phases of a training analysis, an analyst was able to help a student specify and then resolve an unconscious fantasy that had structured many important decisions in his life. The student was much taken with this analytic work. It was only much later in the analysis that he was able to say that this impressive piece of classical analysis had in no way modified—to the contrary—an internal conviction that the analyst was only gratifying narcissistic needs of her own through successful work and was not really concerned with the student's well-being. This was something that the student could not talk about, leaving him with a feeling of "unreality" about the analysis and about his own therapeutic work. The best he could do would be to identify with the analyst and her technique, thereby preventing the internalization of the analytic process. The phase of the analysis in which these issues were finally discussed was initiated by anxiety so intense that the student was certain he was developing a heart problem. (He received a clean bill of health from his cardiologist.) This was an unexpected experience for the student and marked the move from a defensive identification with an idealized analyst to anxiety over internalization of a differentiating process. Such intense anxiety in a neurotic, well-functioning patient is akin to the chaotic fears of differentiation we have seen in the concrete patient. It marks a shift in the basic sense of the reality of the analysis. (I am grateful to a colleague for this material.) I will return to this question in my discussion of internalization anxiety in this chapter and of depressive anxiety in Chapter 4.

9. Earlier, I cited the passage in which Loewald says that repression-defense has a necessary protective function against internalization "going too far," i.e., once more losing the boundary between internal and external. To the extent that Loewald also links repression to the death instinct, to a return to a less differentiated organization, he certainly allows for an oscillating interplay between "life" and "death," between internalizing "expansion" of ego organization and repressive "shrinkage" of it. How-

ever, the only danger he sees in internalization is too great diffusion, the loss of boundaries; he does not link it to the possibility of being overwhelmed by tension. As I will discuss in Chapters 5 and 6, Klein's and Winnicott's understanding of the depressive position and depressive anxiety—the reintegration of that which intrinsically tends to be split off—would have to be integrated with Loewald's understanding of unconscious splitting processes.

10. In Note 6 I contended that any psychoanalytic theory that accommodates itself to an unquestioned subject-object opposition and an equation of perception and reality is protecting itself from a conception of dynamic reality. As the contradiction in Loewald's view of primary narcissism shows, any conception of an "originally undifferentiated state" does the same.

11. Hartmann has his own conceptualization of the ego's conjoint differentiating-integrating function, which is in some ways like Loewald's, although as always he emphasizes adaptation: "differentiations in the ego . . . create specific conditions for adaptation . . . differentiation within the ego leads to an optimal adaptation and synthesis only if the ego is strong and can use it freely; nevertheless, differentiation has an independent role among the adaptation processes. Differentiation is counteracted by a tendency toward a 'closed world,' which may be either an expression of the synthetic function in our sense . . . or a regression to earlier developmental stages of 'fitting together,' to a feeling of being one with the object, to a primary narcissistic state. . . . We are dealing here with the coexistence of *differentiation* and *integration*. . . . The development of the function of differentiation finds psychological expression not only in the formation of the mental institutions, but also in reality testing, in judgment, in the extension of the world of perception and action, in the separation of perception from imagery, cognition from affect, etc. The equilibrium of these two functions may be disrupted, for instance, by precocity of differentiation, relative retardation of synthesis" (pp. 53–54). It is striking that Hartmann notes the tendency to "counteract" differentiation via the "tendency toward a 'closed world.'" He, of course, construes this closed world in the conventional way of understanding primary narcissism. Thus, he cannot see that the "co-existence of differentiation and integration" (Loewald's *conscire*) is itself a disruptive opening that can be defended against by return to a more closed state. Nonetheless, he quite clearly states that "differentiation and integration"

are necessary for the separation of "perception from imagery," which is precisely Loewald's topic here. It is not entirely clear why Hartmann grants differentiation "an independent role among the adaptation processes," but the idea is noteworthy.

12. Moments of sleepiness in sessions are often important clinical markers of the operation of this process. The student analyst's late patient would often fall asleep when the analyst said things she objected to throughout the long period of her treatment dominated by frame violations. Over time, as these violations were addressed and the patient could articulate her extreme difficulties around internalization of the frame, a shift occurred. The patient began to notice that she grew sleepy when she herself said things that indicated internalization of an analytic process. It then became possible to analyze the conjoint withdrawal from herself and from the analysis without the patient feeling that attention to the transference was the "analyst's agenda" and not hers. Similarly, the patient who subtly violated the frame element of lack of visual contact by playing with the tissue box to see my reflection began to report feelings of sleepiness when he spoke to me in ways that indicated a need to understand himself rather than to impose subtle forms of wishful control over the entire analytic process. The patient said, "When I say things that have to do with our working together I feel myself get detached and sleepy. I want to blank out, and go into my own world."

13. In Chapter 1, Note 11, I cited Freud's surprising statement from *An Outline of Psychology* that perception does not guarantee reality testing. This is certainly a move away from a conventional understanding of reality. Given the importance Loewald attaches to Freud's statement in *Outline* that drive as a return to a previous state does not apply to Eros, it is possible to integrate the two ideas. The definition of drive as a return to a previous state is the essence of the closed system model of the psyche within which perception does equal reality testing. Both the exclusive tension-reduction model of the drive and the equation of reality testing with perception are elements of the secondary narcissism that disavows primary narcissism/Eros.

14. In Chapter 2, Note 10, I cited Laplanche's recent statement about psychic conflict in terms of the "sexual death drives" and the "sexual life drives." This is almost the same view that Loewald articulates here. It is compelling that these two great readers of Freud should come to such similar conclusions.

15. The possibility of self-preservation is intrinsically related to the problematic of depressive anxiety as mentioned in Note 8. Self-preservation must be conceptualized in terms of primary narcissism and Eros, such that it always implies the preservation of an other. How this becomes psychically possible and its intrinsic link to aggression are the subjects of the next chapter.

16. In "On Motivation and Instinct Theory" (1971), Loewald makes an analogous statement: "Ego and id are psychoanalytic constructs that . . . make use of the concept of instinctual energy. . . . They also make use of the conception of the equivalence of energy and structure (structure is bound energy and energy is unbound or potential structure), a conception that has been used in physics and has revolutionized it. Psychology has been no less revolutionized by the use of that conception in psychoanalysis, which is not to say that Freud was clearly aware of using it. It is an idea that was 'in the air' and was made use of in various contexts, among them physics and psychoanalysis. In itself it is an idea that does not derive from physics as an established body of knowledge and observations but which, when applied in its investigations, restructures the whole field (compare Freud's introductory paragraph to "Instincts and Their Vicissitudes"). That the same conception has been used in psychoanalysis does not mean that psychoanalysis has taken it over from physics or that it is physical in nature and thus not really applicable in psychological discourse. Neither do the concepts of energy and structure have of necessity physical connotations. They became conventional scientific concepts with specific physical connotations through their use in physics, but they are not by nature physical concepts or entities . . . " (p. 111).

17. In the preface to *Papers on Psychoanalysis* Loewald speaks of how much he owes to his education in philosophy: "Philosophy has been my first love. I gladly affirm its influence on my way of thinking while being wary of the peculiar excesses a philosophical bent tends to entail. My teacher in this field was Martin Heidegger, and I am deeply grateful for what I learned from him, despite his most hurtful betrayal in the Nazi era, which alienated me from him permanently. Freud is close enough to my generation to have been a commanding living force. . . . He has remained for me, through his writings, that living presence" (pp. viii–ix). The trained eye can find the influence of Heidegger throughout Loewald's work, although there is never any direct citation. "Psychoanalysis in Search of Nature" is Loewald's most overtly Heideggerean text, al-

though again without specific attribution. It would take too prolonged an exposition to explicate how and why Heidegger's influence permeates that paper. Suffice it to say that Heidegger's life-long attempt to think through the constraints of metaphysical thought intersects with Freud's reflections on metaphysics and metapsychology, one of Loewald's major topics in the paper.

18. Freud came very close to such a formulation, again in the context of comparisons of progress in psychoanalysis to progress in physics. In "Psychoanalysis and Telepathy" (1922) he justified his own study of "occult" phenomena by speaking of the "the great revolution toward which we are heading and of whose extent we can form no estimate. . . . Some indeed, of the proceedings of the exact sciences themselves may have contributed to this development. The discovery of radium has confused no less than it has advanced the possibilities of explaining the physical world; and the knowledge that has been so very recently acquired of what is called the theory of relativity has had the effect upon many of those who admire without comprehending it of diminishing their belief in the objective trustworthiness of science. You will remember that not long ago Einstein himself took occasion to protest against such misunderstanding" (pp. 177–78). Thus, Freud proposes to integrate psychoanalysis with science by studying "occult" phenomena and compares his stance to the changes in the theory of atomic structure and energy brought about by the discovery of radium (particle emission, the "alchemical" possibility of one element's changing into another) and to the destabilizing of the classical Newtonian universe brought about by the theory of relativity (no absolute points of observation, the temporality of space). Note that Freud makes his comparisons to those advances in physics that most upset the conventional view of nature yet were shown to be "objectively true." The implication is that the psychoanalytic theory of mind must do the same, particularly as concerns mental energy and the relations between "one" unconscious and "another" (telepathy). Freud, of course, was opposed to all forms of obscurantism. If one had to define it, obscurantism would probably be an unquestioned faith in the matching of data to the forms of subjective perception. Freud is quite trenchant on this topic, again using the analogy with physics, in *An Outline of Psychoanalysis*: "The hypothesis we have adopted of a psychical apparatus . . . has put us in a position to establish psychology on foundations similar to those of any other science, such for instance, as physics. In

our science as in the others the problem is the same: behind the attributes (qualities) of the object under examination which are presented directly to our perception, we have to discover something else which is more independent of the particular receptive capacity of our sense organs . . . it is evident that everything *new* that we have inferred must nevertheless be translated back into the *language of our perceptions,* from which it is simply impossible for us to free ourselves. But herein lies the very nature and limitation of our science. It is as though we were to say in physics: 'If we could see clearly enough we should find that what appears to be solid body is made up of particles of such and such a shape and size and occupying such and such *relative* positions" (p. 196, my emphases). This last comparison is crucial, for it is the clearest possible illustration of the difference between conventional objectivity, which matches conscious perception (the chair I am sitting on is solid), and an objectivity that is never available to consciousness (the chair's solidity is formed of atoms made of particles in motion and empty space). The point is that a conception of unconscious processes requires the "objectivity" that always questions perceptual objectivity. For an interesting counterargument, see Cavell, p. 179.

19. In *Narcissistic States and the Therapeutic Process* (1985) Bach makes a similar argument. He is specifically concerned with the question of the difficulty that narcissistic patients display with what Loewald calls the internalization of interaction as the precondition for representational difference, i.e., what is conventionally called the "observing ego." Bach writes: "A bodily sensation, for example, may not be describable simultaneously with a thought or feeling because the boundary between the observed system and the observing instrument is placed differently in each case and cannot be fully defined or controlled. The self observer is inextricably coupled to the self observed, and some feel that introspective 'statements referring to different placings of the partition are complementary in the sense of quantum physics' (Petersen 1968, p. 4)" (p. 160). Bach importantly adds in a footnote: "What I am attempting to point to is an area of ambiguity, transition, or paradox, which exists on both the clinical and theoretical levels and appears to implicate the boundaries between limited perspectives, systems and theoretical positions" (ibid.). Later Bach writes: "It may not be overly fanciful to see some parallel between classical mechanics and classical psychoanalytic technique, both of which begin to break down when applied to those extreme cases which call into

question the very concepts upon which our observations are based" (p. 168). Because Bach cites the idea of complementarity I must say a word about it. The most famous example is that light functions as either wave or particle depending upon the conditions of observation, a contradiction in terms for classical physics. It seems as though Bach might be saying that the narcissistic patient's joining of observer to observed within himself or herself, such that there is no representational "observing ego," is analogous to the relation between complementarity and observation. If so, I think that, like Loewald, he misses the defensive nature of the incapacity to observe oneself. In the view elaborated here, narcissistic or concrete patients cannot tolerate self-observation because unconsciously they repudiate what might be called the complementarity, i.e., differentiating process—intrinsic to self-observation. The "real" transference in which interpretation itself is so strenuously resisted is a prime example of complementarity refused. The patient is made too anxious by the idea that the relation to the analyst might embody supposedly contradictory emotions depending upon the conditions of observation.

20. There is a large literature on this subject. Borch-Jacobsen's *The Freudian Subject* (1988) opens with a compelling analysis of the Cartesianism of the original formulation of the unconscious from a different point of view. Cavell makes a similar argument in *The Psychoanalytic Mind*.

21. In fact, in "The Waning of the Oedipus Complex" (1980) Loewald has a very interesting discussion of what he calls the "intermediate status" of oedipal objects.

The Part Object, Depressive Anxiety, and the Environment

1. In the first section of Chapter 1 I cited Brown. He integrates the Kleinian understanding of the paranoid-schizoid position with dream theory and the ego psychological theory of separation-individuation to explain concreteness.

2. Chasseguet-Smirgel's theory of perversion, for which fetishism also serves as a model, is also based on the idea of depreciation of the father's "powers" and consequent idealization of the child's own masturbatory sexuality. I will return to this question later.

3. One is reminded here of the exemplary position given to obsessional phenomena both by Ferenczi in his paper on the development of the sense of reality and by Loewald in his discussion of the "neurotically distorted" view of reality. In the contemporary literature, Bach, Steingart,

and Chasseguet-Smirgel all emphasize the anal-narcissistic aspects of concreteness.

4. This narcissistic overvaluation of the child's anality is another specific link to Chasseguet-Smirgel's theory of perversion mentioned in Note 2. This entire topic calls for integration with Freud's early view of fetishism as the model of the idealization of an infantile sexual aim.

5. Freud, of course, considered this problem as well. In *On Narcissism* he alleged that the investment of too much libido in the ego was akin to megalomania, predisposing to hypochondriasis, a kind of "damming up" of libido in one's own body—thus, his statement that "we must love in order not to fall ill," i.e., libidinal investment in an external object serves a self-preservative function. Hence, the necessary move beyond autoerotism. As on so many occasions, one regrets that Freud did not link this idea to his original conception of an intrinsic tie to an "external" object. Nonetheless, as discussed in Chapter 2, this idea is essential to his postulation of primary narcissism—precisely what Abraham does not take into account here.

6. "Survival" is an important term for Winnicott. I will explain its relation to the problem of the part object later.

7. See especially "Early Stages of the Oedipus Conflict and of Super-Ego Formation" (1932 [1975], pp. 135, 143).

8. In a series of articles that specifically treat the questions of concreteness, Segal (1957, 1978, 1994) has integrated the Kleinian theories of symbolic equivalence, projective identification, and the depressive position.

9. Recall Renik's idea from Chapter 1 that "use of the analyst as a fetish" implies a magical gratification and reassurance gained from the "actual physical presence" of the analyst. In Abraham's or Klein's terms, this is obviously one aspect of what we can call the "use of the analyst as a part object." Renik's point that such transference configurations entail a thought process in which the "real" purpose of the analysis seems to be forgotten is the key clinical issue that Klein's theory leaves out. Abraham, in his own way, as seen earlier in the paper "A Particular Form of Resistance," was at least highly attuned to this issue.

10. In the Anna Freud–Melanie Klein debates (King and Steiner), Sharpe makes a similar argument about Klein. After giving Klein full credit for her pioneering delineations of infantile fantasies, Sharpe takes up the problem of hallucinatory wish fulfillment in relation to the projective identification of "good" and "bad" objects. She cites Freud's idea

that dreams represent wishes as fulfilled, "in such a way as to command entire belief" (1917, p. 230). In other words, precisely because Klein does link fantasies of "good" and "bad" objects to wish fulfillment, her theory demands that one consider the problem of illusion taken as reality. Sharpe contends that fantasized introjection of the breast is an "illusion or delusion . . . that still there has been no bodily separation from the mother. . . . The entire belief in the good concrete object within, or the bad object within, preserves the illusions of non-bodily separation. Primitive introjection and projection alike are attempts to deny the reality of bodily separation. From this core of belief in the actual good object within proceeds the belief in God immanent, the dweller in the innermost, the ultimate certainty and reality. . . . The ineradicable infantile wishes for *concrete realization* never cease. The acceptance of a symbol, the capacity for mental imagery, means not that infantile wish and hope are relinquished, but that belief in reality separation has occurred and substitutes must be found" (1991, pp. 338–39; my emphasis). What Sharpe calls "bodily separation" is itself a concrete version of what I have called "differentiation," which is not only an oral phase question. Sharpe clearly sees that the good and bad fantasy contents and fantasy process of projective identification are ways of describing illusions taken as realities. These illusions are defenses against "separation." While she does not invoke the theory of fetishism, her reference to belief in "God immanent" as the illusion of having the good (i.e., apparently "whole," apparently "real," and idealized object) inside oneself is exactly what I mean by the possibility of fetishism in the oral phase. Sharpe's point is that without understanding projective identification as a fantasy process, one simply literally posits a transcendent, theological principle—a "god," a "good" object, a fetish—as the "reality" of analytic "cure." Thus, she has given her own explanation of how Klein's metapsychology becomes a theology and has significantly linked it to the wish for concrete realization.

11. In the next chapter I will look at the work of Betty Joseph, a Kleinian who nonetheless understood that certain patients are made most anxious by contact as a function of Eros. Joseph will have important things to say about clinical technique in this context.

12. In *The Shadow of the Object* (1987) Bollas expands Winnicott's thinking about the reality of the environment mother by speaking of what he calls the non-representable, "existential" registration of the "idiom" of the mother's care. He calls such non-representable registrations

"the unthought known." This is a valuable revision of Winnicott because it begins to consider environment in terms of non-representable registrations. However, in an even more extreme way than Winnicott, Bollas thinks of such registrations only in terms of the actual caretaking by the mother in the oral phase. They have no economic connotation of increased tension and are simply repeated in actions not taken to be compromise formations. In my terms, the "unthought known" can be conceptualized as the non-representably registered, which is repudiated by fantasy conflated with reality.

13. I will return to the questions of time and environment, and of changes in the temporality of the frame, in the discussion of Alvarez de Toledo in Chapter 5.

14. In *Sublimation* (1988b) Loewald makes a similar point about transitional phenomena: "when [Winnicott] writes of the transitional object that it is what we see of 'the infant's journey from the purely subjective to objectivity,' he uses terms that in my view are not applicable at this level of experience. The journey does not start from the subjective; it is a journey from a state prior to the differentiation of subjectivity and objectivity to a state when subjectivity and objectivity come into being. . . . One faces a dilemma in that it is the hallmark of such states that they are neutral in respect to subjectivity and objectivity, but scientific language seems to demand or presuppose a decision one way or the other. Therefore scientific language, as commonly understood, is inadequate here . . . " (pp. 72–73). Loewald thus also implicitly links transitional phenomena to the question of primary narcissism. In Chapter 3 I discussed some of the contradictions in Loewald's conception of primary narcissism: because subject and object indeed are not yet differentiated within it, he sometimes tends to see it as an undifferentiated state. To link transitional phenomena to an undifferentiated state out of which the differentiation of subject and object emerge is in a sense absurd, because by definition transitional phenomena are "about" separation-as-relational difference. In fact, it is precisely because transitional phenomena are processively differentiating that they need to be understood in terms of primary reality. But Loewald is right that traditional terminology seems to demand a decision about "subjective" or "objective." Winnicott may simply have succumbed to such usage by assuming that internal and external already exist in respect of transitional phenomena. In general, Winnicott tends to assume the "unit status" he intends to derive. However, one can also ask whether Loewald

could conceive of transitional phenomena in terms of an originally differentiated state not organized in subject-object terms.

15. See also Chapter 2 for a discussion of the fetishistic functioning of the super-ego and Note 12 on the super-ego and conformity to the gender stereotypes castrated–not-castrated.

16. In "The Fetish and the Transitional Object" (1969) Phyllis Greenacre makes a related point. She calls the transitional object "Janus-faced," in that it is both the first not-me possession and a "link to the mother-me state." This makes it more like the fetish than Winnicott suggests, because there is a similar "Janus-facedness in the fetish. . . . The fetish is a conspicuously bisexual symbol and also serves as a bridge which would both *deny and affirm the sexual differences*. Both the fetish and the transitional object . . . serve to bring the current anxiety provoking situation under the illusory control of the individual . . . " (p. 321; my emphasis). Greenacre does not bring the question of depressive anxiety into her understanding of the "current anxiety situation." If both the fetish and the transitional object share the registration of difference, whether the difference between "not-me" and "mother-me" or sexual difference, the transitional object sustains that difference, i.e., is not an indication of traumatized response to either "mother-me" or sexual differentiation. Therefore it does not create the kind of illusory control that the fetish does. Nonetheless, Greenacre has very valuably understood that essentially both have to do with the registration of difference and thus both are "Janus-faced," intrinsically divided. In my terms, transitional phenomena derive from the processive quality of primary reality. The fetish, of course, oscillates between the registration of some aspect of this reality itself and fantasy. Fantasy itself is then divided into an oscillation organized around absence and presence—i.e., "illusory control."

17. This conception has been developed by Steingart (1995), who in fact understands concreteness as "pathological play." Bach (1985) also emphasizes that in "narcissistic states" transition from one state to another is experienced as trauma.

18. Barratt argues powerfully for a "deconstructive" psychoanalysis that takes a critical stance toward all received notions of object, subject, and identity. In his view, psychoanalysis as process is less insight generating than destabilizing of any assumption that an "I" "now" "is." Such a psychoanalysis is also acutely attentive to the privileging of representation, adaptation, and control. However, Barratt's entire effort still presumes

the centrality of repression and seems not to take into account the misfiring of the associative process in enactive remembering or concreteness.

Analysis of Surface, Analysis of Defense

1. Steingart (1995) envisages a technical middle ground between these two extreme positions. He advocates temporary compliance with frame violations within the session as "parameters" that are necessary if the analyst is not to engage in a power struggle with the patient. He gives compelling examples of a patient who had to speak to the analyst while seated on his desk and of a patient who required that the analyst not speak at all. Steingart's assumption is that such parameters are self-correcting over time. While it may indeed be the case that the patient on his or her own will relinquish the specific frame violation, one does not get the impression that Steingart conceives of their global implications. Thus, he does not have an interpretive strategy that grasps the patient's need to create a counter-surface in order to gain total control of analytic time and space. The result is that there would be no clinical focus on how and why the patient is traumatized by the frame but simply an assumption that when the patient relinquishes the violation, one interprets as usual.

2. In a fine appreciation of Gray's contributions, Smith (1993) makes a similar point. He says that Gray "moves us farther than ever before from the reification of named structures toward a surface defined by the most minute phenomenal detail—the shifts in association, attention, and affect that signal the mind 'minding' . . . " (p. 248). He urges that one take Gray's technique one step farther and that analysts focus on "the patient's perception of the analyst's activity or inactivity" (p. 253). The more one does so, he says, "the more apparent it becomes that, at least from the patient's point of view, the analyst is continuously and inevitably participating in an ongoing process of enactment. . . . In this light we might view enactment as ubiquitous, a component of transference that results from the interactive aspect of the analytic relationship" (ibid.). Smith has empirically made the point that Morris made more theoretically: enactment is unavoidable in the analytic dialogue—which again would have to include neurosis. Without explicitly saying so, he extends Gray's principles to a position like Loewald's, i.e., that a scientifically neutral conception of therapy demands that one observe "analyst and patient in interaction," precisely because Gray is right that in such interactions the most subtle, but most important, defensive maneuvers are repeated in the transference.

Abraham, Karl. 1919. A special form of resistance to the psychoanalytic method. In *Selected Papers on Psychoanalysis*. London: Maresfield Reprints, 1927.

———. 1924. A short history of the development of the libido, viewed in the light of mental disorders. In Abraham 1927.

Abraham, Nicolas, and Maria Torok. 1984. *The Wolf Man's Magic Word*. Trans. N. Rand. Minneapolis: University of Minnesota Press.

Adair, Mark. 1993. A speculation on perversion and hallucination. *Int. J. Psychoanal.* 74: 81–92.

Alvarez de Toledo, Louisa. 1996. The analysis of "associating," "interpreting," and "words." *Int. J. Psychoanal.* 77: 291–320.

Bach, Sheldon. 1985. *Narcissistic States and the Therapeutic Process*. Northvale, N.J.: Jason Aronson.

———. 1994. *The Language of Perversion and the Language of Love*. Northvale, N.J.: Jason Aronson.

Barratt, Barnaby. 1993. *Psychoanalysis and the Postmodern Impulse*. Baltimore: Johns Hopkins University Press.

Bass, Alan. 1991. Fetishism, reality, and "The Snow Man." *American Imago* 48: 295–328.

———. 1995. Primary perversion and universal law. *Cardozo Law Review* 16: 1293–1302.

———. 1997. The problem of "concreteness." *Psychoanalytic Quarterly* 66: 642–82.

Boesky, Dale. 1982. Acting out: a reconsideration of the concept. *Int. J. Psychoanal.* 63: 39–55.

Bollas, Christopher. 1987. *The Shadow of the Object*. New York: Columbia University Press.

Borch-Jacobsen, Mikkel. 1988. *The Freudian Subject*. Trans. Caherine Porter. Stanford: Stanford University Press.

Brook, J. A. 1992. Freud and splitting. *Int. Rev. Psychoanal.* 19: 335–60.

Brown, Lawrence. 1985. On concreteness. *Psychoanalytic Review* 72: 379–402.

Busch, Fred. 1995. Do actions speak louder than words? *J. Amer. Psychoanal. Assoc.* 43: 61–82.

Caper, Robert. 1994. What is a clinical fact? *Int. J. Psychoanal.* 75: 903–914.

———. 1998. Psychopathology and primitive mental states. *Int. J. Psychoanal.* 79: 539–51.

Cavell, Marcia. 1993. *The Psychoanalytic Mind*. Cambridge: Harvard University Press.

Chasseguet-Smirgel, Janine. 1984. *Creativity and Perversion*. New York: Norton.

———. 1986. *Sexuality and Mind*. New York: New York University Press.

Chused, Judith. 1991. The evocative power of enactments. *J. Amer. Psychoanl. Assn.* 39:615–39.

Derrida, Jacques. 1986. *Glas*. Trans. J. Leavey and R. Rand. Lincoln: University of Nebraska Press.

Fairbairn, W. Ronald. 1958. On the nature and aims of psychoanalytical treatment. *Int. J. Psychoanal.* 38: 374–85.

Feldman, Michael. 1997. Projective identification: The analyst's involvement. *Int. J. Psychoanal.* 78: 227–41.

Fenichel, Otto. 1941. *Problems of Psychoanalytic Technique*. New York: Psychoanalytic Quarterly.

Ferenczi, Sandor. 1913. Stages in the development of the sense of reality. In *First Contributions to Psychoanalysis*. New York: Bruner-Mazel, 1980.

Freedman, Norbert. Unpub.. Toward a descriptive language of clinical discourse—symbolization and de-symbolization in the course of psychoanalytic therapy.

———. Symbolization and intra-psychic conflict.

Freedman, N., and M. Berzofsky. 1995. Shape of the communicated transference in difficult and not so difficult patients: symbolized and desymbolized transference. *Psychoanalytic Psychology* 12: 363–74.

Freud, Anna. 1966. *The Ego and the Mechanisms of Defense*. New York: International Universities Press.

Freud, Sigmund. 1895a. *Project for a Scientific Psychology*. *Standard Edition*

of the Complete Psychological Works of Sigmund Freud. Ed. J. Strachey.
Vol. 1. London: Hogarth Press.

———. 1895b. *Studies on Hysteria.* S.E. 2.

———. 1896. The aetiology of hysteria. S.E. 3.

———. 1900. *The Interpretation of Dreams.* S.E. 4–5.

———. 1905a. *Fragment of an Analysis of a Case of Hysteria.* S.E. 7.

———. 1905b. *Three Essays on the Theory of Sexuality.* S.E. 7.

———. 1911a. Formulations on the two principles of mental
functioning. S.E. 12

———. 1911b. *Formulierungen uber die zwei Prinzipien des psychischen
Geschehens.* In *Gesammelte Werke.* Vol. 8. London: Imago.

———. 1913. Totem and Taboo. S.E. 13.

———. 1914a. On narcissism. S.E. 14.

———. 1914b. *On the History of the Psychoanalytic Movement.* S.E. 14.

———. 1914c. Remembering, repeating, and working through. S.E. 12.

———. 1915a. Instincts and their vicissitudes. S.E. 14.

———. 1915b. Observations on transference love. S.E. 12.

———. 1915c. Repression. S.E. 14.

———. 1915d. The unconscious. S.E. 14.

———. 1917a. A metapsychological supplement to the theory of
dreams. S.E. 14.

———. 1917b. Mourning and melancholia. S.E. 14.

———. 1918a. From the history of an infantile neurosis. S.E. 17.

———. 1918b. The taboo of virginity. S.E. 11.

———. 1919. A child is being beaten. S.E. 17.

———. 1920. *Beyond the Pleasure Principle.* S.E. 18.

———. 1921. Psychoanalysis and telepathy. S.E. 18

———. 1923. The infantile genital organization. S.E. 19.

———. 1924a. Neurosis and psychosis. S.E. 19.

———. 1924b. The loss of reality in neurosis and psychosis. S.E. 19.

———. 1925. Some psychical consequences of the anatomical
distinction between the sexes. S.E. 19.

———. 1926. *Inhibition, Symptom, and Anxiety.* S.E. 20.

———. 1927a. *Fetischismus.* In Gesammelte Werke. Vol 14. London:
Imago.

———. 1927b. Fetishism. S.E. 21.

———. 1931. Female Sexuality. S.E. 21.

———. 1933a. Feminity. S.E. 22.

———. 1933b. *New Introductory Lectures.* S.E. 22.

———. 1937a. *Analysis Terminable and Interminable.* S.E. 23.

———. 1937b. Constructions in analysis. S.E. 23.

———. 1940a. *An Outline of Psychoanalysis.* S.E. 23.

———. 1940b. The splitting of the ego in the process of defense. S.E. 23.

———. 1985. *The Complete Letters of Sigmund Freud to Wilheim Fliess.* Trans. and ed. J. Masson. Cambridge: Harvard University Press.

Frosch, Allen. 1995. The preconceptual organization of emotion. *J. Amer. Psychoanal. Assoc.* 43: 423–47.

Gray, Paul. 1994. *The Ego and Analysis of Defense.* Northvale, N.J.: Jason Aronson.

Greenacre, Phyllis. 1971. The fetish and the transitional object. In *Emotional Growth*, Vol. 1. New York: International Universities Press.

———. 1970. The transitional object and the fetish. In Greenacre 1971.

Grossman, Lee. 1996. "Psychic reality" and reality testing in the analysis of perverse defenses. *Int. J. Psychoanal.* 77: 509–517.

Hartmann, Heinz. 1958. *Ego Psychology and the Problem of Adaptation.* New York: International Universities Press.

Jacobson, Edith. 1957. Denial and repression. *J. Amer. Psychoanal. Assn.* 5: 61–92

Joseph, Betty. 1989. *Psychic Equilibrium and Psychic Change.* London: Routledge.

Kaplan, Louise. 1991. *Female Perversions.* New York: Doubleday.

King, Pearl, and Riccardo Steiner, eds. 1991. *The Freud-Klein Controversies 1941–1945.* London: Routledge.

Klein, Melanie. 1932. Early stages of the Oedipus complex. 1932. In *The Psychoanlysis of Children.* New York: Delta, 1975.

———. 1986. *The Selected Melanie Klein.* Ed. J. Mitchell. New York: Free Press.

Laplanche, Jean. 1980. *Life and Death in Psychoanalysis.* Baltimore: Johns Hopkins University Press.

———. 1997. Aims of the psychoanalytic process. *Journal of European Psychoanalysis* 5: 69–79.

Laplanche, Jean, and J. B. Pontalis. 1973. *The Language of Psychoanalysis.* New York: W. W. Norton.

Loewald, Hans. 1980. *Papers on Psychoanalysis.* New Haven, Conn.: Yale University Press.

―――. 1988a. Psychoanalysis in search of nature: Thoughts on metapsychology, "metaphysics," projection. In *The Annual of Psychoanalysis*. Vol. 16. Madison, Conn.: International Universities Press.

―――. 1988b. *Sublimation*. New Haven, Conn.: Yale University Press.

McDougall, Joyce. 1986. *Theaters of the Mind*. London: Free Association Books.

McLaughlin, James. 1991. Clinical and theoretical aspects of enactment. *J. Amer. Psychoanal. Assoc.* 39: 595–614.

Morris, Humphrey. 1993. Narrative, representation, narrative enactment, and the psychoanalytic construction of history. *Int. J. Psychoanal.* 74: 33–54.

Opatow, Barry. 1997. The real unconscious: Psychoanalysis as a theory of consciousness. *J. Amer. Psychoanal. Assoc.* 45: 865–90.

Pancheri, Lucia. 1998. What is left of classical interpretation? *Journal of European Psychoanalysis* 6: 3–18.

Panel. 1992. Enactments in psychoanalysis. M. Johan, reporter. *J. Amer. Psychoanal. Assoc.* 40: 827–41.

Renik, Owen. 1992. Use of the analyst as a fetish. *Psychoanal. Q.* 61:542–63.

Rey-Flaud, Henri. 1994. *Comment Freud inventa le fetichisme et reinventa la psychanalyse*. Paris: Payot.

Sandler, Joseph. 1976. Dreams, unconscious fantasies and "identity of perception." *Int. R. Psychoanal.* 3: 33–42.

Schafer, Roy. 1994. The contemporary Kleinians of London. *Psychoanal. Q.* 63: 409–432.

Segal, Hanna. 1957. Notes on symbol formation. *Int. J. Psychoanal.* 38: 391–97.

―――. 1978. On symbolism. *Int. J. Psychoanal.* 59: 315–19.

―――. 1994. Phantasy and reality. *Int. J. Psychoanal.* 75: 395–401.

Silverman, Doris. 1996. Polarities and amalgams: Analytic dyads and the individuals within them. *Psychoanalytic Review* 83: 247–71.

Smith, Henry. 1993. The analytic surface and the discovery of enactment. In *Annual of Psychoanalysis*. Ed. J. Winer. Vol. 21. Hillsdale, N.J.: Analytic Press.

Steingart, Irving. 1995. *A Thing Apart: Love and Reality in the Therapeutic Relationship*. Northvale, N.J.: Jason Aronson.

Winnicott, D. W. 1975. *Through Pediatrics to Psychoanalysis*. New York: Basic Books.

Abraham, K., 6, 8, 146–71, 173, 177–82, 189, 192, 209, 211, 221, 250, 252, 263, 279, 292

Action, acting out, 45, 118, 213–14, 247, 258; dedifferentiating, 220; and obsessional neurosis, 69–70; therapeutic, 41, 52, 91, 128–34, 136, 186

Adair, M., 45

Adler, A., 282

Aggression, 12, 134, 153–54, 170, 173, 176, 178, 203–4, 244, 250, 260, 270, 288

Alexander, F., 3–4

Alvarez de Toledo, L., 231–38, 244, 249, 264, 268, 294

Ambivalence, 46, 157, 159–60, 162, 164–65, 180; ambivalent attitude, 159, 161, 166

Anality, 46–47, 153–58, 164, 185, 292; anal fixation, 153; anal phase, 40, 46–47, 156–58, 165–66; and erotism, 153–54, 156; and fantasies, 46, 156, 251; and sadism, 69, 153, 159, 161

Analysis, classical, 131, 143, 285; dream analysis, 150; ego analysis, 266; super-ego analysis, 244, 283; surface-and-defense analysis, 210–66, 296; transference analysis, 207. *See also* Psychoanalysis

Anxiety, 2, 8–9, 26–28, 30–36, 39, 88, 103–15, 232–33, 236, 238, 243, 252–53, 255, 257–58, 270, 275, 285; castration anxiety, 28–29, 83, 187, 204, 269, 277; and the concrete patient, 42, 245; depressive anxiety, 8, 146–209, 269, 285–86, 288, 295; of integration, 259; internalization anxiety, 114–15, 118, 122–23, 126, 128, 134, 143, 147, 188–89, 195, 198, 203–6, 209–10, 219, 235, 238, 244, 247, 253, 255, 260, 265, 269–71, 285; primal anxiety, 27, 42; separation anxiety, 18, 78; signal anxiety, 26–28, 31, 115, 243; super-ego anxiety, 82

Autoerotism, 55–69, 71, 75, 80–82, 114, 134, 152–53, 157–58, 281–83, 292; autoerotic overvaluation, 57–59, 67, 72; of destructiveness, 176; as global defense, 83; of secondary narcissism, 116, 168; unconscious, 82; and wish fulfillment, 58, 67–68; and wishes, 76–77

Bach, S., 46–47, 53, 278, 290–91, 295

Balint, M., 3

Barratt, B., 295

Biting, 159, 162–66

Boesky, D., 45

Bollas, C., 293–94

Borch-Jacobsen, M., 291

Brook, J.A., 48

Brown, L., 17–19, 21, 25, 34, 275, 291

Busch, F., 245–49, 251, 254, 260–62, 265–66

Cannibalism, 166–67

Caper, R., 13–14, 19–20, 37, 174, 281

Care, 60, 68, 114, 167–68, 177, 187,

189, 192–93, 198, 203–4, 209, 252, 267–68, 284, 293; caretaking, 191, 294

Castration, 30–31, 43, 82, 96, 110, 162–63, 182–83, 188, 192, 204, 279; anxiety of, 28–29, 83, 187, 204, 268–69, 277; complex of, 28, 96, 276; fact of, 30, 34, 227, 229, 276–77; reality of, 83, 86, 128, 153, 182, 187, 208, 227, 231, 268, 279–80; and women, 29–30, 32, 43

Cavell, M., 290–91

Chasseguet-Smirgel, J., 46, 280, 291–92

Chused, J., 45

Compromise formation, 2, 19–21, 27, 36, 95, 111, 115, 133, 161, 194, 211, 225, 262–63, 268, 271, 294; concrete, 40, 115, 278; fetishistic, 102, 109, 154, 269

Concreteness, 11–54, 66–67, 75, 79, 83–86, 95, 102, 115, 118, 146–47, 149, 160, 165–66, 174–76, 192, 198–99, 203–4, 219–20, 227–28, 230–31, 237–38, 245, 247–49, 256, 263, 269–71, 275–80, 291–92; concrete patients, 66–67, 75–77, 83, 88–89, 102–3, 112, 114, 125, 138, 143, 177, 190, 195–96, 210, 213, 220–21, 236, 239, 253, 261, 268, 270, 278, 291

Conscrire (integrative differentiation), 121–24, 128–29, 168, 177, 219, 255. *See also* Loewald

Control, autoerotic, 58, 78–80, 166, 197; illusion of, 58, 103; magical, 204–5, 207–8, 232, 234

Countertransference, 75, 78, 142, 221, 232–34, 258, 271. *See also* Transference

Death, death instinct, 81–82, 109–11, 132–34, 144, 147, 249, 253, 283, 285

Deconstruction, vii–viii

Dedifferentiation, 33, 110, 134, 162, 175–76, 186, 217, 219–20, 246

Defense, global, 54, 83, 151–52, 175, 219, 258; primary, 22–32, 35, 61, 64, 83, 107, 109, 150, 155, 170, 230, 252, 268–69; surface, 237, 243, 249

Depression, 2, 156–69, 162

Derrida, J., vii–ix, xi

Descartes, R., 135, 139, 144

Desymbolization, 39, 175

Difference, registration of, 31, 53, 59, 66, 86, 115, 162, 216, 295; repudiation of, viii–ix, 31, 44, 70, 78, 209, 211, 277; sexual, 31–33, 66, 82, 88, 102, 110, 122, 138, 162, 182, 189, 193, 203–4, 229, 230, 279, 295. *See also* Disavowal

Differentiation, defenses against, 7–8, 32–33, 39–40, 91, 186, 228; sexual, 34, 40, 122, 247, 278, 295

Disavowal (*Verleugnung*), of difference, viii, 32–42, 23. *See also* Splitting
—primary, 32, 34, 36, 38–40, 42, 44–45, 49–50, 53, 62, 67, 69, 75, 79, 83, 88–89, 108–10, 123, 128, 134, 136, 141–42, 166, 195, 210–11, 223, 227, 249, 269, 271, 277–78; of sexual difference, 277–78

Dreams, dream mechanism, 21, 25, 29, 47, 68, 121, 202, 269; dreams as real, 47, 66; theory of, 1, 222

Drives, death drive, 33, 109–10, 134, 170, 175–77, 220, 269; libidinal—self-preservative, 67, 73–75, 77, 79, 81, 85, 88, 90, 94, 96, 128, 153, 158, 168, 170; sexual death drive, 283, 287; sexual life drive, 283, 287

Ego, ego-ideal, 80, 82–83; ego psychology, 283; ego splitting, 20, 30, 48–49, 53, 89, 111, 188, 239–40, 266. *See also* Splitting

Einstein, A., 289

Enactment, 36, 39, 42, 45, 50, 75, 125, 224–26, 229–31, 235, 247, 258, 264–65, 296; enactive interpretation, 138, 142, 177, 221, 231, 238, 242; enactive remembering, 8, 46, 118–28, 124, 138, 142, 146, 148–49, 161, 176–77, 187, 192, 201, 219, 226, 237, 242, 296

Environment, analytic environment, 9, 41, 45, 123, 143, 160, 195–96, 199, 208, 216, 219, 237, 247, 251, 253, 259, 262, 266, 268–69; ego-environment, 94–96, 102, 104, 113, 116

Envy, 151–54, 263–64; penis envy, 277

Epistemophilia, 173–74, 177; sadistic, 176–77, 186, 232, 280

Eros, 33–34, 80–91, 110, 128, 132–33, 136, 141, 160, 170, 175–76, 187–88, 197, 208, 216, 220, 229, 231, 236, 253, 255, 264, 267, 269, 271, 277, 281–83, 287–88, 293; trauma of, 113, 123, 203, 226, 228, 247, 249, 254, 256, 260, 268

Fairbairn, W. R., 262

Fantasy, and reality, 16, 70, 174, 200, 204, 208, 235, 256, 258, 264; opposed fantasies, 33, 44, 82, 123, 142, 154, 262, 265

Feldman, M., 262–66, 268

Fenichel, O., 231, 238

Ferenczi, S., 3–4, 6, 68–70, 75, 86, 98, 116, 133, 188, 204, 208, 213, 262, 282, 291

Fetishism, fetishistic formation, 80, 205, 208–9, 244, 252, 259; fetishistic structures, 34, 38, 42–52, 76, 88–89, 145–46, 160, 168, 247, 269; generalization of, viii, 42, 51, 60, 66, 91–92, 146, 207, 226, 239, 267; theory of, viii, 7–8, 21, 54, 91, 95, 226, 266, 277, 279, 281, 293

Frame, analytic, 14, 78, 128, 134, 143, 231, 238, 271; frame violations, 123, 196, 235, 287, 296; internalization of, 123, 128, 199, 287

Freedman, N., 39, 175

Freud, A., 35, 230, 266, 292

Freud, S., "The Aetiology of Hysteria," 1; "Analysis Terminable and Interminable," 3, 279; *Beyond the Pleasure Principle*, 2, 33, 81, 83–84, 105, 132–33, 196, 216, 253; "A Child Is Being Beaten," 2; *Civilization and Its Discontents*, 93, 132; "Constructions in Analysis," 221, 225; "Female Sexuality," 30; "Femininity," 30; "Fetishism," 179, 279; "Formulations on the Two Principles of Mental Functioning," 59, 62, 66, 69–69, 74, 76, 84, 150, 154, 214, 216; *Inhibition, Symptom and Anxiety*, 2, 172, 240; "Instincts and Their Vicissitudes," 172, 281, 288; *The Interpretation of Dreams*, 1, 22–23; "The Loss of Reality in Neurosis and Psychosis," 221; "A Metapsychological Supplement to the Theory of Dreams," 24; "Mourning and Melancholia," 2; *New Introductory Lectures*, 240; "On Narcissism," 2, 70, 77, 80–82, 93, 132, 292; *An Outline of Psychoanalysis* 48, 60, 82, 132, 279, 287, 289; *Project for a Scientific Psychology*, 2, 22, 24, 33, 42, 61–63, 213; "Psychoanalysis and Telepathy," 289; "Remembering, Repeating, and Working Through," 212, 216, 218, 224; "Repression," 3; "Some Psychical Consequences of the Anatomical Distinction Between the Sexes," 30; "The Splitting of the Ego in the Process of Defense," 227, 279; *Studies on Hysteria*, 2; "The Taboo

of Virginity," 33; *Three Essays on the Theory of Sexuality*, 56–58, 65, 67, 73, 81, 133, 138, 154, 275, 281; *Totem and Taboo*, 282, 284; "The Unconscious," 3
Frosch, A., 18–21, 41, 78, 174, 276

Gray, P., 35, 238–66, 270, 278, 298
Greenacre, P., 295
Grossman, L., 47, 66

Hallucination, positive, 25, 30, 34, 99, 184, 233; negative, 25–27, 29, 32, 34–37, 39, 44–45, 50, 62, 67–69, 75, 88, 99, 115, 184, 233, 278
Hartmann, H., 283–84, 286–87
Heidegger, M., ix, 288–89
Hysteria, 2, 4–5, 282

Idealization, 80, 82, 86, 147, 169, 182–84, 263, 291–92; idealized object, 183–85, 201, 252, 268, 293
Identification, 103–117, 120, 122, 125, 131, 154, 162, 165, 172–75, 177–78, 181, 185–86, 188, 203, 241, 250, 252, 254, 259, 261–62; projective, 147, 170–71, 182, 185–88, 232, 257, 259–63, 265–66, 285, 292–93; time of, 190, 237
Incorporation, 156, 159, 163, 165–66, 178, 180–82, 186
Inertia, 22, 23, 25, 34, 36, 107, 110, 262, 266; and primary process, 33, 42; tendency to, 23, 25, 33
Infantile sexuality, 55–56, 58–59, 68–69, 71–72, 75, 81, 152, 154, 158, 162, 165, 168–69, 171, 283; auto-erotic, 55, 65, 68, 74, 96, 141, 156, 282; narcissism of, 80, 96; theory of, 55, 96, 157–58
Integration, of self-preservation and libido, 76, 260; with environment, 95, 105–6, 111, 123, 133, 146, 188,

190, 192, 194–95, 198, 200, 202–3, 211, 215–16, 220, 229, 237, 247, 251, 253, 262, 268–69, 271; with reality, 98, 201, 204, 259, 267
Interaction, processive, 177, 185
Internalization, of differentiation, 34, 41, 125, 175; of interaction, 105, 117, 131, 290. *See also* Oscillation
Interpretation, resistance to, ix, 6–8, 19, 46, 50, 78, 86, 123, 134, 187, 195, 209, 214, 249–50, 263, 266, 269, 271; content interpretation, 36, 39–40, 79, 198, 211, 251, 255–56, 269
Intervention, processive, 37, 79, 114, 128, 237, 250–51, 270
Introjection, 105, 180, 191, 293; of good object, 181, 190; and projection, 177–78; of whole object, 189, 261

Jacobson, E., 6, 14, 16–21, 25, 34, 43–45, 47, 66, 149, 275–76
Joseph, B., 238–66, 270, 293
Jung, C., 282

Kaplan, L., 283
Klein, M., 3–4, 6, 8, 18, 146–47, 153, 158, 162, 169–92, 209, 232–33, 239, 253–54, 258, 261–63, 266, 285–86, 292–93
Kohut, H., 3–4

Lacan, J., ix, 3–4
Laplanche, J., 281, 283, 287; and Pontalis, J.-B., xi, 54, 226, 270
Loewald, H., 6, 8, 41, 45–46, 51, 91–147, 149, 162, 169, 173, 175–77, 187–88, 190, 192, 195, 206, 208–9, 218–19, 225–26, 235, 253–55, 262, 267–69, 271, 280, 282–91, 294–95

McDougall, J., 53

Mahler, M., 18

Memory, and perception, 25, 29, 67, 115–16, 119, 121, 210, 217, 269; memory traces, 62, 75; representational, 119–20, 124, 126, 131, 224;

Metapsychology, 46, 91, 144, 150–52, 155, 235, 238, 268, 289, 293

Mind, theory of, 1, 4, 6, 24, 43, 49–51, 241, 256, 266, 270, 289

Morris, H., 49, 223–31, 235, 238, 280, 296

Narcissism, destructive, 40, 103, 173, 175, 186; narcissistic equilibrium, 33, 54, 66

—primary, 7–8, 54, 70–90, 92–97, 99, 102–5, 107–9, 113, 115–19, 122, 132–33, 135, 140–41, 168, 177, 191–92, 208, 211, 216, 229, 268–69, 286, 292, 294; and Eros, 84, 91, 132, 136, 141, 188, 229, 267, 281–83, 287–88; concept of, 93–94, 132, 150, 167, 283; derivative of, 89, 105, 119, 143; integration of, 88, 91, 183; organization of, 74, 94, 104, 115, 122, 175

—secondary, 54, 74–76, 78–80, 82, 86, 88–90, 96–97, 102, 104, 106–7, 111–12, 114, 116–17, 141, 155, 163, 177, 185, 208, 211, 216, 220, 269, 283, 287; autoerotism of, 116, 168

Narcissus, 75, 80, 155, 219

Narrative, 226–27, 230; narrative enactment, 224, 230; psychoanalytic narratives, 230. *See also* Morris

Neurosis, 4, 72, 80–83

Neutrality, 20, 38, 41, 130, 198, 244, 271; of analyst, 38, 129–30, 143, 232, 244, 259, 264

Nietzsche, F., ix, 139

Object, and ego, 93, 85, 159, 183; part object, 8, 46, 146–209, 252–54, 261–62, 281, 292; persecutory, 176–77, 184; whole object, 147, 163, 171, 178, 181–82, 186–87, 189, 192, 261–62

Objectivism, 138–39, 142, 170, 186, 188, 239, 254, 267, 271

Obsession, obsessional neurosis, 69, 156, 158, 165, 282, 284

Oedipus complex, 96, 135, 145, 156, 171, 203

Omnipotence, fantasy of, 69–70; of thought, 70, 73–75, 120, 282, 284

Opatow, B., 24–25

Oscillation, between reality and fantasy, 31, 43, 76; between internalization and identification, 203; between primary and secondary narcissism, 80, 90, 97; between two fantasies, 30, 33, 43, 122, 265; between two realities, 31, 106, 171

Overvaluation, 57–59, 71; autoerotic, 57, 59, 67, 72; narcissistic, 65, 292

Perceptual identity, 17, 23–25, 28, 34–36, 39, 64, 119, 121–22, 138, 198, 200, 202, 205, 208, 264, 269; use of, 44, 227, 234

Perversion, 2, 46, 55, 57, 71–72, 168–69, 283; theory of, 280, 291–92

Phallus, maternal, 27–28, 168, 207–08; phallic monism, 31–33, 204; phallic phase, 162, 192, 207, 226

Physics, 135–36, 139, 143–44, 288–90

Piaget, J., 18–19, 245

Pleasure-unpleasure principle, 22, 56, 61, 109

Position, paranoid-schizoid, 18, 147, 171, 178, 186, 190, 261, 291; depressive, 8, 147, 156, 170–71, 178, 180–81, 186–92, 196, 203, 254, 260–61, 286, 292

Projection, *see under* Introjection

Psychoanalysis, vii–viii, 1, 3–5, 7, 30,
41, 54, 71, 91–92, 94, 97–99, 101,
103, 107, 130–32, 135–37, 139–41,
143–45, 147, 149, 151–54, 158,
169–70, 195, 209, 211–12, 216, 224,
227, 230–31, 248, 267, 271, 276,
288–89, 295

Psychosis, 27, 48, 59, 72–73, 121, 179,
221–23, 278

Rank, O., 3

Reality, dynamic, 102, 110, 130, 138,
286; material, 19, 136–37, 144, 236;
processive, 193, 205, 223, 225, 228,
230, 244, 249, 261, 268, 270; reality
effect, 30, 64, 220, 227, 242, 269;
registration and repudiation of, 32,
49, 66–67, 80, 87, 91, 183; static,
102, 162; unconscious registration
of, 9, 59, 63, 95, 97; unreal, 173–78,
180–81

Reference, hyperreferentiality, 245–
46; illusion of, 243, 245; loss of
referentiality, 227, 244; referential
aberration, 229

Renik, O., 20–21, 38, 40, 42, 47–48,
276, 279, 292

Repetition, compulsion, 187, 220,
249, 253–54, 259, 264; transference,
118, 247

Sadism, 153–56, 171–78, 181–82, 189,
209

Sandler, J., 44–46, 51, 64, 121–22, 200

Schafer, R., 255–56

Segal, H., 292

Self-destruction, 134, 155, 170, 220,
246, 260

Self-preservation, 56–57, 59, 72–74,
76–78, 82, 96, 133–34, 155, 187,
283, 288; instinct of, 72–74, 133,
281; and libido, 74, 76, 81, 94,
96, 133, 152, 155, 244, 251, 260,
270

Sexuality, *see* Infantile sexuality

Sharpe, E., 292–93

Silverman, D., 277

Smith, H., 36, 296

Splitting, and disavowal, 7, 49,
109–10, 114, 188, 240, 266; of the
ego, 30, 34, 48–49, 70, 108–9, 183,
240–41, 278; of self-preservation
from libido, 82, 152, 155, 244, 251,
270. *See also* Ego

Steingart, I., 46–47, 291, 295–96

Strachey, J., 63, 276, 282

Super-ego, 80, 82–83, 87, 92, 96, 171,
204, 244, 283, 295. *See also* Analysis

Surface, analysis of, 210–66; surface
resistances, 213, 216, 218–19, 223,
246, 269. *See also* Defense

Symbolism, 19, 171–73, 175–76, 199,
202, 282; symbolic equivalence,
173–78, 182–83, 185–87, 192, 199,
201, 292; symbolization, 175,
235–36. *See also* Desymbolization

System, closed, 76, 89, 103, 114, 118,
130, 132, 208, 244, 262, 287; open,
114, 130, 132, 160, 262, 271

Technique, theory of, 8, 211, 238, 270

Temporal immediacy, 23, 25, 34, 45,
84–85, 105, 202, 269

Time, analytic, 79, 237, 278, 296; conscious, 84–85, 105, 196–97, 237,
250; unconscious, 8, 83–90, 105,
196–97, 229, 235, 237, 267, 269, 271

Transference, global, 45; positive, 87,
130, 151, 155, 161, 241; "real," 143,
147, 166, 217, 220, 291. *See also*
Countertransference

Transitional, object, 199–205, 207,
294–95; phenomena, 148, 199–209,
294–95; space, 8, 18

Trauma, of differentiation, 136, 210,

247, 263; of unconscious time, 229.
See also Eros

Treatment, analytic, 3–4, 6, 11, 16, 20,
100, 107, 129, 131, 208–9, 215, 222,
262, 268, 275; break in, 220, 247;
of the concrete patient, 75, 88, 114,
143, 221; of enactive remembering,
122, 126; of hysteria, 5; of narcissism, 282; of neurosis, 72, 242;
theory of, 1, 3–4, 49, 105

Unconscious, memory, 1, 3, 23, 62,
64, 120, 268; thought, 8, 55–81,
85–86, 90, 94, 96, 105, 141, 150,
154, 176, 214–15, 229, 229, 256,
267, 271; time, 8, 83–90, 105,
196–97, 229, 235, 237, 267, 269,
271; processes, 6, 14, 32, 43, 51, 77,
122, 129, 136–39, 141, 143, 170,
179, 220, 224, 269, 290

Winnicott, D.W., 3–4, 6, 8, 146–48,
158, 188–209, 219, 231, 268, 275,
284, 286, 292–95

Wish fulfillment, 21–23, 25–26, 31,
35–36, 39, 55, 58, 62, 64, 66–70,
78, 97, 99, 104–5, 122, 125, 138,
150, 160, 184, 197, 204–5, 213, 293;
and autoerotism, 58, 67–68; and
defense, 83, 99; dedifferentiating,
50, 115; dream as, 1; and fantasy,
96; and fetishism, 44; hallucinatory,
21, 24, 29, 32, 35, 45, 50, 60, 64,
66, 73, 75, 103–4, 117, 184–85,
187–88, 292; immediacy of, 85,
105; mechanisms of, 118, 200,
269; positive, 24–25, 39; primary,
23, 33–34, 61, 64, 83, 252, 266,
268; processive use of, 35; theory
of, 45, 55

Wolfman, 279